POLICY CHANGE, PUBLIC ATTITUDES AND SOCIAL CITIZENSHIP

Does neoliberalism matter?

Louise Humpage

First published in Great Britain in 2015 by

Policy Press
University of Bristol
1-9 Old Park Hill
Clifton
Bristol BS2 8BB
UK
t: +44 (0)117 954 5940
pp-info@bristol.ac.uk
www.policypress.co.uk

North America office:
Policy Press
c/o The University of Chicago Press
1427 East 60th Street
Chicago, IL 60637, USA
t: +1 773 702 7700
f: +1 773 702 9756
www.press.uchicago.edu
sales@press.uchicago.edu

© Policy Press 2015

British Library Cataloguing in Publication Data
A catalogue record for this book is available from the British Library.

Library of Congress Cataloging-in-Publication Data
A catalog record for this book has been requested.

ISBN: 978 1 84742 965 0 hardcover

Cover design by Policy Press.
Front cover: image kindly supplied by istock
Printed and bound in Great Britain by CPI Group (UK) Ltd, Croydon, CR0 4YY
Policy Press uses environmentally responsible print partners

Contents

List of figures and tables

Figures

Tables

List of abbreviations

ACC	Accident Compensation Corporation
ACTU	Australian Council of Trade Unions
AES	Australian Election Study
AuSSA	Australian Survey of Social Attitudes
BES	British Election Study
BSA	British Social Attitudes
CHE	Crown Health Enterprises
GDP	Gross Domestic Product
GP	General Practitioner
GST	Goods and Services Tax
HSA	Health Savings Account
ISSP	International Social Survey Programme
MMP	Mixed Member Proportional
NGO	Non-governmental organisation
NHS	National Health Service
NZAVS	New Zealand Attitudes and Values Survey
NZES	New Zealand Election Study
NZH	New Zealand Herald
NZVAS	New Zealand Values & Attitudes Study
NZVS	New Zealand Values Study
OECD	Organisation for Economic Co-operation and Development
PADA	Personal Accounts Delivery Authority
PHO	Primary Health Organisation
RCSP	Royal Commission on Social Policy
RHA	Regional Health Authorities
TVNZ	Television New Zealand
UK	United Kingdom
WINZ	Work & Income New Zealand
WWG	Welfare Working Group

Acknowledgements

No book can be written without the support of others and this is no exception.

I am grateful for research funding from the New Zealand Royal Society Marsden Fund (#UOA603), the University of Auckland's Faculty of Arts Research Development Fund and Summer Scholarship programme, as well as the Department of Sociology.

I would like to thank the research participants who took part in my qualitative study about social citizenship in 2007–08. The book, however, would not have been possible without the rich survey data developed by other scholars. Special thanks go to Jack Vowles (for giving me access to the latest New Zealand Election Study data) and Paul Perry (who allowed me to use some of his unpublished New Zealand Values Study data). I also wish to acknowledge all of the people behind the British and Australian social attitudes and election studies I have drawn upon.

The arguments I make in this book are original but I have published articles using some of the same qualitative and quantitative data in *New Zealand Sociology, Policy Quarterly, Social Policy Journal of New Zealand, Kotuitui: New Zealand Journal of Social Sciences Online* and *Australian Journal of Social Issues*. I have also presented related findings at the Annual Conference of the International Sociological Association Research Committee on Poverty, Social Welfare and Social Policy (RC 19), Canadian Political Science Association Annual Meeting, 12th International Conference on Diversity, British Social Policy Association Conference, Australian Social Policy Conference, New Zealand Political Studies Association Conference, Sociological Association of Aotearoa (New Zealand) Conference and at various University of Auckland seminars. I appreciate all the feedback I have been given.

Martin van Randow at the University of Auckland's Centre of Methods & Policy Application, has been particularly helpful, but other colleagues have also read or commented upon parts of the book, including: Maureen Baker, Daniel Edmiston, Peter Skilling, Gerry Cotterell, Bruce Curtis, Charles Crothers and the book's anonymous reviewers. I have also benefited from research assistance on related research projects from: Lis Cotter; Catherina Muhamad-Brandner; Stephen McTaggart; Rebecca Walsh; Tanja Ottaway; Angela Maynard; Ieti Lima; Louise Crehan; Julia Scott and Alex Lee. Appreciation also goes to Emily Watt, Rebecca Tomlinson and Laura Vickers at the Policy Press for answering my many questions.

Finally, thanks must go to my ever-patient partner, Bradley Smith; I have been writing this book almost as long as I have known him and I look forward to seeing more of him now it is complete!

ONE

Introduction: from social citizenship to active citizenship

When I was growing up in New Zealand in the 1970s, we were in the middle of a global economic recession. The impact this had on my family was softened by the confidence that we had a right to healthcare, education and a job paying decent wages. Admittedly, my family would not have articulated this using the language of *rights*; instead, we held an unconscious expectation that the state would play an important role in supporting key aspects of our lives. These assumptions were gendered: my father expected his job as a Post Office telephone engineer would also support his wife and four children, with his union negotiating wages and conditions to this end, while my mother received the universal Family Benefit which recognised the costs and value of bringing up children and the societal impact of poverty among the young. Low interest government loans encouraged home ownership but we lived in a state housing area, where 'fair rent' provisions ensured decent housing for all New Zealanders. When we were sick, we paid only a nominal fee to the local General Practitioner because the state subsidised private doctors. Emergency services at hospital were completely free. My siblings and I also attended the local state primary and secondary schools without charge and, when my brother entered university in the early 1980s, he paid minimal student union fees while the cost of his degree was funded by the state.

As New Zealand settles into the second decade of the 21st century, we are emerging from another significant recession, caused by the global financial crisis of 2008–09. But times have changed. The parents of a child growing up today are likely to find themselves in employment that is far less secure than it was 30 years ago, with part time and casual work common. Most negotiate their wages and conditions directly with their employers because the national wage arbitration system has been abandoned. Low and middle income parents may receive tax credits to relieve the cost of bringing up children but the universal Family Benefit was abolished in 1991, when benefit levels were cut and never resurrected. The unemployed are subject to new disciplinary mechanisms aiming to get them into work, despite poor economic conditions reducing job supply. There are fewer state houses, while the private rental and housing markets have become increasingly unaffordable. The state still subsidises primary and emergency healthcare but the idea of 'user-pays' has become normalised in both healthcare and in education. My brother's degree would now cost him around NZ$18,000 in tertiary tuition fees, even though young New Zealanders have been spared the 2011 increases of almost 275% seen in the United Kingdom (UK) and other recent 'austerity' measures adopted in Europe and North America.

This book tells the story of the significant policy changes that led to these quite different experiences for New Zealand families today. But its major interest is in how these changes have shaped public attitudes about, and expectations of, the welfare state. Policy in democratic countries is often expected to be consistent with public demands, given that governments are formed by parties elected by citizens. But this book has been influenced by growing interest in 'policy feedback' processes which suggest that what the public wants and expects is shaped by the policy settings that structure our lives.

The rights to decent work, healthcare, education and welfare assistance in times of need that my family took for granted are collectively known as 'social citizenship'. Put simply, this refers to the state guaranteeing a basic level of economic and social security to all citizens. Policies institutionalising social citizenship were introduced by governments in New Zealand and other western democracies from the 1930s and 1940s. These assumed that the government would take responsibility for ensuring minimum conditions in education, healthcare, housing and income (usually institutionalised through the 'welfare state') (Roche, 1992; Taylor-Gooby, 2008). Full employment was also a key focus of economic policies and this book builds on the work of key scholars who argue that social rights of citizenship include a right to satisfying work and human self development[1] (Esping-Andersen, 1990; Orloff, 1993; Room, 2000; Stephens, 2010). This is appropriate given that all three countries discussed in this book – New Zealand, the UK and Australia – have been characterised as 'liberal welfare states' where the labour market is considered the first source of welfare, supported by comparatively low levels of social benefits and a restrictive approach to eligibility for and duration of benefits (Esping-Andersen, 1990; Jenson and Saint-Martin, 2003). It is also appropriate since employment has been a key focus of welfare state reform (Vandenbroucke, 2002).

Social citizenship was more an ideal-type than a policy reality in some countries and remained a contested concept (Siltanen, 2002; Bode, 2008; Dean, 2013). But evidence of widespread (if uneven) public endorsement of social rights suggests there is a relationship between the types of policies that governments implement (and the way in which they talk about them) and public attitudes (Mettler and Soss, 2004). A shift in public opinion might, therefore, be expected as significant economic and social changes challenged the socio-political framework that supported social citizenship rights and their realisation from the 1970s.

Following the lead of its British and United States (US) counterparts, New Zealand's fourth Labour government responded to an economic crisis in the mid-1980s by adopting 'neoliberal' policies that opened up its highly protected economy, privatised key state assets, deregulated the labour market and reshaped social policy along market lines. Moreover, citizens became reframed as *consumers* of services who should pay for the benefits they gain as part of a greater focus on *citizen responsibilities*. These reforms are frequently characterised as a radical shift in government thinking about social citizenship rights. But did they have a similarly significant impact on public support for these rights?

A process of neoliberalisation has taken place almost everywhere and neoliberal values dominate most aspects of political and economic life, suggesting this would be the case. But the analysis in this book is informed by theorising that highlights considerable variance in neoliberalism's implementation across time, countries and policy areas:

• Crucially, this book explores whether a new phase of neoliberalism emerging from the 2008–90 financial crisis saw the public 'roll-over' and accept neoliberal norms and values because they were persuaded by the messages coming from the political elites or simply could see no alternative, particularly given the economic context. It finds that early neoliberal reforms usually generated considerable public opposition, leading to policy reversals in some areas. Indeed, as Chapter Two argues, internal crises in part caused by public concern about the negative social outcomes of a neoliberal economic agenda have seen politicians modify neoliberalism to win elections. Recent global protests such as the Occupy movement and anti-austerity protests in countries like Greece, Spain and the UK indicate that such contestation continues today. However, although social rights have traditionally been endorsed and promoted by the ideological Left, support for some aspects of social citizenship diminished more significantly under Third Way Labour governments in the 2000s than they did under harsher, conservative regimes of the 1980s and

1990s. This book argues that this provided a platform for renewed retrenchment in the late 2000s with lesser public resistance than seen two decades earlier, suggesting neoliberal reforms and values have become normalised and accepted by the public.

• However, neoliberalism's impact differs depending on what policy area is being discussed, and sometimes even the specific policy design or the particular discourses used to promote a policy. Thus, there has been a significant hardening of attitudes towards the unemployed but this trend is far weaker when it comes to healthcare, education and superannuation. Attitudes towards economic policy are more mixed.

• Select comparisons between New Zealand, the UK and Australia also highlight considerable coherence in neoliberalism's impact upon public attitudes towards social citizenship; notably, social security is an area where attitudes have hardened significantly across all three countries. But investigating policy variance between the differing countries identifies how policy shapes public views in ways that social citizenship advocates can use to their advantage.

Overall, the book's key findings indicate that neoliberalism *has* had a significant, but *incomplete* and *shifting*, impact on public attitudes towards employment and the unemployed, healthcare, education, pensions, tax and redistribution in New Zealand. The remainder of this chapter indicates the analytical framework used to draw these conclusions prior to providing a brief chapter overview.

Framework for analysis

To what degree and in what ways has neoliberalism shaped public attitudes towards social citizenship? In answering this question, the book follows the tradition of historical institutionalism, which is based on the belief:

> … that political processes can best be understood if they are studied over time; that structural constraints on individual actions, especially those emanating from government, are important sources of political behaviour; and that the detailed investigation of carefully chosen, comparatively informed case studies is a powerful tool for uncovering the sources of political change. (Pierson, 1993, p 596)

In this book, an extended, historical case study of New Zealand is used to explore the relationship between the broad process of policy change known as neoliberalisation and public attitudes towards social citizenship. Chapter Two provides both the theoretical and empirical context for this study, while this chapter simply indicates the methods by which policy change, attitudinal change and the relationship between the two will be analysed.

Analysing policy change

The measurement of welfare state change, in particular welfare state retrenchment, has been a major focus of intellectual interest over the last three decades (Pierson, 1994; Clasen and Siegel, 2007; Starke, 2008). But there has been little standardisation in either the welfare state or political science literatures (Castles, 2004; Burstein, 2010). As discussion below indicates, this book will look at policy change at both the 'big picture' level of neoliberalism and at the level of policy design and discourse in specific areas.

Neoliberalism as a coherent and diverse process

In the first instance, this book explores the deceptively simple question of whether social citizenship matters less to New Zealanders in 2011 than it did in 1990 as a result of the quite differing policy contexts found in each era. However, a novel feature is its adaptation of Peck and Tickell's (2002) argument that the process of neoliberalisation has seen multiple phases of neoliberalism over time.

New Zealand represents an ideal case for such an analysis because its early neoliberal reforms have been characterised as some of the most radical and rapid in the world, given that a unitary parliamentary system allowed a switch in policy direction without broad political consensus (Kelsey, 1997; Esping-Andersen, 2002; Roper, 2005; Starke, 2008). This type of retrenchment of the welfare state has been characterised by Peck and Tickell (2002) as a 'roll-back' phase of neoliberalism. However, public dissatisfaction with such reforms was also a major factor behind the adoption of a Mixed Member Proportional (MMP) representation system from 1996, suggesting that radical policy does not necessarily result in equally radical shifts in public views of social citizenship (Vowles et al, 1995; Schmidt, 2002). Schmidt (2001) further believes that the transformative power of discourse is in its absorption by an opposition party. New Zealand's early period of neoliberal retrenchment was followed by nine years of the Third Way politics of Labour-coalition governments that arguably retained a neoliberal economic agenda but attempted to address public concerns with its social impacts through a focus on 'social inclusion' to be achieved through 'social development'. This characterises the 'roll-out' phase that embeds and legitimates neoliberalism (Peck and Tickell, 2002). This book argues that the return of a conservative National government since 2008 characterises a 'roll-*over*' phase whereby the legitimisation of a neoliberal economic agenda in the 2000s and a further economic crisis has allowed a new wave of retrenchment but one that places a greater focus on social policy than in the 1980s and 1990s.

New Zealand clearly offers a good opportunity to analyse whether neoliberalism's destructive or constructive moments have had a greater effect on the public's views (Brenner and Theordore, 2002). But selective comparisons with the UK and Australia add further depth, indicating where New Zealand's experiences are unique and where there is coherence in both the neoliberal project and its impact. Chapter Two notes some differences in the way social citizenship rights were institutionalised in each country yet all three are commonly regarded as 'liberal welfare states' and have strong historical connections, given that New Zealand and Australia are both former British colonies (Esping-Andersen, 1990; Pearson, 2002). Importantly, each country also alternated between conservative and Labour governments over the past three decades, allowing an assessment of whether any change in New Zealand attitudes is associated with neoliberalism or, rather, a particular political context.

However, *differences* in the timing and the speed of neoliberal reforms in Australia provide an interesting means by which to investigate variation in neoliberalism's effect on public opinion. It is difficult to theorise Australia as having clear roll-back and roll-out phases given that the Labor government's (1983–1996) initial reform period was far more incremental and balanced than that of New Zealand and the UK. The conservative Liberal-National Coalition government's (1996–2007) attempts to complete the roll-back reforms were also hindered by its lack of control in the Federal Senate. It was not until 2007 that a Labor government was returned and began implementing the kind of roll-out policies seen in the UK and New Zealand from the late 1990s. In part this was possible because the global financial crisis had a far lesser impact in Australia than in the latter two countries where, by the late 2000s, conservative governments were adopting austerity measures. This book's analysis of neoliberalism in its 'actually existing' circumstances thus acknowledges the variegated nature of neoliberalism and questions whether this has resulted in an equally varied attitudes towards social citizenship in differing national settings (Brenner and Theodore, 2002; Brenner et al, 2010).

Policy design and discourse

Initial indications that the financial crisis might provide the space for a significant challenge to neoliberalism have not (yet) been fulfilled (Callinicos, 2010; Crouch, 2011; Gough, 2011). I believe debate about alternative economic and political strategies should consider the potential that social citizenship still holds as an organising framework for citizenship, while acknowledging it requires some revision in the 21st century (Dean, 2004a; Taylor-Gooby, 2008). Dean (2013, p S2) notes: 'Social citizenship is best conceptualised as a multilayered process of social negotiation. It is constituted through the recognition and claiming of needs, the acknowledgement of claims as rights and the formulation of rights in specific social contexts'. This book is thus partly driven by a desire to identify how policy design and discourse shapes public views in ways that social citizenship advocates can use to their advantage. It takes seriously arguments that the welfare state cannot be treated as one single object; instead it is necessary to differentiate between distinct policy sectors when trying to understand welfare policies and politics (Mau, 2003; Wendt et al, 2011). This is particularly so given that neoliberalism has been more successfully implemented in some policy areas than in others. It is likely public attitudes on social citizenship issues are loosely integrated at best (Matthews and Erickson, 2005; Bode, 2008; Wendt et al, 2011). Analysing public attitudes across multiple policy sites thus allows us to assess the impact of neoliberalism in different policy realms.

The book focuses on four key policy areas where neoliberal reforms have provided a significant challenge to social citizenship:

- **Economic policy relating to employment**, including economic deregulation and privatisation directly impacting upon work opportunities and thus the right to decent employment and wages;

- **The social security system** (increasingly referred to as 'welfare'), which provides income support to the unemployed, single parents, the sick and disabled. Although the 'worker citizen' has historically been framed as most 'deserving' in liberal welfare states (Turner, 2001), the stigma attached to worklessness has been strengthened by increasing levels of targeting and conditions placed on benefit receipt, as well as a discourse focused on 'active citizenship'. These impact upon the social right to economic and social security;

- **Healthcare, education and superannuation**, which have traditionally been available to a wide population (in some cases through 'universal' access) but have been increasingly marketised and privatised, threatening the right to health, education and economic security in old age;

- **Tax and redistributive policies**, given progressive taxation and direct forms of redistribution have traditionally been used to reduce inequality and poverty. Flatter tax systems and the greater use of tax credits to top up low and middle incomes have challenged the principle of equality.

When analysing policy change in these areas, I am interested not only in shifts in policy *institutions* but also changes in and the effectiveness of *discourses* used to promote policy, given that these are often the most significant aspect of policy change to which members of the public are exposed (Pierson, 1994; Schmidt, 2002). As Chapter Two highlights, public awareness of policy practices and discourses is mediated by the media and is thus shaped by its biases and interests (Gamson, 1992; Stimson, 1999). The main New Zealand empirical case study thus draws upon historical and contemporary news media sources in New Zealand, as well as key policy documents, to identify the political discourses used to promote policy during the neoliberal era.

The book also builds upon arguments that the complexity of the welfare state requires a suite of indicators for measuring policy change (Clasen, 2005). Chapter Two highlights how attitudes towards some policy areas respond to shifts in social spending, so the book draws upon Organisation of Economic Co-operation and Development (OECD) data to note changes in the size of social expenditures as a proportion of Gross Domestic Product (GDP), a common means for measuring 'welfare state effort' (Korpi and Palme, 2003). Where possible, disaggregated expenditure data in specific policy areas is used (Castles, 2004). The public may also be unaware of the specific details of policy but still have sense of its perceived social impacts, even if causal relationships may not be clear. Cross-national comparisons for income inequality are often reported in the media, giving the public a sense of whether citizen outcomes have been improved beyond their own lived experience. As such, the book notes changes in the level of income inequality (as measured by the Gini coefficient) where relevant.

Finally, I am interested in whether *specific* policy programmes have had more impact upon attitudes and why. Investigating the latter draws upon theorising about how policies can have resource, interpretive or normative feedback effects that help shape public opinion, discussed in Chapter Two.

The New Zealand findings are supported by select comparisons with the UK and Australia which focus on key differences in policy design/implementation and their outcomes which may shape attitudes. These include:

- The speed and extremity of the early economic reforms adopted in New Zealand and the UK compared to Australia.

- The implementation of key neoliberal social security reforms, particularly since work for the dole was adopted only briefly in New Zealand and employment services have not been privatised to the same degree as the other two countries.

- The level of universality, given that New Zealand has the only universal superannuation scheme and the British National Health Service is the only fully universal health system across the three countries.

- Trends in income inequality, which grew faster in New Zealand between the mid-1980s and late 2000s than in the UK and, in particular, Australia.

In addition to these specific sites of analysis, attention is paid to two key factors that may mediate the policy impact on attitudes to social citizenship. Chapter Two notes evidence that economic conditions can shape public attitudes. Although change in economic growth and inflation have been used as indicators of economic conditions in other studies (Lewis-Beck, 1988; Crothers and Vowles, 1993; Nadeau et al, 2000; Nadeau and Lewis-Beck, 2001), they appear to have little or no impact on attitudes. The unemployment rate has thus been chosen as the most appropriate indicator and, where relevant, claims made about the influence of policy on opinion are tested by assessing the relationship between shifts in public attitudes and unemployment levels.

Second, the roles that significant alternative public discourses have played in challenging the neoliberal policies, implemented or promoted are considered. These are important because opinion surveys — which are the main source of data for this book — are only one way in which public opinion is expressed (Manza and Cook, 2002). Burstein (2010) argues that many opinion-policy studies ignore such factors or tend to assume that the activity of interest organisations, media coverage and other factors are in competition with each other when instead these factors may overlap or interact with policy. A qualitative analysis allows for deeper consideration of these factors than most studies of public opinion offer, drawing attention to the 'public realm' which Clarke (2004, p 44) believes 'is part of the "grit" that prevents the imagined neo-liberal world system functioning smoothly' and is testimony to the limits of neoliberalism's dominance.

Analysing attitudinal change

More attention has been paid to standardising opinion measurement cross-nationally than policy change, but it remains that opinion surveys do not usually include questions about specific policies, certainly over time (Burstein, 2010). To get around this problem, researchers routinely employ measures of public opinion arguably related to policy issues but not specific to particular policies. For instance, Brooks and Manza (2007) measured the impact of public opinion on social welfare expenditures in 16 democratic countries by considering changes in attitudes towards the government's responsibility to provide jobs and reduce income differences between the rich and poor because there was no specific public opinion data about expenditures.

I have faced a similar problem because surveys do not ask specific questions about 'social citizenship'. To tap into this concept, the book explores responses to questions about government and its responsibility to ensure a decent standard of living for the unemployed and old people, to spend funds gained through taxation on welfare benefits, pensions, healthcare and education and to ensure redistribution of income and wealth. The 'public' represents a multiplicity of intersecting communities, groups and individuals (Clarke, 2004) but when I talk about 'public support' for social citizenship, I refer to the *collective* normative beliefs and opinions of the New Zealand public as recorded in public opinion surveys. Generally discussion focuses on affirmative responses (for example, those who 'agree' and 'strongly agree' with a particular proposition posed in a survey) because this offers the best sense of support for key aspects of social citizenship.

I have also had to draw upon a range of different data sets to make an assessment of public attitudes in this area. The main case study, however, extensively utilises data from the New Zealand Election Study (NZES, 1990–2011). This became a *national* survey only six years after the 4th Labour government began neoliberal reforms in 1984 but it nonetheless provides the most comprehensive and regular data set on social citizenship issues in New Zealand, making it ideal for tracking changes in attitudes over time. This data is supplemented where appropriate by smaller, one-off studies, such as the 1987 New Zealand Attitudes and Values Survey conducted as part of the Royal Commission on Social Policy (1988a), and less regular surveys like the New Zealand Values Study and the International Social Survey Programme.

International data is drawn from electronic depositories or secondary sources providing expert analyses of the British Social Attitudes survey (1983–2011), British Election study (1966–2010), Australian Social Attitudes survey (2003–2011) and Australian Election Study (1987–2010). These studies have asked questions relating to social citizenship that are relatively similar to those in the New Zealand study but direct comparison is complicated by different question wording and survey methodologies. In particular, it can be problematic to compare election surveys drawing a sample from the election roll (as the NZES does) with others that randomly sample the general population. However, compulsory voter registration and regular oversampling for marginalised population groups mean the NZES is likely to be more representative of the total population than many election surveys. More generally, voter turnout has declined (with numerous fluctuations) from the exceptionally high levels apparent in the 1940s and 1950s but around three quarters of registered New Zealand electors generally participate in elections (Vowles, 2012). More details about all of the surveys discussed above can be found in the Appendix.

A further novel aspect of the book is that it draws upon a New Zealand qualitative interview and focus group study involving 87 individuals from a wide range of backgrounds that was conducted in 2007–08 (see Appendix). Following Dean and Melrose's (1999) lead, selected questions from quantitative surveys were used as talking points for the interview and focus group discussions, enabling some 'bench-marking' of attitudes of the qualitative participants against much bigger quantitative samples and further discursive exploration of questions frequently asked in surveys. In that the usual 'global' questions about support for public services often confuse which *groups* ought to be supported with which *services* ought to be supported and do not tease out respondents' reactions to each separately (Crothers, 1988), specific and current policy examples were discussed in the qualitative study. This qualitative research provides a rare depth to the book's analysis of New Zealand attitudes to social citizenship and the role policy and its discourses have had in shaping them. As such, it heeds the call by Mettler and Soss (2004) for more interpretative, citizen-centred approaches to policy feedback.

When analysing this attitudinal data, I am chiefly interested in collective patterns and, as noted, the public is treated as a single unit (Matthews and Erickson, 2008). Many early analyses of public opinion concluded that respondents had no real attitudes, were confused or simply lacked sufficient political knowledge to respond appropriately. But Page and Shapiro (1992) argue that it is possible to accurately measure real and stable collective public opinion, even while the individual responses from which such opinion is constituted may appear unstable. They contend:

> The simple process of adding together or averaging many individuals' survey responses, for example, tends to cancel out the distorting effects of random errors in the measurement of individuals' opinions. And social processes involving division of labor and collective deliberation mean that collective opinion responds — more fully and attentively than most individuals can hope to do — to new events and new information and arguments. (Page and Shapiro, 1992, p 15).

Shifts in the attitudes of sub-groups of the population are thus explored only where this helps to theorise about neoliberalism's impact.

For instance, it has been argued that ideological distinctions between political parties are narrowing and, in particular, the Third Way represents a shift away from the 'Old Left' values, associated with socialist, social democratic and working class parties and support for state intervention, ownership and control, along with social justice. I am therefore interested in whether NZES respondents self-identifying as having a 'Left' or 'Centre' position on the ideological spectrum have begun to adopt values traditionally associated with the 'Right', that is, conservative parties supporting the free market and individual freedom (Gold and Webster, 1990; Vowles and Aimer, 1993; Plant, 2004). Although not without some issues (see Chapter Two), self-placement on an ideological scale has been widely used as a measure of ideological position (Kumlin and Svallfors, 2007; Cook and Czaplewski, 2009; Wilson et al, 2012). New Zealand's MMP context means multiple smaller parties have come and gone across the 1990–2011 period, making the Left-Right measure more useful than party affiliation. Analysis shows that the largest proportion of NZES respondents identified with the ideological Centre in all eight election years studied. More respondents tended to associate with the Right than the Left and this was particularly noticeable in 1996. However, it is also difficult to argue that the proportion of respondents affiliating with the Left declined overall, given this was smallest in 1996 but Left affiliation then grew through the late 1990s and early 2000s, peaking in 2005, before diminishing again. Ideological affiliation in New Zealand thus appears to shift over time (see Chapter Two).

The book also considers differences between four age cohorts (<30 years, 31–45, 46–60 and >61 years), paying particular attention to whether the youngest group of respondents in the 2010s offered less support for particular propositions than their counterparts in 1990. This provides a means for assessing whether differences in attitudes found between younger and older NZES respondents are generational rather than associated with different stages of the life course. As such, the assumption that older New Zealanders might support social citizenship more than younger people because they have personal memories of the Keynesian welfare state can be assessed. These findings are clearly important given political decisions protecting superannuation at the expense of working age social security entitlements in recent years are often said to be related to the greater political participation – and thus electoral power – of older citizens (Duffy et al, 2013).

Given theorising that neoliberalism may have changed individual conceptions of self-interest by reducing support for social rights even among those who have the most to gain from an expansive welfare state, Chapter Five also analyses whether attitudes towards social security have hardened most among benefit recipients who are subject to increasing levels of work-related obligations under neoliberalisation. Shifts in their views are compared to those of superannuitants and students (who receive income support with relatively few conditions attached) and wage/salary earners. Finally, Chapter Seven considers whether shifts in attitudes towards tax, redistribution and inequality have differed among respondents on low, middle and high incomes, as identified by dividing self-reported respondent household incomes into three bands for each survey year.

Influenced by the work of Page and Shapiro (1992), Table 1.1 indicates the indicators of change in public attitudes used in this book. The percentage change indicated refers to an *absolute* percentage point increase or decrease in support for a particular proposition in each time period. A 'fluctuation' is said to occur when there are reversals in the direction of opinion change within a given time interval. The

Table 1.1: Indicators of change in public support over three key time periods

	3 year period	3–14 year period	15 year + period
Significant (%)	5+	10+	15+
Moderate (%)	3–4.9	5–9.9	10–14.9
Slight (%)	2–2.9	3–4.9	5–9.9
Steady	Fluctuations of less than 2% across entire period	Fluctuations of less than 3% across entire period	Fluctuations of less than 4% across entire period

smallest period over which change is examined is three years, given the majority of the New Zealand data comes from the NZES, which is tied to the three-yearly election cycle. The book's major focus will be on significant changes over as long as period as possible. In many cases this is 21 years, but some questions were included in the survey only for a shorter time period. Although the 3–14 year period indicated in the third column may seem rather broad, it accommodates the period of time a particular government was in power across all three countries. No government was in power for 15 years or more, allowing the final key time period to reflect broader attitudinal change.

Assessing the relationship between policy change and attitudes

The greatest hurdle in understanding how neoliberalism may have influenced attitudes is that there is also no one established way of measuring the relationship between policy and attitudes, with widespread recognition that it is difficult to trace concrete causal linkages between policy and public attitudes (Pierson, 1993; Hills, 2002; Gusmano et al, 2002; Burstein, 2010). When researchers have focused on effects on public opinion, they have usually done so by examining how policies affect the political attitudes and behaviours of policy 'target populations' (Edelman, 1971; Skocpol, 1992; Pierson and Hacker, 2005; Soss and Schram, 2007). Even then it is often difficult to separate policy out from other key explanations of how political dispositions are determined by an individual's self-interest (with rational choices based on expected utility), position within social structures, contexts and networks and underlying identities, beliefs, values, attitudes and symbolic predispositions (Cook and Barrett, 1992; Mettler and Soss, 2004).

Emerging from an intellectual tradition which explains mass opinion and behaviour via the interplay of state structures and institutions, political actions and communication flows, mobilisation and demobilisation, this book thus focuses on the public as the unit of analysis and treats public opinion as emerging from an overtly political context. I aim to assess whether there is congruence between attitudes and policy over time. There are multiple ways of assessing congruence (Burstein, 2010) but I follow the lead of Page and Shapiro (1983) who adopted a 'covariation' approach, which is possible when the public in a particular political unit is asked about the same policy more than once, or publics in different political units are asked about the same policy. If differences in policy preferences over time are associated with comparable differences in policy, then there is covariance between opinion and policy and opinion is seen as potentially having affected policy.

Plan of the book

Chapter One has identified the key policy shift that drives the book and provided a framework for analysing the impact neoliberalism has had on public attitudes to social citizenship. Chapter Two explores how neoliberalism challenged the institutional and normative framework that supported social citizenship in most western countries during the post–World War II period in some detail, before reviewing what previous empirical studies tell us about the relationship between policy and attitudes. Chapter Three tells the fascinating story of New Zealand policy and politics between the mid-1980s and 2011. Discussion of the three key phases of neoliberalism as they played out in New Zealand is punctuated by analysis of key policy differences in the UK and Australia, providing the basis for comparison with the New Zealand case study data presented in Chapters Four to Seven, which each deal with one of key policy areas studied. Chapter Eight draws together findings from these four chapters, considering patterns across the three case study countries, as well as across policy areas and phases of neoliberalism. It concludes that neoliberalism *does* matter and by the 2010s the public *had* rolled-over and accepted some of its key tenets. But there is also evidence of 'grit' that could destabilise neoliberalism in the future. These broader findings are used to engage with recent proposals aiming to revitalise social citizenship in the 21st century.

Note
[1] T.H. Marshall (2000), a key intellectual figure in conceiving social citizenship, identified work as a basic civil right.

TWO

Social citizenship, neoliberalism and attitudinal change

The pivotal shift from a Keynesian policy regime that institutionalised social citizenship to one driven by neoliberal values is central to this book. Providing important background to Chapter Three's more specific discussion of how this shift played out in New Zealand, discussion here first highlights the importance of social citizenship as an intellectual concept. Importantly, however, this concept was widely institutionalised and – according to the limited evidence available – widely supported in the period following World War II. By the 1970s and 1980s, however, significant economic and political challenges threatened the institutions supporting social citizenship. The major focus here is on the process of neoliberalisation and how it transformed citizenship, making it more market-focused and oriented towards active labour market participation. The second part of this chapter outlines this process, which I understand to have been implemented across three phases but with differing levels of success in varied policy areas and countries. Drawing upon existing empirical evidence, a third section explores what the empirical literature tells us about neoliberalism's potential impact upon public opinion. It also highlights good reasons why these findings may not necessarily be applicable to the New Zealand case, illustrating why the kind of historical, multi-faceted analysis that this book provides is required.

The rise and fall of social citizenship

Although the earliest discussion of social citizenship emerged in the late nineteenth century, British sociologist Marshall (2000[1]) was the first to theorise social rights as part of a combined package alongside civil and political rights that formed modern citizenship. His historical account aimed to explain why the post-war welfare state emerged in the United Kingdom (UK) in the late 1940s, extending to citizens the universal right to an extensive set of state-guaranteed social and economic provisions; that is, social citizenship (Roche, 1992; Dwyer, 2004a). For Marshall (2000) it was necessary to meet an individual's basic economic and social needs not only to reduce poverty and inequality but also to activate civil and political rights that ensured full participation in society. As an ideal-type, social citizenship therefore 'stands for a set of institutionalised ties between members of a (political) collectivity that are grounded in common rights and duties, with the former being a prerequisite to the fulfilment of the latter' (Bode, 2008: 193).

Many commentators have challenged Marshall's (2000) model, in part because what 'citizenship' actually entails is debated. When we speak of citizenship, we generally imply membership of some type of community, usually a 'nation state' (such as New Zealand, the UK or Australia). Citizenship can also refer to a social status (for instance, being a citizen rather than a permanent resident or a temporary visitor) that allows people to make claims in relation to the state (Dwyer, 2004a). However:

> Citizenship, broadly defined, is not simply a way to identify subjects with political rights in any abstract way. It is also an important political tool for the state, which, in defining citizenship, sets the conditions for full membership in the political community. In addition, it is a way for political actors who may use citizenship vocabulary to seek inclusion in the polity. (Jenson and Papillon, 2001, p 2)

This dual relationship (between individuals who are members of a community and between individuals and the state) means there is often conflict around the purpose of citizenship: should it promote solidarity among citizens or protect the rights of individuals? Although noting this is a rather simplistic distinction, Dwyer (2004a) argues that the two major traditions theorising citizenship have different responses to these questions. Liberalism, for instance, stresses the importance of individually held rights. In contrast, communitarianism or civic republicanism focuses on individuals' commitments and obligations to a wider community.

Marshall's (2000) views on social citizenship emerged from the liberal tradition, incorporating both classical and social liberal notions of citizenship rights. Liberalism developed in the 17th century, promoting civil and political rights as the means by which the limited state guaranteed the freedom and formal equality of the individual who is sovereign (Lister, 2003a). According to Marshall (2000), civil rights were institutionalised in the 18th century, political rights in the 19th century, and social rights in the 20th century, as part of a constant search for stability and equilibrium between democratic equality and guarantees of individual freedom (Jenson and Papillon,

2001). Regarding rights as embedded in developing social institutions and material conditions, Marshall (2000) characterises modern, democratic-welfare-capitalist societies as 'hyphenated societies', where citizenship consists of three interdependent components: a political democracy; a welfare state; and a market economy. He argues that all three must exist in equilibrium with each other in order to guarantee full citizenship status (Dean and Melrose, 1999; Dwyer, 2004a).

Marshall (2000) recognises the relationship between capitalism and citizenship to be dynamic and contradictory, given a permanent tension between the principles of equality that underpin democracy and the de facto inequalities of wealth and income that characterise the capitalist market place. But the redistribution of resources based on one's status as a citizen could mitigate the negative effects of economic class within capitalist society: if the state ensures citizens a decent standard of living when unemployed, sick or old, for instance, they are freed from dependency on wage labour (Gilbert, 2002). Later scholars refer to this as 'decommodification' or the degree to which welfare states substitute transfer payments and public services as social rights of citizenship for income and services to be allocated by the market (Esping-Andersen, 1990; Orloff, 1993; Room, 2000; Stephens, 2010).

If all citizens of all social classes received the same protections, Marshall (2000) argues, they would also be engaged in the same collective project grounded in state-based assurances of citizen equality and social progress with other members of a shared (national) community (Turner, 2001; Dwyer, 2004a). In this way, social policy could improve the possibilities for inclusive democratic politics and redefine the scope and meaning of citizenship. Although the view that universal social rights which accrue equally necessarily promote solidarity and inhibit stigma has been challenged (Gilbert, 2002; Hartman, 2005), Esping-Andersen's (1990) empirical work on welfare regimes certainly demonstrates how social policies can impose class stratification, foster new kinds of equality or inequality, promote solidarity to different degrees and alter citizens' dependence on states and markets (Mettler and Soss, 2004).

This highlights that social citizenship is not just an intellectual concept but became institutionalised through the development of a comprehensive welfare state to varying degrees across most western countries in the post-war period. Many governments established age pensions and public compulsory education from the late 19th century but welfare benefits and services were not properly considered citizenship rights in any meaningful sense at that time. The Great Depression saw unemployment and poverty increasingly attributed to structural factors, such as international business cycles, rather than individual idleness (Marshall, 2000; Gilbert, 2002; Dwyer, 2004a). Working class mobilisation through unions and Left-wing parties also contributed to the development of welfare states during this period (Myles and Quadagno, 2002). Social democratic governments gained power in many countries, promoting a socialist society through incremental change via democratic elections and a parliamentary Labour Party (Cheyne et al, 2008). As a result, a kind of equilibrium was attained in the form of 'welfare capitalism' and a 'mixed economy' between the late 1940s (earlier in some countries, like New Zealand) and the early 1970s, whereby the 'interventionist state had a crucial role in negotiating agreements with large capital and organised labour so a "class compromise" could be reached' (Bottomore, 1992, p 74).

This compromise was facilitated by the macroeconomic policies advocated by Keynes (1936), the British economist who did not believe economies are automatically self-correcting and advocated a counter-cyclical approach stimulating the economy in times of recession, for example through unemployment insurance and public works programmes, and weakening demand through taxation and control of money supply in times of potential inflation. He regarded the welfare state as a necessary means for ensuring a healthy and well-educated (and thus productive) population (Roche, 1992). Many countries were further influenced by British developments, including Beveridge's (1942) *Report of the Inter-Departmental Committee on Social Insurance and Allied Services*, which proposed the construction of what was effectively, although not explicitly or in principle, a new system of social rights to unemployment, disability and retirement income and to healthcare services (Roche, 1992). In this way, the welfare state was conceived as a collective strategy for managing the social and economic risks that citizens all faced (van der Veen, 2012a). The 1948 United Nations Universal Declaration of Human Rights, which incorporated substantive social and economic entitlements, helped extend the idea of social rights internationally, with all advanced industrial welfare states spawning a proliferation of claims to a range of increasingly generous social benefits with relatively little discussion of social responsibilities (Dean and Melrose, 1999; Dwyer, 2004a).

Peck and Tickell (2007, p 29) note that 'the Keynesian consensus of the post-World War II period was, in retrospect, a broad and variegated one'. There were certainly key differences in New Zealand, British and Australian policy and politics. Known as a 'social laboratory' at the end of the 19th century, New Zealand and Australia developed a system of occupational 'awards' (from 1894 in New Zealand and 1907 in Australia) that determined wages and governed employment relations. In the context of this 'wage-earners' welfare state', the two former colonies focused more on (male) *wage* security than *social* security but achieved extremely high standards of living during the post-war period, despite offering more 'residual' and less universal welfare state entitlements than found in the UK[2] (Castles, 1996; Ramia and Wailes, 2006; O'Connor and Robinson, 2008). It is also notable that social democratic Labour parties gained a much earlier hold in both colonies. New Zealand elected the world's first majority Labour government in 1935, something the UK did not achieve until 1945 (Alcock and Craig, 2001; Bryson, 2001).

While variation was clearly apparent, Table 2.1 highlights considerable coherence in the range of key policy settings supporting social rights (commonly referred to as the 'Keynesian welfare state'[3]). US President Nixon's 1971 declaration that he was also now a Keynesian shows how even the most liberal of countries developed some of the key institutions supporting social citizenship, even if social rights had little place in welfare debates in that country (Fraser and Gordon, 1994; Harvey, 2007). Bipartisan support for Keynesian

Table 2.1: Keynesian policies and values

Policy	Values
Keynesian economic management, including: • management of aggregate demand through fiscal (budgetary) policy • tight regulation of financial sector and international capital flows to ensure low-cost credit available for productive investment • tight control of foreign trade to manage balance of payments and protect/promote domestic manufacturing • controls on migration to exclude low wage labour and/or manage labour shortages • a policy of full (male) employment	Collectivism, focused on the interdependence of individuals within society Solidarity, based on common goals, experiences, interests, and sympathies, as well as the sharing of social risks (for instance, through unemployment insurance)
A 'welfare state', including: • education and healthcare services (often more or less free of charge) • entitlements to unemployment benefits and basic pensions (often via social insurance-based schemes but in some cases funded through general taxation)	Universalism, with all citizens having the right to access the same set of benefits and services
Redistribution of wealth and opportunity through: • 'horizontal' redistribution (between life stages) • 'vertical' redistribution (between richer and poorer groups)	Equality, with citizens sharing a common status in respect to the rights and duties they hold Altruism, with the welfare state providing the mechanism for a 'gift relationship' between citizens who are strangers

Sources: Titmuss, 1970; Jessop, 2002; Dwyer, 2004a; Bode, 2008; Cheyne et al, 2008; Taylor-Gooby, 2008.

policies certainly indicates a degree of political consensus that social rights were important, even if debate remained about how they were to be achieved (Roper, 2005; Harvey, 2007). But did this necessarily mean that the general public supported the notion of social citizenship? Taylor-Gooby (2008) has argued that for the welfare state to function and maintain popular support, it must endorse three key values underpinning social citizenship:

- Reciprocity, as indicated by a willingness to support horizontal redistribution between groups among the mass of the population.

- Inclusion, as indicated by an acceptance of vertical redistribution between the mass of the population and disadvantaged minorities.

- Trust that welfare services and provisions will work effectively and efficiently, other citizens will maintain their commitment to horizontal redistribution across different life stages when assistance is needed and that an inclusive benefit system targets those in need accurately. This nourishes the legitimacy of the system as a whole.

To a large degree these values were endorsed during the Keynesian era. The long boom saw incomes and living standards rise. Labour unions and the political Left had a very real influence on the state and most citizens benefited from interventionist policies in some way, encouraging a sense of solidarity (Taylor-Gooby, 2008). In providing 'an ideal citizenship against which achievement can be measured and towards which aspiration can be directed' (Marshall, 2000, p 36), Roche (1992) argues that a key post-war political objective was to construct and promote a 'myth' of social rights. Together with its associated ideas of equal membership status and social justice, this served an ideological function that became socially real and powerfully effective. He believes social citizenship reflected 'a personally and existentially real moral trust and political hope for many citizens in modern Western politics' (Roche, 1992, p 224), becoming an idea people felt it personally necessary to believe in, even when it did not necessarily match policy reality.

Relatively little is known about public opinion towards social citizenship prior to large data sets becoming common in the 1980s, but the available evidence indicates strong and relatively stable support for responsibility being taken by the government in a range of social policy areas (Taylor-Gooby, 1985; Page and Shapiro, 1992; McAllister, 1997; Svallfors, 2012). Coughlin (1980) undertook one of the most comprehensive early studies, reanalysing survey data from eight North

American and European countries across the post-war period with a focus on public support for particular welfare state provisions, satisfaction with services and support for welfare state spending. He found more similarities than differences across these countries and across time, noting a striking absence of hard-core laissez-faire ideology in public opinion. But his findings nonetheless hint at the complexity of understanding public attitudes towards social citizenship, even in the Keynesian welfare state period. Despite strong support for assuring minimum standards of employment, healthcare, income, and other conditions of social and economic wellbeing, he concludes that '[t]he prevailing ideological climate in each of the eight nations is mixed and is not dominated by extremes of ideology' (Coughlin, 1980, p 31). An ideological orientation towards 'collectivism' was thus attractive only in so far as it did not appear to threaten the cherished values and beliefs of individualism. Svallfors (2010) also notes that clear support for welfare policies coexisted with considerable ambivalence, notably towards welfare abuse/cheating and bureaucratic inefficiencies in the public sector. Public attitudes in the post-war period were thus not ideologically pure even as they, overall, endorsed the types of Keynesian policies adopted across the advanced industrial world.

By the mid-1970s, the economic and social context that had helped institutionalise social citizenship was changing. Deindustrialisation saw jobs shift from manufacturing to the service and knowledge industry sectors, diminishing the ability of workers to find a collective interest and to promote them through union mobilisation (Huber and Stephens, 2001; Pierson, 2001; Jessop, 2002). Alongside rapid technological innovation and the expansion of welfare rights, many workers became relatively 'affluent' or 'middle class' in terms of quality of life and values (Bottomore, 1992). 'Old politics' focused on material concerns and the state ownership and intervention that drove welfare state expansion was challenged by a 'new politics' associated with 'post-material' issues, such as environmental preservation, women's equality and identity politics. This new politics is thought to have reduced ideological distinctions between Left and Right (Inglehart, 1997; Clark and Lipset, 1991; Vowles et al, 1995).

Bourdieu (1998, p 34), however, regards the globalisation of production, finance and the labour market across national boundaries as 'the main weapon in the battles against the gains of the welfare state'. In refocusing governments on enhancing economic efficiency and international competitiveness, countries with minimum wage protections and strong trade union mobilisation were pitted against those who did not, diminishing support for national industries through trade protections and subsidies (Hall, 2002; O'Connor and Robinson, 2008; Taylor-Gooby, 2008). Globalisation is not merely an effect of economic change but involves societies conceptualising themselves as part of a global order, both in terms of identity and in regards to who they perceive responsible for protecting and enforcing social rights (Beck, 2000; Held, 2006). Indeed, increasing levels of governance and policy-making at the supra-national level reshaped the way in which rights were conceptualised and activated (Jessop, 1999; Mishra, 1999; O'Connor and Robinson, 2008).

From the 1960s, new social movements certainly drew upon an international human rights discourse to focus attention on inequalities in accessing citizenship rights, which was often restricted or conditional for women, ethnic minorities and other marginalised groups (Williams, 1989; Turner, 2001; Lister, 2003a). The extension of social rights had provided the state with a new means for governing citizens through bureaucratic modes of administration and the professionalisation of social service provision, with many citizens feeling alienated by large welfare state bureaucracies whose entitlements were based on universalistic notions of citizenship (Dean, 2007; Wacquant, 2012). Government attempts to recognise difference, however, provoked concern that the material disadvantage experienced across all groups would be marginalised, weakening altruism and hampering the formation of a common political consciousness along class or labourist lines (Gitlin, 1995; Taylor-Gooby, 2008).

Given the wider range of social identities claimed and occupied, and with individuals less likely to be members of trade unions, churches and other traditional social institutions, responses to social risks are said to have become highly individualised rather than institutionally predetermined (Giddens, 1991; Bauman, 2001; Achterberg and Raven, 2012). This shift has been facilitated by a lifeworld marked by 'endemic insecurity', even among the middle classes, given the new social risks associated with globalisation, economic growth and technology (Beck, 1992; Bode, 2008; Taylor-Gooby, 2008).

These challenges suggest that not only did the goal of class solidarity become less important, but citizens became less focused on collective issues more broadly, while universal rights were increasingly challenged by particularist claims for improved recognition of difference. Such societal shifts coincided with the economic crises of the 1970s, which saw high inflation, weakening economic growth and rising unemployment, provoking arguments that the welfare state was not sustainable, requiring cost cutting and reductions in state services (Dean and Melrose, 1999; Jessop, 2002). Public expenditure was already under pressure from demographic changes, such as the baby boom and ageing populations, and growing expectations about the quality of public services (Piven and Cloward, 1971; Harvey, 2007). It is in trying to make sense of how such escalating public demands threatened welfare state legitimacy that scholars began to show interest in how 'public opinion matters' to welfare state development. The next section highlights that such challenges coincided with and contributed to an important new policy direction that totally reshaped the way governments conceived citizenship.

Citizenship transformed: markets, work and community

Neoliberalism can be understood as a theory and intellectual movement; a set of policies; a social practice; and a broad strategy to restructure power relations and institutions towards capitalist interests (Larner, 2000; Brand and Sekler, 2009; Mudge, 2011). This book is largely concerned with what Brand and Sekler (2009, p 6) call the *political* dimension of neoliberalism; that is, 'concrete neoliberal policies, practices and political discourses representing the compromises arising from the struggles of different social forces'.

This focus on struggle and compromise is important because the implementation of neoliberal policies in almost every country in the world appears to give credence to the 'there is no alternative' political rhetoric used to persuade electorates of the necessity of neoliberal reforms since the late 1970s. Neoliberalism is frequently ascribed a hegemonic, all-powerful status in much of the academic literature, being framed as 'a common sense of the times' (Peck and Tickell, 2002, p 381) and a 'planetary vulgate' aligned with major sources of political-economic power (Bourdieu and Wacquant, 2001, p 1). It was this view of neoliberalism as a 'strong discourse' (Bourdieu, 1998: 95) that initially drove this author's interest in the relationship between policy change and public attitudes towards social citizenship. Although Table 2.2 highlights a high level of coherence in the policies introduced under neoliberal forms of political-economic governance, analysis of public attitudes over time and space requires an understanding that neoliberalism is capable of diverse strategies and tactics between and within different countries (Larner, 2000; Harvey, 2007). Neoliberalism has been implemented:

> ... under conditions of military dictatorship as in Chile, imposed as so-called structural adjustment in line with the Washington Consensus, articulated with conservative

Table 2.2: Neoliberal policies and values

	Roll-back	Roll-out	Roll-over
Macro-economic policy	**Policy** Focused on reducing inflation Deregulation of trade, finance, labour market		
	Values Laissez-faire, with state intervention limited only to ensuring the same laws governing the market are applied to all		
Public expenditure and programmes	**Policy**		
	Significant cuts/targeting, leading to extensive welfare state retrenchment but not necessarily less social expenditure	Selective spending growth and welfare state expansion	Strategic cuts and greater targeting, leading to some welfare state retrenchment
	Values		
	Small government, limiting bureaucratic waste and inefficiency and decentralised decision-making	Social inclusion, requiring strategic social investment to build human capital	Small government, limiting bureaucratic waste and inefficiency and decentralising decision-making
Privatisation	**Policy**		
	Public assets sold Shift towards private provision of social services Introduction of user-pays	Public-private partnerships Continuing private provision and user-pays but some attention paid to equity	Renewed public asset sales/public-private partnerships Continuing private provision and user-pays
	Values		
	Choice and competitiveness, ensuring individuals are best able to pursue their self-interest	Service efficiency and effectiveness	Choice and competitiveness, ensuring individuals are best able to pursue their self-interest
Social security	**Policy**		
	Reductions in benefit eligibility/generosity Introduction of conditionality	Extension of conditionality but with greater focus on training/education	Extension of conditionality (sometimes supported by training/education)
	Values		
	Individualism, with citizens framed as responsible for ensuring their own wellbeing Active citizenship focused on citizen responsibilities, especially participation in paid labour market		
	Neopaternalist views on the family and causes of poverty	Neocommunitarian views about the balance between responsibilities and rights	Neopaternalist views on the family and causes of poverty

Sources: Etzioni, 1998; Larner, 2000; Peck & Tickell, 2002; Dwyer, 2004a, 2004b; Parker, 2004; Hartman, 2005; O'Connor & Robinson, 2008; Springer, 2010.

policies as in the US and UK, implemented in post-socialist countries in Eastern Europe or in more social-democratic ways as in Germany or the Scandinavian societies. (Brand and Sekler, 2009, p 5)

This diversity is due both to the existing institutions and national values found within each country and the ability of interest groups and electorates to mobilise around and against neoliberalism, at times mediating or even blocking its expression in policy (Schmidt, 2002; Mudge, 2011).

Neoliberalism has also had differing impacts *within* differing countries, being more successfully implemented in some policy areas more than others. Bode's (2008, p 207) study of social citizenship in the UK and Germany found both 'conceptual fragmentation', where universal rights still existed in some policy areas while a market model was apparent in others, and 'procedural fragmentation' resulting from the uneven outcomes in terms of coverage and quality produced by marketisation, despite a new discourse on rights to 'consumer empowerment'. This twofold process generated a 'hybrid configuration', whereby governments selectively retained parts of the social citizenship agenda, while at the same time following a market model elsewhere. Indeed, despite much intellectual debate about the 'crisis' of the welfare state, even the most regressive reforms of the 1980s and 1990s did *not* completely dismantle welfare institutions and in many cases social spending continued to increase, particularly as economic conditions improved (Mishra, 1990; Pierson, 1994, 2001; Taylor-Gooby, 2008; Clarke and Newman, 2012).

This is why this book adopts the view that neoliberalism is a process constituting differing phases (Peck and Tickell, 2002; Hall, 2005; Craig and Cotterell, 2007; Brenner et al, 2010). Favouring a more nuanced, dynamic conception of neoliberal*isation* over static notions of neoliberal*ism* allows a focus on 'the prevailing pattern of regulatory restructuring, driven by a family of open-ended social processes and associated with polymorphic forms and outcomes' (Peck et al, 2009, p 101). Peck and Tickell (2002) argue there was an early 'proto' phase of neoliberalism, based in the abstract intellectualism of Hayek (1944) and Friedman (1962) which endorsed the principles of individual freedom, universalism as opposed to social and cultural particularisms, the primacy of the free market and small government. Although not widely known outside economic or political circles, these ideas were articulated prior to the sharp shift in policy from the late 1970s and may have begun to influence public opinion.

Social citizenship's failure as a paradigm to fulfil the promise of reciprocity, inclusion and trust (evident in rising social spending, public expectations and concern about the effectiveness of bureaucracy) certainly set part of the context but it was the economic crises of the 1970s that provided fertile ground for neoliberal ideas to be used to attack the welfare state. This gave rise to a 'roll-back' phase of neoliberalism whereby Keynesian institutions were dismantled through deregulation, dismantlement and discreditation. Low inflation and reducing public expenditure replaced full employment as the goal of macroeconomic policy. Trade, finance and labour market deregulation removed 'unnecessary' state involvement in the economy, while market logics were extended to almost all realms of policy, including healthcare and education via user-pays charges and the use of private providers (Larner, 2000; Peck and Tickell, 2002). Individuals were now responsible for unemployment, with reductions in the generosity of, and eligibility to, the social security system providing 'incentives' for the shift into paid work. Comparing the key roll-back policy reforms and the values driving them noted in Table 2.2 with those associated with the Keynesian welfare state (see Table 2.1), it is easy to see why the shift from a Keynesian to a neoliberal policy setting is frequently characterised as radical and transformative (Gilbert, 2002; Jessop, 2002; Starke, 2008).

Importantly, this retrenchment phase is said to have not only fundamentally reformed major post-war welfare institutions but also to have challenged the normative foundations of social citizenship in two key ways (Gilbert, 2002; Dwyer, 2004a; Bode, 2008). First, citizens were no longer regarded as holders of social rights but as consumers in the market. They thus had a right to information and to complain if a service did not meet set standards but could no longer rely on the state to guarantee particular rights and act on certain responsibilities (Dwyer, 2004a; Dean, 2007). This may have changed public expectations about citizenship entitlement, the collective provision of social needs and the efficacy of the welfare state in ways that works against the self-interest of users of public services (Larner, 2000). According to this marketised form of citizenship, the state was no longer directly responsible for delivering particular services or benefits, but instead indirectly accountable through the funding contracts held with non-government service providers (Dean et al, 2000; Freedland, 2001). Such providers were, however, governed through New Public Management technologies such as budget disciplines, accountancy and audit that made service outputs more open to the public. It is possible that a focus on consumer choice and agency has actually *enhanced* citizen expectations and motivated them to challenge perceived inadequacies in service, even if consumer rights have largely focused on 'choice' over modes of delivery not 'voice' in terms of democratic participation (Le Grand, 2003; Clarke and Newman, 2006).

Second, recognition of collectivist social rights was replaced by a focus on individual responsibility, given that inequality and social risk were understood as emerging from individual inadequacies rather than structural factors that the government could and would regulate (Dwyer, 2004a; Henman, 2007). With citizenship redefined as a contract rather than a status, entitlement became increasingly contingent upon a person's attachment to the labour market (Handler, 2004; Dean, 2013). Citizens were thus not only *re*commodified but their social rights became conditional on the fulfilment of compulsory responsibilities or duties. Usually achieved through coercion and surveillance, this arguably created a 'second-class' form of citizenship for benefit recipients and may have reshaped conceptions of self-interest by convincing those subjected to conditionality of its need and appropriateness (Gilbert, 2002; Dwyer, 2004b; Hartman, 2005; Wacquant, 2012). Conditionality principles are also thought to have impacted more broadly upon social solidarity and cohesion in the long term, with collectivism more likely to be conceived only in terms of a family's standard of living or individual prospects for career advancement than across society (Beck and Beck-Gernscheim, 2001; Shaver, 2001). This individualising of responsibility is said to constrain reciprocity, contradict inclusion and undermine important aspects of public and political trust (Taylor-Gooby, 2008; Wendt et al, 2011).

The idea that these significant shifts in government thinking around citizenship will have diminished public support for social rights is endorsed by arguments that neoliberalism's power as an ideological tool stems from its ability to mobilise support in a number of different ways and thus 'makes sense' to people in a range of different social positions. This is possible because neoliberalism draws upon traditions that sit in tension with each other in a shifting and multi-layered manner (Hall, 1988, 2005; Larner, 2000; Harvey, 2007; Peck et al, 2009). Neoclassical economic theories of consumer sovereignty, for instance, were central to the roll-back phase, employed to argue that individuals have the best knowledge of their needs in the market, and that state provision inhibits their freedom of choice. Yet the rolling back of social security was framed by a neopaternalist view that some individuals lack the right values and attitudes to choose the *right* thing and thus should be disciplined through work obligations, so as to overcome intergenerational welfare dependency and poverty (Murray, 1984; Mead, 1997; Dean and Melrose, 1999; Henman, 2007). Giddens (1994) notes a further tension in neoliberalism's hostility towards tradition (reflected in marketisation and individualisation) yet its dependence on the persistence of tradition for legitimacy in areas of nation, religion, gender and family. In liberal welfare states, some commentators regard Keynesianism and neoliberalism as representing different points on a liberal continuum, highlighting continuity in the values promoted under both that may have made the significant policy shifts that occurred less visible to the public (Siltanen, 2002; Craig and Porter, 2005; Dean, 2007; O'Connor and Robinson, 2008).

Neoliberalism's power further stems from the way it is not constituted and exercised exclusively on the terrain of the state (Leitner et al, 2007). The roll-back of state provision was accompanied by a contracting out process that subjected a range of profit and non-profit providers to neoliberal agendas and gave them a stake in maintaining the neoliberal order. Decentralisation and privatisation made it more difficult to know where neoliberal governance began and ended and less likely that citizens saw themselves benefiting from national or collective institutions (Larner and Butler, 2005; Craig and Porter, 2006; Taylor-Gooby, 2013). Alongside the consumer orientation noted, the privatisation of social services also likely addressed some of the public's frustrations with the mass bureaucratic approach of one-size-fits-all, universal services that could not be tailored to individual needs (Harris, 1999; Parker, 2004; Clarke and Newman, 2006; Humpage, 2008).

Springer (2010) indicates that first wave reforms were often introduced rapidly, as a purported response to collective crises or disasters at precisely the moment when societies were too disoriented to mount meaningful contestation. This undermined collective institutions (such as trade unions and the voluntary sector) that traditionally led claims against the state (Taylor-Gooby, 2013). Viewing neoliberalism as a process not an end state, however, means our analysis does not conclude with the period of retrenchment that characterises 'neoliberalism' for many people. Importantly, while the first shift from proto- to roll-back neoliberalism was associated with an *external* economic crisis, *internal* contradictions and tensions provoked a further shift towards what Peck and Tickell (2002) refer to as a 'roll-out' phase focused on the purposeful construction and consolidation of neoliberalised state forms, modes of governance and regulatory relations. While neoliberal economics largely succeeded in reducing inflation and public debt, it created new problems (high levels of private debt, income inequality and child poverty) over which governments have limited influence in a deregulated, globalised world (Roper, 2005). As the negative social and economic outcomes emerging from a narrow focus on marketisation became evident in the late 1980s and early 1990s, so did the institutional and political limits of roll-back neoliberalism.

In this book, the Third Way politics – at least in liberal welfare states – are conceived as representative of roll-out neoliberalism, rather than a new 'post-neoliberal' era (Green-Pedersen et al, 2001; Brand and Sekler, 2009). Hall (2002, p 36) argues that 'the new social democracy is conditioned by globalization and deeply committed to it', maintaining the fundamentally 'business friendly' economics of neoliberalism. Third Way governments thus made minor modifications to the deregulated regime established in the 1980s and 1990s but macroeconomic policy was still fundamentally concerned with low inflation and free trade. Advocates like Giddens (1998) argue that changes in socio-economic organisation, modes of cultural identities and ways of communicative interaction made a state-centred approach of traditional social democracy and a focus exclusively on distributive justice no longer feasible. The failure of social democratic policies to solve the economic crises of the 1970s and 1980s appeared to confirm that new responses were needed, not least to boost the popularity of social democratic parties among middle classes. This diversified their constituencies from largely traditional blue collar workers with a relatively homogenous social background and subsequent political preferences (P. Hall, 2002; Schmidtke, 2002; S. Hall, 2005).

Worried about the electoral ramifications of public disgruntlement with continued retrenchment, Third Way governments positioned themselves as recognising and attempting to ameliorate the human costs of roll-back neoliberalism. Increased spending in key social policy areas like healthcare and education was justified as sustainable because 'social investment' in welfare state institutions was essential for building human capital. Distancing themselves from 'excessive' involvement of state in civil society and thus drastically redefining the traditional social democratic commitment to protecting people from the market, Third Way governments also reframed the state as a facilitator ensuring individuals are offered opportunities to successfully compete in the market without necessarily providing such services itself and while redirecting resources away from transfer payments and means-tested entitlements. Middle class citizens, meanwhile, remained significant beneficiaries of the welfare state but were encouraged to opt into the private welfare market, usually through tax incentives (Giddens, 1998; Esping-Andersen, 2002; Schmidtke, 2002).

—

31

Critics argue that these attempts to reduce the threat that roll-back reforms represented for 'social inclusion' were driven less by genuine political concern about social inequalities and more by an interest in running a market economy more effectively and with fewer crises (Schmidtke, 2002; Dwyer, 2004a). As such, they had the effect of embedding, legitimating and securing neoliberalism (Porter and Craig, 2004). Hegemony is said to be achieved through an ongoing process of contestation and struggle that ultimately changes political thought and argument (Leitner et al, 2007). Acknowledgement of public concern about the roll-back reforms was thus not so much a political back-step but a way of containing resistance that threatened the neoliberal economic agenda. For this reason, the roll-out phase 'represents *both* the frailty of the neoliberal project *and* its deepening' (Peck and Tickell, 2002, p 390, italics in original).

Such an argument is supported by the Third Way's reworking of citizenship. Roll-back neoliberalism's extreme hostility to collective forms of welfare, which in liberal welfare states was heavily influenced by neopaternalist ideas about welfare dependency, was softened by a neocommunitarian[4] focus on 'no rights without responsibilities' for all citizens (Giddens, 1998, p 65; Deacon, 2005). Although reframed by the language of 'active citizenship', paid work was still considered the best form of welfare, individual responsibility remained the key to ensuring welfare needs were met and welfare recipients still faced penalties for not fulfilling their obligations (Dwyer, 2004b). While active citizenship in a liberal sense focused mainly on the poor and socially excluded, at another level it drew upon neocommunitarian views that an individual's potential can be achieved through citizens meeting their responsibilities towards each other that arise independently of the claims they make on the government (Selznick, 1998; Selbourne, 2001; Deacon, 2005; Johansson and Hvinden, 2005). This focus on communities, social capital, local governance and partnership-based modes of policy development and programme delivery aimed to mobilise and gain further buy-in from non-government organisations and civil society wishing to find 'local solutions to local problems' (Graefe, 2005; Humpage, 2005; Larner and Butler, 2005).

The electoral success of many social democratic parties in the 2000s suggests an explicit emphasis on 'the social' helped bolster support for the status quo, while continuing to shifting the boundaries of responsibility for outcomes away from the state and onto individuals and communities (Porter and Craig, 2004; Humpage, 2005). Voters who regard themselves as supporters of a party and consider it as a trustworthy source of information can usually be expected to replicate its position when asked about their own political views (Svallfors, 2006; Curtice, 2010). Members of the public who normally associate with the political Left may thus have endorsed a Third Way view even though it arguably reflected a radical change in values of the political Left (Schmidtke, 2002).

Evidence supporting this argument is found in events following the financial crisis of 2008–2009. Writing in the early 2000s, Peck and Tickell (2002) were already noting that roll-out neoliberalism had created new strategic targets and weak spots but:

> Neoliberalism's persistent vulnerability to regulatory crises and market failures is associated with an ongoing dynamic of discursive adjustment, policy learning and institutional reflexivity. As long as collateral damage from such breakdowns can be minimized, localized or otherwise displaced across space or scale, it can provide a positive spur to regulatory reinvention. (Peck and Tickell, 2002, p 392)

The global financial crisis initially provoked new doubts about neoliberalism, with many governments temporarily intervening to bail out private financial institutions and assist businesses through pseudo-Keynesian stimulus packages, while also providing tax relief and lower interest rates for householders. But Peck et al (2012) argue that these not only failed fundamentally to challenge a neoliberal economic agenda, but crisis conditions provided the space for a further entrenchment of market-disciplinary modes of governance. There were 'dramatic conservative resurgencies, affirmed by electoral victories and promptly followed by new rounds of righteous budget slashing' (Peck et al, 2012, p 266) in the US and the UK, while European policy settings ranged from fiscal restraint to enforced austerity (Hemerijck et al, 2012; Vis et al, 2012). In the UK, for instance, cuts to welfare state spending and services were justified by the growing public debt that resulted from bank bail-outs and renationalisation (Gough, 2011). Toynbee and Walker (2011) suggest Labour's legacy was so easily dismantled after 2010 not only because the new Conservative-Liberal Democrat government blamed Labour for the deficit but also because Labour had failed to try to convince the public why spending was needed and why increased taxation was necessary to sustain it.

However, Vis et al (2012) note that while the big (welfare) state was regarded as a primary cause of the 1970s and 1980s crises, this latest phase of neoliberalism saw the welfare state positioned as part of the *solution* to the problems caused by the financial sector and their aftershocks. Both a consumer orientation and a focus on community and partnership provided new ways for citizens to mobilise to defend the welfare state and social rights, while the financial crisis of the late 2000s provoked a new wave of global mass protest. It is unlikely such contestation was sufficient to be characterised as a form of 'push-back' neoliberalism (Peck and Tickell, 2002). But nor did this most recent phase simply represent a return to the roll-back period of the 1980s and 1990s and renewed retrenchment in some policy areas was combined with a limited focus on the 'social'. Aside from assistance for those recently unemployed, electoral politics in some countries meant continued, significant investment in healthcare and education given that Third Way politics (re)built expectations around government responsibilities in these policy areas. However, in some countries this sat alongside a new wave of privatisation and a return to explicit neopaternalist concerns about welfare dependency, bringing a further tightening of eligibility and a raft of new obligations (Callinicos, 2010; Gough, 2011; Vis et al, 2012; Harper, 2013).

The impact of this latest phase of neoliberalism is still emerging but recent trends in attitudinal data are one means for exploring whether the public have 'rolled over' and accepted neoliberal logics. The anti-austerity protests and Occupy movement of 2010 and 2011 suggest public acquiescence is incomplete, especially as these explicitly attacked neoliberal economics rather than simply defending popular institutions like education and healthcare (Levitas, 2012). But, more generally, the global dominance of neoliberal governance and the external economic crisis may have led the public to endorse neoliberal values or at least accept their inevitability. Where recent retrenchment has been offset by a limited focus on social policy and outcomes, some members of the public may simply be grateful that there has been no wholesale return to the roll-back reforms of the 1980s and 1990s — without necessarily recognising that the fundamental economic transformation is already complete and the last two decades of politics and policy have focused on ensuring the legitimacy and continuity of this economic agenda.

How do policies matter? Neoliberalism's potential impact on attitudes

My interest in neoliberalism's impact upon public attitudes towards social citizenship emerges from recent scholarly interest in policy feedback, an approach emerging from historical institutionalism that views policy as exerting an influence over the sources of welfare state support and the strategies of actors seeking to shape policy (Page and Shapiro, 1992; Gusmano et al, 2002; Brooks and Manza, 2007). Importantly:

> Policies can set political agendas and shape identities and interests. They can influence beliefs about what is possible, desirable, and normal. They can alter conceptions of citizenship and status. They can channel or constrain agency, define incentives, and redistribute resources. They can convey cues that define, arouse, or pacify constituencies. (Soss and Schram, 2007, p 113)

In these ways, policies do more than satisfy or dissatisfy, generating electoral reward or punishment, but are political forces that can change basic features of the political landscape (Skocpol, 1992).

The 'policy learning' of political elites (politicians, bureaucrats and policy experts) or organised interest groups has been the main focus of policy feedback studies (Skocpol, 1992; Pierson, 1994; Heclo, 2001). A developing research interest in how policy shapes *public* attitudes, however, has produced mixed empirical results (Mettler and Soss, 2004; Barabas, 2009; Wendt et al, 2011). Table 2.3 provides a visual map of potential policy feedback effects to frame the following discussion of what the empirical literature tells us about neoliberalism's potential impact upon public attitudes. These effects run parallel to each other and at times offer competing ideas about policy's effect on public opinion. At the macro-level, many political scientists have been influenced by Wlezien's (1995) 'thermostatic' model of political preferences, which suggests that the electorate has a preferred (or ideal) policy point in relation to specific policy domains and reacts to the general policy direction or public expenditure in a way that *opposes* the current policy setting (that is, negative covariance). Welfare state studies' scholars, on the other hand, tend to focus on how different sets of welfare institutions (or 'regimes') produce differing levels of welfare state effort that, in turn, impact upon public support for the welfare state.

It has also been argued that policy design and discourse can shape public attitudes through normative and interpretative effects, which are more likely when policies are designed in ways that make them highly visible, traceable and proximate to members of the public (Pierson, 1993; Soss and Schram, 2007; Svallfors, 2007). This highlights that

Table 2.3: Potential policy feedback effects on public attitudes

Policy mood effects	Thermostatic effects	Normative effects	Interpretative effects	Resource/ incentive effects
Aggregate opinion shifts in response to general policy direction in a counter-cyclical fashion	Aggregate opinion shifts in opposite direction to social spending	Individuals are cued to some idea of what society will look like through an appeal to values	Individuals are cued about how the world works	Individuals gain some material benefit and/ or incentive to endorse a policy
		Visibility Individuals know about a policy and are given clear signals about how it fits with their interests and what political strategies are promised		*Lock-in* Incentives encourage individuals to develop particular skills or make the kind of investments that makes them resistant to policy change
		Traceability Individuals link policy outcomes to some government action and apportion credit or blame		
		Proximity Policy has a tangible presence in individuals' immediate lives or to those in their networks		

Sources: MacKuen et al, 1989; Arnold, 1990; Pierson, 1993; Soss & Schram, 2007; Svallfors, 2007; Bartle et al, 2011.

policy feedback effects may change over time but, in that policies also often provide individuals with resources or incentives to support the status quo, the public may become resistant to policy change. As will become evident, the impact of such effects on public attitudes depends on the policy area and other factors that may mediate the policy's influence (Mettler and Soss, 2004; Soss and Schram, 2007). These factors are noted where relevant as the following discussion explores what is already known about how policy may encourage or discourage support for social citizenship as a starting point for this book's unique study of New Zealand.

General policy direction

If neoliberalism is a 'strong discourse', public views would be expected to have moved to the political Right over time. However, the work of MacKuen et al (1989), Stimson (1999, 2004) and Erikson et al (2002a) suggests there is a generalised 'policy mood' underlying specific opinions on policy issues which is counter-cyclical to policy activity and moves over time and circumstance. Believing that individuals are enmeshed in a social environment and thus do not function as individuals when it comes to political matters, they used a composite indicator of the public's policy views as they fall on the liberal[5]-conservative continuum and found that aggregate policy preferences respond to the government over time by demanding *less* of the direction of policy that they are currently receiving. This is not necessarily because the electorate dislikes a particular piece of legislation; rather, when politicians respond with different policies, the mood eventually moves back in the opposite direction.

Representing the *relative* judgement of the electorate, the policy mood among the American public was most conservative in 1952 and around 1980 and most liberal in early 1960s and the mid-1990s. Not all issues align themselves with this policy mood dimension but most domestic policy issues do, including social security and tax (Erikson et al, 2002b). Only recently have these findings been corroborated elsewhere. Bartle et al (2011) tracked the policy mood or 'preferences' of the 'political Centre' in the UK between 1950 and 2005, reporting a similarly thermostatic response: Centre preferences moved to the Right between the 1950s and 1979, to the Left between 1979 and 1997 and back to the Right from 1997.

These findings indicate that we need to study public support for social citizenship over time to determine whether they have been *irretrievably* changed by neoliberalism. Notably, Erikson et al (2002a) found Americans slightly more liberal than conservative overall, which is the opposite of what studies considering self-identification with these ideological labels have found since the 1980s. Stimson (2004) argues that thermostatic shifts may result from some voters being 'operationally liberal' when it comes to desiring and responding to actual policies, even though they are 'ideologically conservative' at the symbolic level (Page and Jacobs, 2009). Although a third of Americans provided no response to ideological orientation questions, suggesting they do not think in those terms or do not know what they mean, Stimson (2004) also notes that the symbols and meaning of being liberal or conservative may have changed over time. This is an important point, given the argument that the Third Way fundamentally redefined what it means to be Left or Right (Schmidtke, 2002). Changes in policy mood may well hide significant shifts in ideological orientation.

As noted earlier, many voters keep the transaction and opportunity costs of participation low by acquiring only a minimum amount of factual information about political parties and changes in their policies. Having developed a generally favourable image of one particular party early in their political lives, most only change that image radically as a result of a major external shock (Curtice, 2010; Sanders, 2000). There is little evidence that ideological and class interests are weakening (Svallfors, 1997; Clarke et al, 1999; Edlund, 1999; Korpi and Palme, 2003). But British Attitudes Survey data suggests the British public reacted differently to Labour than the Conservatives, taking a more decisive turn to the Right – particularly towards welfare – under a Labour government. While noting other possible influences, Curtice (2010) and Sefton (2003, 2009) argue this attitudinal shift began in 1994 when Blair took over the leadership of the Labour party but occurred most obviously after Labour was elected. Padgett and Johns' (2010) study of five European countries also supports the claim that Labour's ideological retreat had an effect on public opinion. The biggest swing in attitudes was among Labour's own supporters, as might be expected given that they would be likely to be influenced by their own party's ideas (Sefton, 2009; Curtice, 2010). In Australia, Wilson et al's (2012) research finds public attitudes moved towards the Left during a period of conservative government, suggesting a similar trend might be apparent there.

The impact policy has on public attitudes at the macro-level may, however, be mediated by economic conditions. Bartle et al (2011) argue that, while it is tempting to associate the thermostatic public responses they found with variations in the size of the state – which generally expanded in the first period they studied, contracted in the second and then rolled forward again in the third – more directly economic factors, such as the unemployment rate, were also probably at play. The British public have tended to be more sympathetic to the unemployed in times of high unemployment but this economic effect is thought to be weakening (Sefton, 2003; Taylor-Gooby, 2005; Clery, 2012a; Pearce and Taylor, 2013). Vis et al's (2012) content analysis of recent news items nonetheless suggests that the 2008–09 financial crisis *increased* support for the welfare state. Page and Shapiro's (1992) review of US public opinion data between the 1930s and early 1990s also found that recessions and high unemployment increased support for domestic welfare spending and concerns about foreign competition, leading the public to favour tariffs and other protectionist trade restrictions.

Blekesaune and Quadagno (2003) note that generalised collective concern with the national economy has a stronger effect on public attitudes than being unemployed oneself (Page and Shapiro, 1992; Crothers and Vowles, 1993; Nannestad and Paldam, 2000). Economic voting studies nonetheless show that public perceptions of the national economy are general, future-focused and not always accurate (Lewis-Beck, 1988; Sanders, 2000). These economic effects are often weaker in contexts where the economy is very open and where there is an extensive state sector (Duch and Stevenson, 2008) or where there are multiple-party governments (Lewis-Beck, 1988). Nor will the same economic issue necessarily have the same effect in differing countries (Crothers and Vowles, 1993; Nadeau et al, 2000). This book focuses on unemployment rate, the most common economic effect (probably because citizens' limited economic knowledge is usually more accurate about unemployment than other issues), when assessing whether economic conditions mediate neoliberalism's influence on public support for social citizenship (Dunleavy and Husbands, 1985; Nannestad and Paldam, 2000).

Level of welfare expenditure and welfare effort

The view that the public act as a 'weathervane' of government actions, having been persuaded by and thus aligning their views with a neoliberal policy direction, has also been challenged by other studies finding that aggregate public opinion responds thermostatically (that is, moves in the opposite direction) to the *specific* spending priorities of governments (Curtice, 2010). Thus when the public perceives the government as spending 'too little', demand for additional expenditure increases and, when it spends 'too much', the demand for additional expenditure declines (Soroka and Wlezien, 2005; Wilson and Meagher, 2007; Clery, 2012a).

Importantly, healthcare and education have been identified as policy areas where this thermostatic effect is apparent. There shifts in opinion are thought to be associated with levels of dissatisfaction with the quality of services and perceptions about the levels of individual benefits and the extent to which these are perceived (often inaccurately) to be adequate (Sefton, 2003; Wilson and Meagher, 2007; Taylor-Gooby, 2008; McAllister and Pietsch, 2011; Wendt et al, 2011; Clery, 2012a, 2012b; Soroka et al, 2013). Importantly, Soroka and Wlezien (2004) found stronger thermostatic responses in the UK where a unitary parliamentary system makes responsibility for policy more traceable than in the US and Canadian federal systems. Given New Zealand also has a unitary system, attitudes towards social spending in healthcare, education and pensions might be expected to be thermostatic rather than permanently transformed by neoliberalism, but this might not be true in Australia's federal context.

Coming from a completely different theoretical perspective, Esping-Andersen's (1990) seminal work categorised different types of welfare regimes based, in part, on their differing levels of welfare effort, and one would expect that the variances in historical development that led to such differences would result in disparate levels of support for social citizenship that either reinforce or make attitudinal change more resistant. This is because policy incentives 'encourage individuals to develop particular skills, make certain kinds of investments, purchase certain kinds of goods, or devote time and money to certain kinds of organizations', in turn 'locking in' a particular path of policy development (Pierson, 1993, p 609).

The evidence that general welfare effort shapes public attitudes towards social citizenship, however, is mixed (Svallfors, 2010; Wendt et al, 2011). Coughlin's (1980, p 51) early work found '[w]here social welfare institutions are most developed – as measured by relative budgetary effort, program coverage, and program duration – the collectivist components of mass ideology are strongest'. More recently, Jaeger (2006) assessed the impact of regime type by four different indicators and found only modest support that regime matters although, notably, higher public social expenditure encouraged greater support for redistribution. This may be because greater welfare effort is usually associated with improved (and potentially visible) social outcomes (Korpi and Palme, 1998). Svallfors' (2010) review of the literature similarly indicates support for equality, redistribution, and state intervention remains strongest in social democratic regimes, weaker in conservative regimes and weakest in liberal welfare regimes. Although roughly correlated with welfare policy commitment, he nonetheless argues that differences and similarities between countries are too complex to be summarised as 'worlds of welfare attitudes'.

Indeed, a study of European countries in the 1990s unexpectedly found that support for an extensive and intensive welfare state was higher in *liberal* rather than social democratic welfare states, arguably because once a high level of income equality or welfare standards is reached, the public becomes less supportive of government policies aiming to achieve an even higher level (Gelissen, 2002; Huseby, 1995; Forma, 1997; Wendt et al, 2011). Esser's (2009) research on employment commitment among individuals across several countries found that those living in 'basic security states' (including New Zealand, the UK and Australia) in 2005 demonstrated *less* employment commitment than those from corporatist or 'encompassing welfare states', countering neoliberal arguments that generous welfare states create serious disincentive effects that make people lazy. Notably, the level of employment commitment was stable over time in most countries, but declined in the UK between 1989–1997, as retrenchment occurred, then steadied from 1997.

It is important to stress that cross-national institutional differences in welfare state effort are likely mediated by the way different welfare systems instil different norms and ideas about reciprocity, obligation and responsibility and hence create different 'moral economies' of the welfare state (Lipset, 1963; Mau, 2003). Blekesaune and Quadagno (2003) found egalitarian nations have more positive attitudes towards active welfare state policies for the unemployed, while attitudes towards the sick and old varied little across countries. This is likely tied to notions of deservingness, which appear to be quite stable across time and across different countries: the elderly are generally regarded as the most deserving, followed by sick and disabled people, and finally the unemployed (Coughlin, 1980; Taylor-Gooby, 1985; Forma, 1997; Appelbaum, 2001; Larsen, 2006; van Oorschot, 2008). Concluding that both situational and ideological factors play a role at the national level, Blekesaune and Quadagno (2003) believe nations generate different public beliefs about national social problems and about the relationship between individuals, the state and other institutions and eventually these normative effects influence popular attitudes about the policies the government should pursue and who should benefit. This challenges the traditional belief that collective attitudes are a product of *institutional* characteristics of welfare policies in different countries, rather than the other way around (van Oorschot, 2006). Brooks and Manza's (2007) 'embedded preferences' approach also views policy preferences as having multiple social foundations that confer a degree of stability at the aggregate level, resulting in public preferences changing slowly and in a monotonic fashion.

Because collective constructions of meaning are produced and reproduced by the social practices of social actions and through negotiation processes and discourses between social actors, such moral economies are not always necessarily ordered or logically consistent and they *can* eventually change over time (Page and Shapiro, 1992; Dean and Melrose, 1999; Pfau-Effinger, 2005). But this section's findings generally challenge the idea that attitudes towards social citizenship will have changed significantly in New Zealand as a result of neoliberalisation; not only was the country already a liberal welfare state that put comparatively poor effort into the welfare state but it was also strongly shaped by notions of deservingness.

Policy design

Neoliberalism, particularly in its roll-back phase, is associated with targeting and user-pay charges that reduce the resource/incentive effects of formerly universal policies (Gelissen, 2002; Taylor-Gooby, 2008; Wendt et al, 2011). Diminishing support for social citizenship might therefore be expected because there is significant evidence that universal social programmes, such as old age pensions and universal healthcare schemes, tend to garner higher levels of public support than targeted programmes like unemployment insurance (Coughlin, 1980; Bean and Papadakis, 1998; Gelissen, 2002; Blekesaune and Quadagno, 2003; Svallfors, 2004; van Oorschot, 2008). Universal programmes are proximate to and directly benefit almost all citizens, providing an incentive for all members of the public to support them (Pierson, 1993). Citizens also trust universal schemes more than selective, means-tested schemes because the latter are regarded as more open to abuse and partial administrative practices, while universal programmes tend to be better at controlling costs, guaranteeing equity and efficiently improving population outcomes (Elola, 1996; van Oorschot, 2008).

Importantly, support for formerly universal policies remains high despite the introduction of targeting and user-pays (Gelissen, 2002; Taylor-Gooby, 2008; Wendt et al, 2011). This is likely because universal programmes also embody symbolic values and beliefs about 'us', who we are, what we stand for, and what we expect of one another (Mau, 2003; Mau and Veghte, 2007; Pfau-Effinger, 2005; Soss and Schram, 2007; Svallfors, 2007, 2010). For instance, the universal National Health Service (NHS) in the UK is not only accessed by virtually every citizen but it evokes strong emotional ties to post-war welfare state development (Taylor-Gooby, 2008; Hall, 2012). Dean and Melrose (1999) argue that policy changes will rarely force the abandonment of old myths about the state unless new frames of understanding are introduced. Gelissen (2002) also found support for an all-encompassing healthcare system especially high in countries with well-developed national health services, but support was also significant in countries with fewer social services for children and the elderly and a larger proportion of female (part-time) employment. The perceived *need* for universalism may thus also influence opinion.

However, Soss and Schram (2007) suggest that some universal policies (old age pensions, for instance) exist as a potent but *distant* symbol for mass publics; those not directly affected at the time will rarely pay close attention to changing policy realities and therefore remain unaware of significant changes. This may explain why Matthews and Erickson (2005, 2008) found support for universal pensions/old age security fell more significantly than that for universal healthcare and education between 1988 and 2000 in Canada. They also highlight how some political discourses framing universal programmes are more effective than others, with an emphasis on their redistributive impact actually reducing their credibility and acceptance that the general population (including the rich) may benefit. Neoliberalism's impact upon public support for social citizenship might thus be expected to vary across policy domains, as well as across the three case study countries, especially given that the UK traditionally offered greater levels of universalism than New Zealand and Australia.

It seems likely, however, that neoliberal welfare policies may provide negative political learning experiences for benefit recipients subject to conditionality. Although Campbell (2003) found policy-based mobilisation to be strongest among low income recipients of old age insurance, the group most likely to be dependent on Social Security income, Soss (1999) notes considerable evidence that benefit recipients are less politically active than other citizens. This is not only because they tend to come from population groups with less abundant political resources and skills but also because benefits themselves discourage political involvement by cultivating personal traits of dependence and because social provision can divert or temper political demand-making through its discourse and images of 'helping' such citizens. In the US, for instance, individuals receiving Aid to Families with Dependent Children in the 1990s faced a directive and threatening programme which offered negative policy learning about government's responsiveness to people like them. In contrast, Social Security Disability Insurance recipients had their policy demands at least partly met, bolstering their external political efficacy as a group.

It is difficult to ascertain whether the regime of conditionality, coercion and surveillance that now characterises the social security system has already reshaped support for social citizenship among benefit recipients. Although holding virtually the same core values and beliefs as those not receiving welfare (Dean and Taylor-Gooby, 1992; Gallie and Alm, 2000), the unemployed tend to be more supportive of government intervention than wealthier, employed people (Hasenfeld and Rafferty, 1989; Eardley et al, 2000; Sefton, 2003; Svallfors, 2003). Presumably this is because they are more likely to benefit from such assistance, although notably altruism, a moral commitment and collective values often outweigh individual self-interest in shaping attitudes (Gelissen, 2002; Orton and Rowlingson, 2007; Matthews and Erickson, 2008). There is some indication that the recession of the late 2000s saw British attitudes towards the unemployed harden more quickly among those *least* affected (Clery, 2012a), but during Labour's term the attitudes of the *unemployed* hardened the most (Sefton, 2003; Barnes and Tomaszewski, 2010). This may be linked to Labour's neocommunitarian framing of welfare reforms begun under the Conservatives and it is possible a similar trend may be apparent in New Zealand.

Means of funding policy programmes

How a policy is funded can also influence its level of public visibility and thus public support for it (Gelissen, 2002; Pierson and Hacker, 2005; Wilson et al, 2009). Wilensky (1976) and Kangas (1995) argue that higher support for government intervention is found in countries where the tax system has low visibility, focusing more on indirect taxes such as sales and value-added taxes than on direct income or property taxes to finance the welfare state. In fact, Wilensky (2002) found significant resistance to tax to be more commonly seen in countries reliant on direct taxes, simply because tax payers are more aware of such taxes. Although indirect taxes have played a greater part in tax regimes under neoliberalism, cuts in direct forms of taxation like business and income tax have been widely promoted and thus visible. Importantly, Wilson et al's (2009) Australian research found that many voters make judgements about both tax and welfare priorities from a common set of norms about the most suitable role for the government.

Contributory insurance schemes can also garner greater support than tax-financed schemes, again because of the greater visibility and traceability of citizen contributions to unemployment, healthcare and pension funds (Duffy et al, 2013; Mulheirn and Masters, 2013). Resource effects may likewise be apparent because public support for a scheme is shaped by people's perceptions of its fiscal burden, which is related to perceptions of its generosity and the number of claimants (van Oorschot, 2008). There has been significant debate about the cost of welfare in a neoliberal policy context, particularly regarding pensions (Gelissen, 2002). But it remains that social security in New Zealand and Australia is based largely on flat-rate benefits financed directly from the General Exchequer, with only New Zealand's accident compensation scheme and Australia's retirement programme including a contributory component (Davey, 2001; Bryson, 2001). This contrasts with the UK's mix of universal flat-rate insurance with occupational income-related or private insurance cover and a means-tested safety net for those without insurance entitlements (Castles, 1996; Svallfors, 2004).

Private versus public provision

Gusmano et al (2002) note that a highly visible policy may encourage a belief that government involvement is appropriate and that the government is obligated to take responsibility for that domain, while one lacking visibility may do the opposite. Neoliberal reforms have contracted out many social services and programmes to non-government organisations and privatised social assistance in the form of accounts-based policies. This has made them less visible and less proximate, reducing the likelihood that the public is aware of policy changes (Mettler and Soss, 2004).

However, Barabas (2009) highlights the importance of examining programmatic details and experiences before assuming privatisation will have necessarily reduced support for social rights. He found that holding a Health Savings Account (HSA) *reduced* American public support for healthcare privatisation because participation experiences (involving considerable attention, risk and little voluntary motivation) were ambivalent. However, the more positive participation experience of Individual Retirement Account owners meant they tended to favour Social Security privatisation. Cook and Czaplewski (2009) also found that initial, significant US support for partial privatisation of Social Security in the late 1990s plummeted as the public learned more about the trade-offs involved in implementing such reforms. Wendt et al's (2011) European study further notes the amount of private out-of-pocket payment as a factor positively related to public support for a strong state role in healthcare; presumably this is why high income earners in Gelissen's (2002) cross-national study were also most supportive of a public health system. Finally, British research found an association between private health care and lower support for the *principle* of free universal provision but not support for the NHS specifically, with non-users of healthcare having more egalitarian attitudes than users of either private or public services (Burchardt and Propper, 1999).

Sefton (2003) offers evidence of a growing acceptance of private provision in housing and pensions, but Taylor-Gooby (2008) explains why offering British NHS consumers greater choice in using private providers had a relatively small effect on public satisfaction and trust compared to other objective (staffing levels and waiting times) and subjective factors (the commitment to care of frontline staff). He argues that demands for 'having a greater say' in the health system were not completely met, probably because this relates more to citizen voice than market-driven consumer choice. The latter is appreciated when it leads to quicker and better provision but dissatisfaction and distrust may continue if overall productivity gains and a reversal of significant social inequalities remain illusive. These findings strongly suggest that public frustration with neoliberalism, particularly in its early roll-back phase, will have encouraged stronger, not weaker, support for social citizenship.

Political discourse

If neoliberalism's power is at least partly bound to its use of multiple discursive frames to promote policy change, it is clearly important to consider the interpretative effects of political discourse on public opinion (Dunleavy and Husbands, 1985; Zaller, 1992). Political elites usually adopt a particular set of ideas and symbols to construct meaning about a specific policy or general policy direction, giving the public cues about how to view a policy by how they name and classify social problems, identify 'enemies' or 'crises' said to threaten society, use statistics and draw upon 'public opinion' to justify policies (Edelman, 1977; Gamson, 1992; Jacobs and Shapiro, 2002; Manza and Cook, 2002). For instance, Dunleavy and Husbands (1985) indicate how the British Thatcher government reduced the unemployment rate by 1% by changing the measure to include only those claiming a state benefit, then repeatedly told the public that unemployment had never fallen over the term of a Labour government. This factually incorrect belief became widespread. In contrast, Nadeau et al (2000) found that the Canadian Liberals' *in*effective discourse on job creation almost lost them their parliamentary majority in 1997, despite a decrease in unemployment rate during the Liberal's term.

Burstein's (2010) analysis of the research evidence suggests that it is more difficult for elites to manipulate public opinion than one might think (see also Duffy et al, 2013; Taylor-Gooby, 2013). Page and Shapiro (1992) certainly found American public opinion on *domestic* issues was highly resistant to manipulation by politicians and/or the media when compared to foreign policy or national security matters. Nonetheless, many events cannot be known personally and, even when they are, an individual may not know their full magnitude or their political significance except via mass media. As such, public ideas about policy are often shaped by how they are reported in the media and the level of coverage given to an issue.

The policy debates that tend to spark media/public interest are often controversial ones tapping into a variety of values, creating debate about the policy problem and solution (Edelman, 1971; Page and

Shapiro, 1992; Stimson, 1999). The promotion of neoliberal beliefs about unemployment in the UK, for example, was aided by an existing deep-rooted hostility towards the unemployed (Deacon, 1978). Wendt et al (2011) note that support for state responsibility for unemployment benefits and social assistance is much more variable than healthcare and other areas of policy because it involves pronounced conflicts over social values. Given the public lacks detailed information about policy matters, emotional reactions that draw upon stock frames (such as the deserving versus the undeserving) or an appeal to values (for example, national solidarity or the public good) are likely to play a salient role in shaping public attitudes towards government policy (Edelman, 1977; Gusmano et al, 2002; Schmidt, 2002). Svallfors' (2010) overview of the attitudinal literature found *general* support for the welfare state is more dependent on changes in the public discourse and general ideological dispositions (and thus public support is more volatile at this level) than *specific* support for concrete welfare policy programmes which, being rooted in everyday life experiences, tends to be more stable.

Schmidt's (2002) six-country analysis contends that the welfare reform discourses framing new policy initiatives differed not only in the:

> ... ideas and values to which they may appeal but also in how they are constructed and where they are focused. This is because different institutional contexts tend to frame the discursive process, determining who is involved in the initial elaboration of the policy program and discourse and toward whom the discourse is directed. (Schmidt, 2002, p 171)

Notably, Schmidt (2002) found all countries studied had both a 'coordinative discourse' (a common language and framework through which key policy actors agree to construct a policy programme) and a 'communicative discourse' (whereby policy actors seek to persuade the general public, via discussion and deliberation) but the balance between them differs. Communicative discourses were more dominant in single-actor systems where power is concentrated in the executive, such as the UK and New Zealand. This is because such governments have the capacity to impose reform without impediment and if debate and deliberation over a major policy initiative occurs at all, this happens in the wider public sphere, often in adversarial fashion. In multi-actor systems where governmental power and/or societal representation is more dispersed, such as Australia, policies are the product of a much wider cross section of policy-related elites. A coordinative discourse is required because the government generally lacks the capacity to impose reform and communicative discourse is often weak except during election periods or when the coordinative discourse breaks down. Australia's institutional settings may thus shape attitudes towards social citizenship in differing ways to New Zealand and the UK.

Government discourses, however, are not the only ones that can shape public opinion. Blyth (2002) demonstrates how business and labour have attempted to persuade the public of a particular understanding of economic uncertainty and its institutional solutions, while Skocpol (1992) found voluntary associations played an important role in lobbying for both Civil War pensions, social policies for mothers and certain protective labour regulations for adult female wage earners in the US. Under the right circumstances non-governmental organisations and protest groups can offer alternative viewpoints and shape public views on policy, even though they usually lack the same resources available to political elites for promoting their viewpoint. Less formally, most individuals rely on others within their social groups, as well as politicians' and others' views transmitted through the media, to work out what they want in politics (Edelman, 1977; Gamson, 1992).

Policy, however, can shape differing levels of civic engagement among citizens. For instance, Mettler (2002) contends that the extension of generous social benefits to returning World War II veterans conveyed different messages than the stigmatised relief programmes of their childhood, with individuals from less advantaged backgrounds finding themselves included as esteemed members of the polity. This generation responded by engaging in civil society more than expected. In that neoliberalism has been accused of trying to *shut down* opposition both by discrediting and co-opting alternative discourses, organisations and individuals, it seems likely it had a negative impact upon civic engagement. This is especially so since individuals who have been politically socialised during periods in which these elite messages are most intense and visible may demonstrate views different to those of previous or later generations (Gusmano et al, 2002). Certainly, British evidence finds citizens growing up in the 1980s under Thatcherism are less supportive of the welfare state than their older counterparts (Sefton, 2003; Hall, 2012; Duffy et al, 2013).

Conclusion: studying neoliberalism's impact in New Zealand

This chapter has traced the significant shift from Keynesian to neoliberal policy settings which reshaped the way in which governments regarded their role in guaranteeing the social rights of their citizens from the late 1970s. While much theorising around neoliberalism suggests this policy shift will have produced an equally radical change in public views about social citizenship, in fact the existing research indicates much public opinion has remained surprisingly stable over the past three decades (Taylor-Gooby, 1985; Page and Shapiro, 1992; Bean and Papadakis, 1998; van Oorschot et al, 2008; McAllister and Pietsch, 2011; Wendt et al, 2011; Wilson et al, 2012). The long-term impact of neoliberalism has not been assessed, however, and this chapter's empirical review has highlighted that:

- Diminishing ideological distinctions between Left and Right political parties may have reduced the visibility, traceability and normative effects of policies supporting social citizenship. Yet evidence suggests the electorate swings from Left to Right over time in response to government activity/direction and ideological orientations remain important (although what these mean may have changed over time).

- The roll-back and roll-over phases of neoliberalism promoted the need for significant reductions in social expenditure but research shows that actual spending cuts tend to encourage an *increase* in support for more spending.

- Neoliberal targeting, user-pays and privatisation may have reduced policy proximity and visibility, as well as resource/incentive effects, but this likely *increased* rather than decreased support for universalism and public ownership in some policy areas. Moreover, transforming citizens into consumers offered a limited but active opportunity to articulate perceived inadequacies in service.

- Greater use of indirect taxes and of tax credits may have reduced the public visibility of tax policy but, in the latter case, increased its proximity and the likelihood of resource/incentive effects. Neoliberalism has also favoured more visible and traceable contribution-based programmes which are associated with stronger public support.

- Despite reductions in benefit generosity and greater conditionality decreasing policy proximity and resource/incentive effects for some groups of benefit recipients, there is little evidence that conditionality has reshaped unemployed people's conceptions of self-interest.

- More broadly, neoliberal discourses around welfare dependency, individual responsibility economic efficiency and – in more recent phases of neoliberalism – social inclusion, community and 'no rights without responsibilities' likely produced strong interpretative and potentially normative effects. But their impact on public attitudes may depend on the effectiveness of communicative discourses of a particular government and may be mediated by the media and alternative public discourses. In liberal welfare states, long-standing normative effects around individual responsibility, deservingness and work may also mean the shift from Keynesianism to neoliberalism did not provoke a sharp or immediate shift in attitudes.

These findings are insightful and have helped identify key sites for this study's analysis. But it cannot be assumed that they are relevant today or in New Zealand, for two reasons. First, many of the studies cited above, particularly the cross-national comparisons which rely on infrequently run surveys, draw upon data from the 1980s and 1990s or, at best, the early 2000s. They can thus largely inform us only about public responses to the first wave of roll-back reforms. Yet earlier theorising suggests that, despite early public resistance, these reforms produced lock-in effects that hardened attitudes over time, with the Third Way legitimating and embedding neoliberalism in ways that appeased public concerns. To understand such effects, one must consider the impact of the third phase of roll-over neoliberalism provoked by the global financial crisis of 2008–09. Drawing upon qualitative data also allows consideration of how the public interpret both their policy context and the survey propositions posed.

New Zealand's particular experience of neoliberalism offers a second reason why the empirical findings cannot be assumed to apply. This country's economic reforms were particularly rapid and radical in the 1980s and 1990s, with the disjuncture between elite and public support contributing to the adoption of Mixed Member Proportional representation in 1993 (Kelsey, 1997; Starke, 2008). Although this shift saw coalition governments become the norm from 1996, potentially making it difficult for the public to trace responsibility for policies, it suggests a stronger level of public resistance than found elsewhere (Schmidt, 2002; Vowles, 2004). These and other differences in policy and politics are explored in the next chapter, which traces the process of neoliberalisation in New Zealand, offering select comparisons with the UK and Australia to set a context for the an indepth, qualitative analysis of New Zealand public attitudes towards social citizenship that follows.

Notes

[1] Marshall's essay 'Citizenship and social class' was originally published in 1950.

[2] The level of universalism in the UK during the post-war period has, in fact, led to some debate about whether it is correctly categorised as a 'liberal welfare state'.

[3] This book uses this term in a broader sense than simply referring to the ideas of John Maynard Keynes.

[4] The Third Way has drawn largely upon neocommunitarian ideas (see Etzioni, 1998; Selznick, 1998; Putnam, 2000) concerned with the balance between: social forces and the person; the community and autonomy; the common good and liberty; and individual rights and responsibilities. This contrasts significantly with classical or radical communitarians, whose focus is more on the significance of social forces, community and social bonds (see Etzioni, 1998; Deacon, 2005).

[5] Here 'liberal' is used in the North American sense, referring to a progressive politics on the Left of the ideological spectrum.

THREE

Implementing neoliberalism

The previous chapter's discussion of the international empirical literature challenged theoretical assumptions that public attitudes to social citizenship will have shifted comprehensively and coherently over the last three decades. It did so by highlighting the varied policy feedback effects known to shape public opinion. Building on this discussion, the present chapter provides an overview of New Zealand's turbulent political and policy history between 1984 and 2011. Exploring neoliberalism's shifting nature over its roll-back, roll-out and roll-over phases, it finds good reason to believe New Zealand attitudes towards social citizenship may also fluctuate over time. Discussion of each key phase in New Zealand is punctuated by brief analysis of significant variances in the type, strength and/ or timing of policies implemented in the United Kingdom (UK) and Australia, identifying where trends in public attitudes may also differ across geographical space. In focusing on four key policy areas – economic policy relating to employment; social security; healthcare, education, pensions; tax and redistribution – the chapter also stresses that neoliberalism's implementation has been far from uniform, even within one time period or country. Nor has it gone uncontested, with both political divisions within government and public demand for electoral reform and policy reversals providing a final reason why we cannot assume that New Zealand attitudes towards social citizenship have been comprehensively and coherently transformed. Indeed, while economic crises were behind the earlier and later phases of neoliberalism, the electoral impacts of this public concern contributed to the internal crises driving the roll-out period. This background provides a crucial context for the following chapters, which each examine how neoliberalism – in all its diversity – shaped attitudes towards social citizenship in one of four key policy areas.

Roll-back neoliberalism: 1984–1999

Neoliberalism's 'destructive' moment is said to have been facilitated by external economic crises justifying government-led restructuring projects that dismantled Keynesian institutional frameworks and subordinated social welfare policies to economic considerations

(Brenner and Theodore, 2002; Peck and Tickell, 2002). Both New Zealand's Labour (1984–1990) and National (1990–1999) governments certainly used economic conditions to justify the rolling back of institutions supporting social citizenship. An unexpected foreign currency crisis rationalised the newly elected 4th Labour government's immediate macroeconomic reforms from 1984. One of the most protected economies in the world, New Zealand was transformed as Labour removed all price and quantitative import controls, assistance to agriculture and manufacturing and most barriers to foreign investment. This left only low, steadily reducing tariffs. By 1987, New Zealand also had one of the flattest and simplest tax systems in the developed world and a new comprehensive value-added Goods and Services Tax (GST). These changes were only partly offset by narrowly targeted benefits and taxation dispensations for low income earners (Vowles and Aimer, 1993; Davey, 2001; Roper, 2005).

Although Labour had campaigned on a traditional economic and social policy agenda, opposition to economic reform was relatively muted from within both the Labour Party and the trade union movement as economic conditions improved (Roper, 2005; Starke, 2008). Importantly, Labour restored compulsory unionism in 1985 as promised, while the 1987 Labour Relations Act abolished compulsory arbitration in the private sector and offered employer's more flexibility but retained compulsory union membership and permitted wage bargaining through national awards. Only weeks before the 1990 election, Labour also agreed to consult unions on social and economic policies in exchange for a low 2% wage path for two years (Vowles and Aimer, 1993; Roper, 2005; Ramia and Wailes, 2006). Full employment, however, was abandoned as an economic goal in 1985, when direct job creation and wage subsidy schemes were abolished (Higgins, 1997). The 'no fault' approach to accident compensation was retained but employers' contributions were reduced, an employees' premium introduced and lump sum compensation payments abolished (Davey, 2001).

Two months after the next election in 1987, a share market crash precipitated a deep recession and rapid growth in unemployment. Minister of Finance, Roger Douglas, used this new crisis to promote more tariff reductions, local government and telecommunications reforms and an extensive privatisation programme. The latter was not part of Labour's policy manifesto, causing huge disagreement within the party, but all major state trading organisations were privatised by 1990, drastically reducing the size of the public service and further increasing unemployment. Labour won the 1987 election with an increased share of the vote, however, at least partly because Labour's economic policies initially appeared to work and there were widespread expectations it would place greater emphasis on social policies benefiting Labour's 'traditional supporters' in its second term (Davey, 2001; Roper, 2005).

In fact, Douglas had plans to significantly reform the welfare state. Although some delays resulted from Prime Minister David Lange establishing a Royal Commission on Social Policy in 1986, Labour had already broken an election promise by introducing income testing on New Zealand Superannuation in 1985. It backtracked after a public outcry, establishing a 25% tax surcharge on additional income that was then reduced to 18% in 1986 due to its extreme unpopularity. But further negative reaction was provoked when Labour partially restructured New Zealand Superannuation (renaming it Guaranteed Retirement Income), increased the surcharge to 20% and raised the eligibility age to 65 in 1989 (Vowles and Aimer, 1993; St John, 1999a; Davey, 2001; Roper, 2005). Labour was reluctant to implement pro-market reforms in health but policy advice was placed in the hands of the Ministry of Health while service delivery was undertaken by 14 new Area Health Boards. These changes fuelled existing public concern that primary healthcare subsidies covered less than 10% of the usual adult fee by the mid-1980s (Roper, 2005; Cheyne et al, 2008). In addition, responsibility and accountability for the delivery of educational services were decentralised to school level Boards of Trustees from 1989. Reframed as a private good, tertiary education saw massive increases in student tuition fees, the partial means-testing of student allowances and bulk funding based on student numbers which resulted in declining government expenditure in tertiary education. Large protest marches and mass occupations against rising fees and student debt and inadequate living allowances led National to pledge it would scrap the tertiary fees Labour had just introduced. A teacher wage strike and media attention on compulsory education funding and quality further ensured that education – like superannuation and healthcare – was a major election issue (McQueen, 1990; Vowles and Aimer, 1993; Boston, 1999a; Roper, 2005).

Indeed, the 1990 election result is widely regarded as a rejection of neoliberalism. Schmidt (2002) believes the communicative discourse Labour used to persuade the public was effective, retaining some 'collectivism' and increasing spending on social assistance but arguing that competition was needed to make the welfare system more sustainable. However, ideological disorientation resulted from *Labour* initiating the reforms with support from both business *and* unions.

Labour itself was also divided about the policy direction taken. Douglas and the Minister of State Owned Enterprises, Richard Prebble, lost their seats in cabinet for attempting to implement extremely regressive tax reforms in 1988. When they regained power within the party, Lange resigned and there were two further leadership changes before the 1990 election. The most prominent opponent to neoliberalism, Jim Anderton, also left Labour to form the New Labour Party, taking approximately one third of Labour's membership (Vowles, 2004; Roper, 2005). The Māori Council of Churches' call for a boycott of the election, due to disillusionment with the political system, indicates the impact these unsettling moves had on the New Zealand public (Sullivan and Vowles, 1998).

Vowles and Aimer (1993, p 184) contend that 'National actively sought to mobilise conservative opinion by playing on the widespread sense of confusion and insecurity felt by many people as a result of the very rapid pace of change since 1984'. Its election focus on 'fairness' and a 'decent society' and its attack on Labour's economic management suggested Labour's policies would be reversed. The poor economy saw National elected in 1990, but the continuation of monetarist policies and radical social policy reforms saw its support fall to 22% by late 1991. Labour's polling also suffered as a new Alliance Party, formed by the New Labour, Green, Democrat and Mana Motuhake and Liberal parties, surged ahead based on its consistent criticism of neoliberalism. National won the 1993 election but a hung parliament was only narrowly avoided, and continuing public dissatisfaction saw 84.7% of referendum voters support the replacement of the majoritarian, First-Past-the-Post system with a Mixed-Member Proportional (MMP) representation system in 1992, despite little public interest in electoral reform when a Royal Commission recommended MMP in 1986 (Vowles and Aimer, 1993; Vowles et al, 1995; Roper, 2005).

Schmidt (2002) argues that the implementation of radical reforms without regard to public opinion led to this transformation of its governing institutions, yet the introduction of MMP also made it difficult for future governments to reverse reforms already instituted. This is because negotiating with a much wider range of policy elites requires an elaborate coordinative discourse alongside a communicative one focused on persuading the public. However, the rate of reform did slow in National's second term and, as economic conditions improved and business confidence increased, it argued the short-term pain of reform was over (Roper, 2005). The 1996 election nonetheless remained centred on neoliberalism's social impacts. Although bringing some important social policy gains, as further discussion highlights, this election caused further political disillusionment when the New Zealand First Party – which had campaigned on an anti-neoliberalism agenda – unexpectedly formed the country's first coalition government with National, whose policies radically diminished social rights (Davey, 2001).

Being the only economic policy area where Labour had not implemented significant reform, National quickly introduced the 1991 Employment Contracts Act to replace compulsory arbitration and collectivism with voluntarism and individualism (Ramia and Wailes, 2006). Unions mobilised up to half a million New Zealanders against the law during a 1991 Week of Action, but vigorous lobbying from the business sector also saw further cuts to employers' Accident Compensation Corporation (ACC) levies, while those of workers increased in 1992 to make the scheme more 'insurance based'. Once the coalition with New Zealand First broke up, National also opened ACC to competitive provision in 1999, making accident compensation the only social policy arena where National was able to successfully deliver more market-driven reforms (St John, 1999b; Roper, 2005; Duncan, 2007).

From 1997, work capacity assessments reframed ACC recipients as 'welfare dependent' (St John, 1999b), a move in line with the broader communicative discourse of fairness, self reliance, efficiency and greater personal choice used to justify 'the most radical reform of the welfare state in the nation's history' in 1991 (Vowles et al, 1995, p 81). National had indicated that some change was impending during the 1990 election, but not that it would cut benefit levels directly for the first time in history and abolish the universal Family Benefit, reducing the disposable income of benefit recipients by up to 30%. The deficit blowout and fiscal costs associated with increased benefit numbers provided a pretext for the benefit cuts but they were also framed as reducing the income margin between welfare and full-time employment. When economic growth and falling unemployment did not result in all unemployed people finding work, this 'proved' that coercion was needed. Formal job search testing and sanctions, longer stand-down periods and the extension of unemployment benefit youth rates to the age of 25 were introduced after 1994. Those receiving support were no longer 'citizens' but individual 'clients' and they received 'income support' not 'social security'. 'Welfare' itself became a term of abuse and 'need' was translated as 'dependence', suggesting this group were not deserving of assistance (St John, 1999c; Roper, 2005; Lunt, 2008; St John and Rankin, 2009).

In 1997, work-test requirements became even more stringent and included possible participation in a voluntary 'work for the dole' scheme called the Community Task Force (Higgins, 1997). Full-time education or training requirements were also extended to sole parents with children aged over 14, while those with children aged 7–13 faced part-time obligations. Child care subsidies were modified to facilitate this expectation of work, but many low income children were excluded from increases to the income-tested, child-related tax rebate called Family Support in 1996 because most of it was separated off as an Independent Family Tax Credit not available to parents on a benefit (Dale et al, 2010). Work for the dole became mandatory in 1998, with all unemployment benefits replaced by a Community Wage received in return for 20 hours per week of 'public good work' in the non-profit sector (Higgins, 1997). National also introduced a two-year trial of work capacity assessment for Invalid's and Sickness benefit recipients (Lunt, 2006a).

These social security changes were mostly proximate and visible to affected benefit recipients but concern widened when a Department of Social Welfare (1998) public discussion document reframed citizenship around reciprocal *obligations* rather than social *rights*. Intended as the basis for a contract between the state and its citizens, this Code of Social and Family Responsibility threatened direct monitoring of benefit recipients but viewed *all* New Zealanders as active subjects responsible for their own social wellbeing. Widespread public resistance meant the Code was never implemented but, alongside a 'benefit fraud' media campaign from 1998, it contributed to an explicit communicative discourse focused on welfare dependency (Larner, 2000; Roper, 2005). National denied that poverty existed until late in 1994, when access to highly targeted, means-tested special benefits and special needs grants was eased. It then framed growing poverty and income inequality as illustrating the need to eliminate welfare dependency and implement personal income tax cuts in 1996 and 1998 (Boston and St John, 1999; Davey, 2001; Dale et al, 2010). National largely ignored the considerable public protest and academic debate challenging these views in the late 1990s (St John, 1999c; O'Brien, 2008).

The National government was more responsive to public discontent about superannuation. Despite promising to abolish the unpopular surcharge, its harsher abatement policy for the elderly effectively turned New Zealand Superannuation into a tightly targeted benefit. Public opposition saw New Zealand Superannuation reinstated in 1992 but the surcharge increased to 25%. An Accord was forged between the major parties to avoid further policy lurches but this lasted only between 1993 and 1996. New Zealand First negotiated the abolition of the surcharge in 1998, making superannuation fully universal again (but at 60% instead of 65% of net average wages) and a 1997 public referendum on superannuation saw 91.8% of participating voters reject fundamental reforms to the basic pension (St John, 1999a; St John and Rankin, 2009).

In other areas of social policy, a market model was introduced. From 1993, Labour's 14 Area Health Boards were replaced by four Regional Health Authorities (RHAs) intended to be quasi-markets, receiving funding from central government to purchase healthcare services for their region's population from contracted health providers (Davey, 2001; Cheyne et al, 2008). Publicly-owned hospitals became Crown Health Enterprises (CHEs) required to make a 'profit', provoking widespread resistance from clinical professionals and health sector unions. As formerly universal healthcare subsidies were restricted to low income families from 1992 and user charges were introduced, large street protests opposed the decreasing accessibility and affordability of healthcare, contributing to hospital part charges being removed after only four months in 1992. Despite increased income from user charges, some CHEs were forced into debt to keep operating as real per capital expenditure on health fell (Ashton, 1999; Roper, 2005; Duncan, 2007).

New Zealand First negotiated a slight increase in health expenditure and free primary healthcare for children under six after 1996 and the removal of some part charges in 1997 and some income/asset tests for elderly patients in 1998 (Ashton, 1999). More fundamentally, the Coalition agreement reoriented the health system towards 'co-operation and collaboration rather than competition' (New Zealand Government – NZG, 1996, p 34). RHAs were merged into a Health Funding Authority in 1996 and the quasi-commercial profit motive removed from hospital management. Despite these changes, a 1997 national petition called for a referendum to increase annual spending on health services, and street protests expressed public dissatisfaction with government's management of the public healthcare system (Ashton, 1999; Duncan, 2007; Cheyne et al, 2008).

Marketisation was also introduced in tertiary education. National 'abolished' Labour's tertiary fees as promised but restricted the fees subsidy and allowed tertiary institutions to set their own fees, resulting in increased costs for most students. From 1992, they could finance their study through a new student loan system at significant interest rates and repaid through the tax system, a necessary move given only a third of enrolled students were eligible for National's more highly targeted student allowances as the level of funding per student fell to 75% from close to 100% in the mid-1980s (Kelsey, 1993; Boston,

1999b; Roper, 2005). In compulsory education, National abolished school zoning, compulsory teaching registration, Labour's Parent Advocacy Council and Boards of Trustees equity requirements. Public funding to private schools increased and a trial of bulk funding for teacher salary costs became mandatory in 1992 (Kelsey, 1993). As Peters and Olssen (1999) note, Labour's reforms embodied the twin notions of 'devolution' and 'community' but the latter focus was abandoned under National, leaving a dominant discourse centred on efficiency, equity and consumer choice. In this context, socio-economic disparities in education grew and schools become heavily reliant on fundraising activities and 'voluntary' school fees (Thrupp and Irwin, 2010). With both the cost of tertiary education and poor teacher wages causing discontent, New Zealand First also negotiated a small increase in education spending in the late 1990s (Davey, 2001; Roper, 2005).

New Zealand First's credibility was, however, heavily reliant on its opposition to further privatisation of state assets. A sharp Right-turn after Jenny Shipley became Prime Minister in November 1997 saw National decide to sell the government's majority shareholding in Wellington Airport, leading to the breakup of the coalition government in 1998. National cobbled together sufficient support to continue governing until the 1999 election, calming business community nerves about the stalling of neoliberal reforms under the coalition. But as the election drew closer, the media uncritically relayed business opposition to Labour's planned policy changes, proclaiming a crisis of business confidence (Aimer and Miller, 2002; Roper, 2005).

Nonetheless, with the economic crises used to justify radical economic and social restructuring largely resolved, the internal crisis of public dissatisfaction became more important given low levels of trust in politicians and democracy meant '[t]he 1990s were the most electorally unsettled decade for more than fifty years' (Aimer and Miller, 2002, p 1). Policy reversals (notably in superannuation and healthcare) occurred when the electoral risks got too high and multi-party agreements (such as the short-lived superannuation Accord) were used to depoliticise controversial issues and secure greater political stability. Importantly, National *failed* to implement: an integrated system of targeting across social security, healthcare and student allowance assistance; a system of competing private healthcare purchasers and any substantial privatisation of healthcare funding; a voucher system to charge tertiary students the full cost of their courses; and the reconstitution of universities as Crown companies in preparation for privatisation (Kelsey, 1993; Boston, 1999a, 1999b).

Roper (2005) argues that by the mid-1990s many of the social movements reacting against neoliberalism had run out of steam but, despite being demoralised by the first coalition result, they turned to the electoral system as the avenue for change. He therefore views the election of a Labour-Alliance government in 1999, despite high levels of financial backing for National and the Right-wing ACT Party, as evidence of the working class and some sections of the urban middle class becoming more conscious of, and strongly opposed to, the pro-business ideology of neoliberalism. It is possible the public came to accept neoliberalism over time as significant policy changes reducing their social rights became locked in, particularly in economic policy where there was less policy reversal. But examining the politics surrounding policy change strongly suggests neoliberal retrenchment likely *strengthened,* rather than significantly diminished, public support for social citizenship.

Rapid, radical reform versus incrementalism

There are good reasons to believe that public resistance to neoliberalism may have been more significant in New Zealand than in the UK and Australia during the early reform period. Schmidt (2002) believes British governments tried harder than New Zealand's to win over the electorate through a stronger communicative discourse legitimating the need for reform. Many Britons expressed jubilation upon the death of former British Prime Minister Margaret Thatcher in 2013, suggesting her desire to have everyone believe what she believed as she imposed reform in the 1980s was unfulfilled. But New Zealand's Roger Douglas expected the public simply to come around once reforms had been implemented. That New Zealanders opted to change the parliamentary system supports an argument that the level of political disillusionment was even greater than that found in the UK (Boston et al, 1996; Quiggin, 1998; Rawlinson and Quine, 2013). Australian academics, policy makers and commentators, in contrast, largely agreed that reform was necessary by the early 1980s and support for reform broadened once the economy improved, even if disagreement remained about its pace (Bryson, 2001; Taylor, 2009). While Quiggin (1998) contends that Labor is primarily remembered for economic deregulation not social policy innovations, Schmidt (2002) believes Labor's balance between economic reform and the strengthening of key social rights (notably regarding health and superannuation) distinguished it from other countries. Indeed, it has been argued that Labor's policies set a precedent for the Third Way (Pierson and Castles, 2002).

The greater level of public disgruntlement in New Zealand and the UK in comparison with Australia is also likely associated with the more rapid and extreme reforms implemented in these two countries. Their unitary parliamentary systems gave the Executive considerable powers to implement policy without the need for public consensus. Not only does the Australian federal system offer states autonomy and primary responsibility for many policy areas, but Federal Labor lacked a majority in Senate in the bicameral national parliament (Bryson, 2001). Labor's reform agenda was thus necessarily more incremental but also experienced virtually no backsliding. This encouraged steady business expectations and high levels of investment, reducing the need for more dramatic economic changes (Ramia and Wailes, 2006; Taylor, 2009).

These political differences resulted in significant policy variances in the early reform period that potentially shaped public attitudes towards social citizenship. Overall, the early neoliberal reforms in the UK and New Zealand were more economically and socially disruptive than Australia's, making the reforms themselves and their impacts upon citizens more visible and traceable. Economic deregulation not only occurred more rapidly in New Zealand but, given the country's relatively small size and geographical isolation, its impact was arguably greater and may have contributed to the 'there is no alternative' discourse becoming more normalised than in the other two countries (Kelsey, 1997; Roper, 2005; Starke, 2008). More specifically, industrial relations reforms in New Zealand and the UK were implemented quickly and comprehensively and, in the latter case at least, existing public dissatisfaction with industrial relations encouraged acceptance of these and other economic changes (Edwards and Sayers Bain, 1988; Castles, 1996; Schmidt, 2002). In contrast, Australian Labor established a series of Accords with trade unions and the Liberal-National government's plans in industrial relations were hindered by its lack of control over Senate until 2005 (van Wanrooy, 2007).

Chapter Two found that targeting is associated with weaker support for a particular policy. Although the number of New Zealanders with private health insurance *decreased* and public protest saw policy reversals after 1996, New Zealand's market-led reforms may have lessened support for healthcare more than in the UK and Australia, where there was greater universalism. In the UK, the National Health Service (NHS) remains the most salient of welfare state services, defining what the welfare state means for many Britons. Although healthcare was underfunded and attempts were made to introduce competition and business models, Thatcher repeatedly indicated the NHS was safe from radical reform (Parker, 2004; Taylor-Gooby, 2008; Ham, 2009). Meanwhile, Australia *introduced* the largely universal Medicare in 1984, providing free public hospital care and meeting 85% of private General Practitioner (GP) fees. This may have encouraged Australians to believe that the government was responsible for ensuring access to universal healthcare (Quiggin, 1998; Lewis et al, 2010).

In contrast, we might expect New Zealanders' views on superannuation to differ from those expressed in the other countries during the first phase of neoliberalism because strong lobbying and public protest *resurrected* universal superannuation and rejected compulsory private superannuation by the end of the 1990s. In the UK, a two-tier system of pensions became increasingly targeted and privatised during its early period of reform, while Australian Labor's 1992 Superannuation Guarantee *introduced* a two-tier system, maintaining the means-tested age pension but also requiring employers to contribute to individualised accounts in a private sector superannuation fund (Dwyer, 1998; Bryson, 2001; Lewis et al, 2010).

In the case of social security, both the New Zealand and British governments adopted an explicit welfare dependency discourse to frame early reforms (Roper, 2005; Starke, 2008). Individual responsibility and reciprocal obligations were an important part of Australia's social policy regime from 1987, but Labor also talked of the *right* to employment when extending labour market programmes and guaranteeing six to 12 month job placements for the long-term unemployed (Eardley et al, 2000; Shaver, 2001; Wright et al, 2011). Chapter Two indicated that contributory social insurance schemes may encourage support for social rights. Only the UK had such a system but the British Conservative government's unprecedented focus on means-testing and wage supplementation for low income earners reversed the post-war idea that social insurance benefits were the primary channel for social protection during this period (Hills, 1998; Korpi and Palme, 2003). Indeed, the Australian welfare state remained more redistributive towards lower income earners than most countries. Australia's one truly universal benefit – the Child Benefit – became means-tested but an *increase* in Australia's overall welfare effort and improved anti-poverty measures partially offset the increases in income inequality associated with free market reforms (Saunders, 1994; Whiteford, 2006; Harding et al, 2009). For these and the other reasons cited, Australia's early period of reform probably had a less dramatic impact upon attitudes towards social citizenship when compared with New Zealand and the UK.

Roll-out neoliberalism: 1999–2008

It is argued that internal contradictions and tensions associated with roll-back reform provoked both a general questioning of the neoliberal agenda and new forms of 'exclusion'. Roll-out neoliberalism thus aimed to calm public concerns and give the 'excluded' some stake in the wider neoliberal order by offering a 'human face' to economic rationalism (Peck and Tickell, 2002; Porter and Craig, 2004). In New Zealand, Labour moved to address this internal crisis after its resounding 1993 election loss, electing Helen Clark as leader and repositioning itself on the Centre-Left. This put it in direct competition with the Alliance Party, which laid claim to Labour's ideological traditions and part of its electoral constituency. With the Alliance overtaking Labour in the polls by late 1995, it is no surprise both parties prepared their memberships and the public for a coalition government prior to the 1999 election (Aimer and Miller, 2002; Vowles, 2002).

However, the Alliance's failure to ensure key policies were traceable to it rather than Labour and a party crisis over Anderton's leadership allowed Labour to call an early election and improve its polling. It formed a minority government with Anderton's tiny new Progressive Coalition Party from 2002, supported by the United Future Party on the Right, the Green Party on the Left and, after 2005, New Zealand First (Levine and Roberts, 2003). The coalition mix was notably more conservative after 2002, allowing Labour to focus on recapturing the attention of low and middle income 'Kiwi battlers' to whom it had discursively reached out during the 1999 election but had thus far paid little policy attention (Armstrong, 1999; Roper, 2005).

These shifting political concerns shaped the Labour-coalition's policy agenda, encouraging criticism that the Third Way was intellectually vacuous and driven by the polls (Kelsey, 2002). With an improving economy reducing pressure to continue with a programme of neoliberal structural adjustments, the new government tried to disassociate itself from neoliberalism with talk of a 'new social democracy' (Maharey, 1999a). The previous government's hard-line monetarist approach *was* moderated through acknowledgement that fiscal policy could counteract cyclical economic fluctuations. But Schmidt (2001) suggests the transformative power of discourse is found in its absorption by an opposition party and the coalition government retained all main features of the neoliberal economic policy regime and went to great lengths to shore up business confidence (Roper, 2005).

This helped ensure industrial relations were far less divisive than in the early 1990s. The Labour-coalition's 2000 Employment Relations Act maintained individual agreements for employees whose job could be covered by a collective agreement but the union movement supported its softening of some of National's restrictions on union membership (Rudman, 1999). Moreover, government policy delivered substantial improvements to workers through: the introduction of paid parental leave and a fourth week of annual leave; nine increases in the minimum wage in eight years (compared to four in nine years under National); the right to request changes in working hours and improved worker conditions around rest breaks and infant feeding; and the renationalisation of ACC in 1999. While these government-led initiatives had positive outcomes for many workers, they may have discouraged some New Zealanders from viewing union membership as necessary (Rasmussen and Lamm, 2005; Rasmussen et al, 2006; Burton, 2010).

The only economic policy which really distinguished the new government from National, however, was the emphasis on maintaining key industries in New Zealand ownership, thus securing profits and jobs stayed in the country. Financial troubles at Air New Zealand, privatised in 1989, saw the Labour-coalition buy back 80% of the airline in 2001. In the same year it repurchased the Auckland suburban rail network, followed by the national Tranzrail network in 2003–04 and, finally, all rail and ferry assets in 2008. The Alliance coalition partner also negotiated the establishment of Kiwibank as a subsidiary of the state-owned enterprise New Zealand Post in 2002 and Television New Zealand was restructured as a Crown Entity in 2003, requiring the broadcaster to maintain commercial performance while also following a new public service Charter (Roper, 2005).

That Labour-coalition policy represented a *continuation* of a neoliberal economic agenda was blurred not only by these economic policy reversals but also by the adoption of a communicative discourse focused on 'social inclusion' and 'social development'. Framing the 'socially excluded' (those involuntarily deprived of the opportunity to participate and belong) as constituting both an economic and social cost justified 'social investment' in policy initiatives aiming to improve social wellbeing *and* raise the human and social capital needed for a globally competitive economy (Ministry of Social Policy – MoSP, 2001; Porter and Craig, 2004).

In this context, Labour attempted to reduce educational inequalities that had developed through the 1990s by reintroducing zoning to prevent over-subscribed state schools picking off middle class students from poorer schools, capping private school subsidies and discontinuing bulk funding for teacher's salaries, instead redistributing these funds through a decile system favouring schools in low socio-economic areas (Thrupp, 2007). There was also less dogmatic reliance on 'the market' in the Labour-coalition's tertiary education strategies, alongside a shift towards funding based on outcomes rather than just outputs (Roberts and Codd, 2010). The most visible and traceable policy shift, however, was the Labour-coalition's exemption of student loan interest from all full-time students still studying from 2001 and all borrowers resident in New Zealand from 2006. Having also frozen tuition fees from 2000 to 2003, these changes significantly improved the affordability of tertiary education (Roper, 2005; St John and Rankin, 2009).

Labour also reformed the health sector, replacing CHEs with democratically-elected District Health Boards in 2000. The Health Funding Authority was abolished and the Ministry of Health re-established with responsibilities for funding as well as policy advice. A shift away from hospital-based service outputs towards health status via population-based objectives led to the introduction of community-based Primary Health Organisations (PHOs) in 2002 (Duncan, 2007; Cheyne et al, 2008). These improved access to primary healthcare and reduced user charges. By 2004, 91% of the population were enrolled in the 82 PHOs, suggesting such improvements were highly visible and popular among the public (Quin, 2009).

The Labour-led government not only restored New Zealand Superannuation to 65% of average wages in 1999 but also invested government surpluses in a newly established New Zealand Superannuation Fund from 2001, with withdrawals expected to help pay for superannuation benefits from 2020. Such planning provided reassurance that universalism would continue but individual responsibility for private retirement savings was encouraged through a voluntary work-focused, auto-enrolment private savings scheme called KiwiSaver, introduced in 2007 with no prior warning. Automatic enrolment for workers changing jobs and generous government subsidies, however, facilitated high take up and suggested superannuation was at least partially a government responsibility (St John and Rankin, 2009).

Given low unemployment during the 2000s, those remaining on income support had significant caring responsibilities, disabilities or faced multiple disadvantages. The new government initially softened work capacity, testing and sanction regimes, most notably by abolishing the Community Wage and reinstituting named unemployment benefits in 2001 (Roper, 2005; St John and Rankin, 2009). But, focused on both the rights *and* responsibilities associated with citizenship, the Labour-coalition introduced Job Seeker Agreements setting out a benefit recipient's employment-related responsibilities and the penalties for non-compliance while at the same time placing a much greater focus on case management, education and training to support the unemployed moving into work. In 2002, work tests for Domestic Purposes benefit or Widows benefit recipients were replaced by compulsory Personal Development and Employment Plans, and pilot projects from this time made greater support available for people with ill health or disability who wished to work (NZG, 2001; Benson-Pope, 2006; Lunt, 2006b).

As the 2000s progressed, it became increasingly apparent that the Labour-coalition's concern with inclusion was driven by a belief that 'work in paid employment offers the best opportunity for people to achieve social and economic well-being' (NZG, 2007, n.p.). With an enhanced case management system in place, work-focused assistance was extended to *all* clients regardless of their benefit type in 2007 and benefit recipients were streamed according to work status. Domestic Purposes benefit recipients found their planning and activity requirements and sanctions strengthened and those on Sickness and Invalid's benefits became subject to them for the first time. These changes were driven by a belief that every unemployed person should receive the same, generic benefit and be subject to the same work-testing conditions, with only additional payments acknowledging special circumstances. Labour abandoned its generic benefit policy when the economy slowed in 2008 but the 2007 Social Security Amendment Act further strengthened work testing, including a new *pre*-benefit activity requirement for the unemployed, and revised the fundamental principles behind social security to reflect the 'work-first approach' already adopted (St John and Rankin, 2009). Public debate and discussion about these changes was limited, being largely visible and proximate only to benefit recipients who, given the strong economy at the time, were relatively small in number and lacked the power to actively resist such policy changes.

There was far more debate about the Working for Families package introduced in 2004. Aimed at low and middle income families with dependent children, it included increases to Family Support, a new In-Work Tax Credit, changes to abatement rates and thresholds for the Accommodation Supplement and increased childcare subsidies (St John and Rankin, 2009). Child poverty was a significant issue during the 2002 election and, although no specific targets were established, Working for Families explicitly aimed to reduce child poverty by 'making work pay'. Evidence suggests it did contribute to falling child poverty between 2004 and 2007 for children in 'working' households (Perry, 2010). But the Child Poverty Action Group (Dale et al, 2011) prominently argued that the strategy's impact was limited by the exclusion of benefit recipients from the In-Work Tax Credit. With benefit purchasing power falling and with hardship provisions tightened after 2005, Working for Families thus further enhanced the discursive distinction between deserving low and middle income families who were working longer for less and undeserving benefit recipients, for whom this package provided a monetary incentive to gain employment (Roper, 2005; Humpage and Craig, 2008).

Although this discourse attempted to justify the redistributive effects of Working for Families, the political Right called it 'middle class welfare' and promoted tax cuts instead. The Labour-coalition had increased the top marginal tax rate on income from 33% to 39% in 2000 but tax did not become a significant issue until after 2002 (Levine and Roberts, 2003). Mounting political pressure for tax cuts during the 2005 election saw the government extend Working for Families to provide further 'tax relief' for low and middle income families in lieu of a general tax cut, but it eventually gave in to demand and reduced top tax rates in 2008 (St John and Rankin, 2009). The election campaign that year was dominated by the country's descent into recession and, although statistics showed inequality and poverty were on the rise again after improvements in the mid-2000s, these immediate economic worries framed the National Party's return to power (Perry, 2010; Roper, 2011).

Overall, the Labour-coalition government addressed some of New Zealand's concerns, modifying the harshest restrictions on union activity, attempting to 'make work pay' through regular increases to minimum wages and the Working for Families strategy, renationalising ACC and returning a small number of state assets to public ownership. Its attempts to tackle growing social inequalities and reluctance to adopt a neoconservative welfare dependency discourse distinguish it from the previous National government and were factors behind the diminishing level of public protest (Roper, 2005). But, as critics elsewhere have noted, the Third Way's interest in inequality stemmed more from its potential impact on future economic progress than a genuine desire for social justice (Schmidtke, 2002; Dwyer, 2004a). Certainly, paid work was considered the best form of social inclusion, justifying greater levels of conditionality for benefit recipients and diminishing the social rights of this group, even as it strengthened those of deserving workers contributing to the economy.

—

Third Way versus Howard's way?

Giving the public a little of what they wanted while at the same time consolidating and embedding most of the broader neoliberal economic agenda is also a criticism made of the British Labour government between 1997 and 2010 (Lister, 2003b; Hall, 2005). But Australia is more complicated to characterise during this period, being governed by John Howard's conservative Liberal-National coalition government (1996–2010) which further retrenched social rights in some policy areas. Notably, however, 14 of 16 individual pieces of industrial relations legislation were blocked in the Senate between 1996 and 2004 by minor parties and the Liberal-National coalition only gained the majority needed to complete labour market deregulation in 2005. The more incremental nature of the Australian reforms probably reduced the kind of lock-in effects experienced in New Zealand and the UK, where labour market deregulation occurred early and rapidly. Certainly the significant public protest provoked by the 2005 WorkChoices legislation suggests that unions were still considered crucial for protecting employment rights in Australia (Taylor, 2009; Lewis et al, 2010). However, it is also interesting to note that Australian reforms in 1997 and 2005 *increased* state intervention, with greater regulation of union workplace access and on union elections and strike ballots, potentially leading to a greater sense of government responsibility in this area than in New Zealand or the UK (Wilson et al, 2013).

All three countries undertook significant privatisation in the early years of reform (Pusey and Turnbull, 2005). But New Zealand stands out for renationalising ACC, Air New Zealand and Kiwi Rail and establishing Kiwi Bank in the 2000s. In the UK, the Post Office was further commercialised and public-private partnerships developed so that private companies could take responsibility for key infrastructure. Several such partnerships failed in key areas, resulting in private companies seeking financial assistance from the government, potentially shaping British attitudes towards privatisation (Parker, 2004). Australia's privatisation programme was only *completed* in 1999, after years of Senate resistance, when the Liberal-National government was re-elected despite campaigning on a platform of further privatisation for Telstra (Pusey and Turnbull, 2005).

New Zealand also diverged from the other two countries by significantly strengthening social rights in two key social policy areas. The highly popular and visible PHO system is likely to have enhanced public support for the idea that the government should take a responsibility in healthcare during the 2000s, given that it significantly increased the affordability and universality of primary care. In the UK, health similarly benefited from significant spending increases, which saw waiting times drop to an historic low in 2007 and a strong emphasis on primary care. However greater use of financial incentives for individuals and organisations, including the option of using private services, drove reforms to improve patient choice and competition (Appleby and Phillips, 2009; Ham, 2009). The Australian Liberal-National government recognised the electoral advantage of maintaining Labor's Medicare but introduced incentives for low and middle income individuals and families to take up private health insurance in the late 1990s. This increased the number of Australians covered privately from around 30% in 1998 to 45% by 2009, the highest of the three countries (Bryson, 2001; Lewis et al, 2010; Organisation for Economic Co-operation and Development – OECD, 2013; Wilson et al, 2013).

New Zealand's interest-free tertiary student loan policy, which reframed tertiary education as a public good, also diverged from the trends apparent in the two other countries. British Prime Minister, Tony Blair's (1996, n.p.) mantra 'education, education, education' brought a substantial increase in spending on education but Labour further marketised education when *introducing* tertiary fees in 1998 (Sefton et al, 2009; Zimdars et al, 2012). The Australian Liberal-Coalition, meanwhile, significantly reduced public funding to tertiary education, stimulating rapid tuition fee increases. In 2001, a loans scheme for the private cost of fees was introduced, contributing to a further significant shift in the ratio of public to private contributions (Brennan, 2005).

Although New Zealand's universal superannuation still set it apart from the UK and Australia, Labour's KiwiSaver private superannuation scheme was in line with international trends that saw governments encourage increased private savings for retirement. In 2002, British Labour replaced the State Earnings Related Pension scheme with a new State Second Pension, providing higher earnings-related benefits for low and middle income pensioners but, when modified to include a system of credits, the basic pension shrank and pensioner poverty grew from 2004. It also created the Personal Accounts Delivery Authority to enrol employees automatically into a qualifying workplace pension scheme with a minimum employer contribution (Sefton et al, 2009; Stewart, 2009a). The Australian Liberal-National government offered generous tax concessions for mandatory private superannuation and liberalised age pension income and asset tests but did not prioritise spending on pensions overall (Harding et al, 2009; OECD, 2013).

New Zealand also diverges from the other two countries because it did not significantly privatise employment services. Australia conducted one of the most radical experiments in the world when replacing the long standing government-operated Commonwealth Employment Service with an integrated quasi-market of employment services. These linked the federal government purchaser with the two providers, Centrelink (the former Department of Social Security) and Job Network, a system of over 200 for-profit and non-profit human service agencies (Marston and McDonald, 2007). Wright et al (2011) note, however, that Australia's mixed welfare economy had long offered a well-developed role for both for-profit and non-profit organisations than found in the UK, making the creation of the British Jobcentre Plus in 2001 even more radical. By 2006 Jobcentre Plus provided a single national gateway to services from the former Employment Service, Benefits Agency and other welfare providers, including those in the private sector.

The differences are more subtle when it comes to specific social security policies, given that conditionality increased in all three countries. Both the New Zealand and UK governments articulated an interest in rights *and* responsibilities but with greater focus on training and support than found in Australia where the Liberal-National government's communicative discourse was more explicitly neopaternalist, consistently contrasting undeserving 'dole bludgers' with deserving 'Aussie battlers' (Eardley et al, 2000; Marston and McDonald, 2007). There a work for the dole programme became central to Australian social security from 1998. British Labour's New Deal programme required participation in either training or subsidised or voluntary work (Gu, 2011) but New Zealand's Labour-coalition government abolished the programme established by National. Welfare dependency rhetoric was also more racialised in Australia, with indigenous Australians in remote communities becoming the focus of income quarantining trials from 2007 (Mendes, 2009). The political opposition framed Māori as 'privileged' by biculturalism, but the Labour-coalition government did not racialise welfare dependency in this way (Humpage, 2006).

Indeed, although many policies attempted to address ethnic socio-economic disadvantage, New Zealand's focus on social inclusion conspicuously avoided acknowledging race and ethnicity (Elizabeth and Larner, 2009). Overall, this social inclusion discourse, as well as those focused on 'making work pay' and child poverty, were less visible than in the UK, where Labour established the first ever national minimum wage, introduced a wider range of tax credits, set ambitious targets to reduce child poverty and increased the universal Child Benefit (Hills, 1998; Harker, 2006; Waltman and Marsh, 2007; Stewart, 2009a, 2009b). In Australia, Labor-led state governments articulated an interest in social capital and inclusion and even the federal Liberal-National government used this language by the early 2000s, but no effective communicative discourse was established (Norton, 2004; Mendes, 2005). Australia's core focus on welfare dependency also did nothing to encourage discussion about poverty and, in extensively using tax incentives to garner support from the 'aspirational' middle class, the family payment system's anti-poverty goals were lost (Smyth, 2010; Wilson et al, 2012). However, although the UK spent more than the other two countries on family benefits, Australia remained the most highly redistributive towards lower income earners (Whiteford, 2006; Harding et al, 2009; Wilson et al, 2012). In this sense, there were not only ideological differences between the Liberal-National government and its Labour counterparts in New Zealand and the UK during this period but also differences in the extent and visibility of the negative social outcomes driving the internal crisis of public dissatisfaction that New Zealand and British Third Way policies explicitly tried to address.

Roll-over neoliberalism: 2008–

This book argues that neoliberalism's vulnerability to regulatory crises and market failures led to further discursive and institutional adjustments in the late 2000s, opening up opportunities for further entrenchment of market-disciplinary modes of governance (Peck et al, 2012). In New Zealand, the economy shaped both the 2008 election result and National's first term, with the need to reduce the internal deficit justifying zero budgets two years running, significant public sector job cuts and highly visible plans to partially privatise state assets. Importantly, however, National bolstered spending in some areas by making cuts elsewhere and a series of national disasters (including the Canterbury earthquakes, Pike River mine disaster and the Rena oil spill) helped build a sense that reduced spending in some areas was necessary (Roper, 2011). By 2011, economic concerns were weakening but the deficit remained a major justification for significant reforms in social security and industrial relations.

Nonetheless, the new government tried to appease voters by going ahead with promised tax cuts in 2009, 2010 and 2011 that disproportionately benefited middle and high income earners and a rise in GST to 15% that negatively affected low income earners.

While these endorsed the National Party's (2008, p A12) election slogan – 'its time to choose a Government that is focused on what matters to you' – a new Independent Earner Tax Credit targeting full-time workers receiving below-average wages indicated a concern with neoliberalism's social impacts that had been largely missing during the 1990s (St John and Rankin, 2009; National Party, 2011). Similarly, National offered relatively generous redundancy and wage supplement packages for individuals temporarily affected by the recession in 2008 and the Canterbury earthquakes in 2010–11. These were short term and excluded those already unemployed but recognised that structural factors can affect employment opportunities (Key, 2008).

In response to rapidly growing youth unemployment, National also introduced a Youth Opportunities package subsidising six-month job placements in businesses or community programmes for low skilled young people, while a Youth Guarantee aimed to keep 16 and 17-year-olds engaged in learning by allowing them to study towards free school level qualifications at a range of public and private learning institutions, including newly established Trades Academies for trade and technology training. Although a new bootcamp-style Limited Service Volunteer programme for 18 to 24-year-olds indicated the neopaternalist drivers behind the National Party's (2011) interest in young people, these policies exemplify Vis et al's (2012) view that the welfare state was seen as part of the *solution* to the problems caused by the latest economic crisis.

What National did *not* do in its first term provides further evidence that this was a new phase of neoliberalism. Although repealing the Employment Relations Act was National's official policy for some years, in 2008 it promised only less prescriptive bargaining processes and a more business-friendly focus. This meant radical employment relations reforms were not high on the political agenda for the first time in nearly three decades (Rasmussen and Anderson, 2010). Several policies detrimental to the right to decent employment – most controversially a 90-day trial period for new employees – were introduced, but National's first term reforms were very incremental. The Labour-coalition's flexible working hours legislation was retained and minimum wages continued to increase, although allowed to fall relative to average weekly earnings (Burton, 2010; Wilkinson, 2010; National Party, 2011; Wilson et al, 2013).

Despite earlier criticism of Working for Families, National not only retained this strategy but extended the associated 20 hours free early childhood assistance to under-fives and to a wider range of providers (National Party, 2011). The need for recessionary cost cutting, however, provided the rationale for reducing the income threshold and increasing abatement levels. Thomas (2008) argues that a steep drop in the number of Domestic Purposes benefit recipients, following the introduction of Working for Families, suggests that the widening of the financial gap between work and non-work provided a bigger incentive to get this group into work than conditionality. Nonetheless, at a time of relatively low unemployment, the Domestic Purposes and Sickness benefits were a more fruitful focus for reform than the Unemployment benefit, explaining National's election promise to reinstitute work testing for Domestic Purposes benefit recipients once their youngest child turned five and introduce conditional medical checks for those on the Sickness benefit. In contrast, National clearly announced it would *not* reintroduce work for the dole and, with the media offering cautionary reminders of the social costs of roll-back reforms, was careful not to develop an extreme position on welfare in its first term (New Zealand Herald – NZH, 2008a, 2008b; St John and Rankin, 2009). From 2010, however, an explicit welfare dependency discourse was used to frame significant reforms aiming 'to ensure a fairer system of social assistance with an unrelenting focus on work' (NZG, 2010, p 1). National imposed a work test of 15 hours per week on sole parents whose youngest child was aged six and on Sickness benefit recipients deemed able to work part time with sanctions of reduced benefit payments for non-compliance (Dale et al, 2010). It also required unemployment benefit recipients to reapply every 12 months, while the Sickness benefit was subject to yearly reviews and eight-week medical certificates (National Party, 2011).

In addition, National established a Welfare Working Group (WWG, 2010) to examine ways to reduce long-term benefit dependency for people of working age. Its terms of reference excluded income adequacy, New Zealand Superannuation, the tax benefit interface and Working for Families tax credits, ensuring discussion was primarily on benefit recipient behaviours. Following two rounds of public submissions, the WWG (2011) proposed: Jobseeker Support, a new single work-focused welfare payment to replace all existing categories of benefit; a new outcomes-focused delivery agency called Employment and Support New Zealand; and an actuarial approach to measuring the forward liability of welfare dependency, including numerical targets for reducing the number of income support recipients. An Alternative Welfare Working Group (Welfare Justice, 2010a, 2010b) established by non-governmental agencies attempted to counter this welfare dependency discourse but public debate was more limited than that evident in the 1990s.

The National Party (2011) used the election to seek a mandate to implement the WWG's recommendations, promising both to protect welfare for those who deserved it and to clamp down on benefit fraud. Once elected, National drip-fed its responses to the WWG (2011) recommendations to the media, finally indicating some were too strong, thus making the government's reforms look moderate in comparison. The WWG (2011) process had done much of the discursive work in trying to shape public attitudes by the time 16 and 17-year-old benefit recipients and 18-year-old parents were subjected to income management controls over their benefit in 2011. National also announced that three new benefits (Jobseeker Support, Sole Parent Support and Supported Living Payment) would replace the existing seven in 2012. This 'simplified' benefit system was similar to that proposed by the Labour-coalition in the mid-2000s; National also borrowed Third Way language when talking about an 'investment based approach' tailoring support to individuals based on their likelihood of becoming long-term welfare dependent (National Party, 2011). Labour attempted to highlight the negative impact of a renewed emphasis on welfare dependency would have on child poverty during the election but National was more interested in a new Children's Action Plan targeting 'vulnerable' children and parents at risk of abusing or neglecting them (Barron, 2011; Ministry of Social Development, 2012). National did form a Ministerial Committee on Poverty (2011, p 1) as part of its 2011 confidence and supply agreement with the Māori Party but the committee's scope was very much framed by the mantra 'work is the primary route out of poverty'.

Superannuation was the other big social policy issue of the 2011 election but, in contrast to welfare, no significant communicative discourse was developed. National made no regressive changes to universal superannuation in its first term, while reducing government-funded incentives and contribution rates for KiwiSaver and pausing New Zealand Superannuation Fund payments until the country was back in surplus. These moves were not particularly controversial. Then, four weeks after the election, Labour announced it would retain universality and the current rate of 66% of the average wage but gradually lift the age of New Zealand Superannuation eligibility from 65 to 67, starting in 2020. Labour also promised to make KiwiSaver compulsory and to immediately resume contributions to the Superannuation Fund, a policy said to cost NZ$6.1 billion over four years. In response, Key pledged the age of eligibility would not change while he was Prime Minister and accused Labour of adding extra debt that was unaffordable and illogical (Barron, 2011; Hartevalt and Vance, 2011a).

National also did not tamper significantly with tertiary education. Framed in terms of improving value for money, it retained the interest-free loans policy for tertiary students resident in New Zealand but incentivised repayments (with enhanced penalties) and placed time- and grade-based performance limits on borrowing. National also linked funding to tertiary institutions to performance rather than just student numbers. In compulsory education, National increased spending on school infrastructure and ultra-fast broadband but also increased funding to private schools and introduced National Standards in 2009, with the latter causing considerable protest among both teachers and parents (Thrupp and Irwin, 2010; National Party, 2011). Notably, National did not implement the policies it promoted during the mid-2000s: a voucher system for extra tuition in reading and maths; compulsory bulk funding; performance-based teachers' salaries; and an end to rigid zoning (Clark, 2010).

National also maintained the Labour-coalition's PHO system and increased health spending in its first three years in an attempt to reduce waiting lists, raising no spectre of 1990s-style restructuring. The 2011 election even saw National promise free after-hours GP visits for children under six, an after-hours telephone health advice service, improved home support services and the extension of a voluntary bonding scheme for health graduates agreeing to work in hard-to-staff specialties or regions (National Party, 2011). Furthermore, National tried to win support for its plan to partially privatise a number of key public assets by announcing it would fence off funds gained from such privatisation for future infrastructure investments, including hospitals and schools. Labour made 'no asset sales' a major part of its 2011 campaign, rightly assessing that many New Zealanders supported this view. But the election result suggests that National's fencing off of privatisation funds and its conscious attempts to address public concerns about assets being sold to foreign owners by prioritising 'average' New Zealanders in the first round of share allocation were successful (Barron, 2011).

New Zealand's most recent phase of neoliberalism thus represents a unique hybrid form of governance. National retained policies supporting key social rights in health and education and indicated there was still a role for the government in employment through further minimum wage increases, recession-focused redundancy and subsidy packages and its youth employment strategies. The word 'redistribution' was not used but keeping Working for Families and a new Independent Earner Tax Credit suggested National thought it appropriate to assist low to middle income workers. Was National re-elected in 2011 because this emphasis on economic *and* social objectives blurred the distinction between it and Labour and was effective in reassuring some of the New Zealanders concerned about the social impact of neoliberalism? That National tactically avoided promoting some of its more controversial policies until after its 2011 win certainly implies it had learned that rapid, radical reform provoked a negative public reaction. Yet at the same time, National extended both the neopaternalism of the 1990s through further social security reform and its neoliberal economic agenda, via incremental industrial relations changes and partial privatisation of state assets. With further retrenchment planned, these facts indicate roll-over neoliberalism was under way.

Retrenchment versus stability

Although the global economic recession helped justify such retrenchment in New Zealand, National's reforms were comparatively moderate compared to those implemented in the UK under the Conservative-Liberal Democratic government formed in 2010. Facing its first double dip recession since 1975, the UK's bleak economic situation was used to rationalise more radical reforms than implemented in New Zealand, Australia or, indeed, most European Union countries (Cameron and Clegg, 2010; Taylor-Gooby and Stoker, 2011). Aiming to cut an average of 20% from government spending over four years, the new government eliminated 490,000 government jobs, cut benefits, abolished 'unnecessary' programmes and froze public employee salaries (Clarke et al, 2012).

An 80% cut to overall tertiary teaching funding was particularly controversial. This saw the top level of tuition fees which could be charged by English universities increase by almost 275%, provoking opposition within parliament and large-scale public demonstrations during 2011 (Levitas, 2012; Zimdars et al, 2012). There was also heavy criticism of plans to devolve the management and ownership of the NHS by establishing clinical commissioning groups led by GPs to buy healthcare services on behalf of their local populations in place of Primary Care Trusts. These would take control of around 60% of the total NHS budget, which saw no real increase between 2011 and 2015 in England and real reductions in Wales and Scotland (Appleby and Lee, 2012; Clarke et al, 2012). A highly visible dispute over public sector pensions also emerged, involving major union mobilisations in

2011. The government protected many key benefits for older people and restored the earnings link for the basic state pension from 2011, but established an independent commission to review the long-term affordability of public sector pensions and the age of eligibility for state pensions (Cameron and Clegg, 2010; Levitas, 2012). After being allowed to stagnate for some time, the minimum wage was increased in 2011 but younger workers were disadvantaged and a range of other reforms and consultations intended to reduce the impact of employment regulation on businesses were introduced (Carley, 2011; Hall, 2012). The new government also used the financial crisis to propose targeting the universal Child Benefit, the Sure Start childcare and early education programme and some tax credits (Harrop, 2012).

The British experience of retrenchment sits in stark contrast with Australia, which did not technically enter a recession during the financial crisis. Under a Labor government from 2007 (with Green Party and independent support), Australia's increase in social spending in response to the global recession was above the OECD average, while New Zealand sat around the average and the UK was below it. Education and health infrastructure were a key focus of Labor's early stimulus spending and pension rates were increased (OECD, 2012; Starke, 2013). Labor's reversal of the unpopular WorkChoices legislation in 2009, however, was what really set it apart from the UK and New Zealand, where the right to decent work and conditions was further diminished. A new body, Fair Work Australia, was established as a national workplace relations tribunal with wide-ranging powers relating to setting minimum wages and conditions, bargaining and dispute resolution (Lewis et al, 2010). Despite the relatively low take up of enterprise bargaining, Taylor (2009) argues that this was the first backslide in the neoliberal reform agenda in 30 years.

New Zealand's economy was weaker than Australia's but did relatively well in a global context, meaning policy was far more stable in both countries when compared to the UK. Just as in the 1980s and early 1990s, Britons protested against the rapid and radical spending cuts and we might therefore expect British support for social citizenship to have responded by increasing support for spending, as Chapter Two indicated has happened in the past. However, the British coalition government's strong 'austerity' discourse alluded to the period of enforced austerity between 1940 and 1955, invoking nostalgic sentiment about being 'in this together'. In addition, an emphasis on the Big Society and social action at the local level shared some similarities with Labour's focus on community and social exclusion, calling for a revival of civil society as a counterweight to neoliberalism.

These multiple communicative discourses may have persuaded the public of the need for reform, particularly since the Conservative-Liberal Democrat government's devolution of power and responsibility downwards framed civil society and the voluntary sector as supporting the kind of values that would counter welfare dependency (Macleavy, 2011; Clarke et al, 2012; Clarke and Newman, 2012; Levitas, 2012). As in New Zealand, many key reforms were not passed into law until 2012 but, in being touted as some of the biggest changes in the welfare system for more than 60 years, the coalition's social security reforms were highly publicly visible before this (Clery, 2012b).

National's communicative discourse centred on welfare dependency and economic austerity was not as multi-layered nor as strong as the Conservative-Liberal Democrat government's, while in Australia Labor used comparatively neutral language to talk about benefit recipients and established a new Minister for Social Inclusion and a Social Inclusion Unit to assist the most disadvantaged geographic areas and communities to re-enter mainstream economic and social life (Harding et al, 2009). Despite easing income tests for some benefits and a focus on job subsidies and training initiatives, Labor did not improve the generosity of unemployment benefits (which are low by international standards) and it maintained and, in some cases, strengthened its predecessor's paternalist and authoritarian regime, notably by extending compulsory income management to all benefit recipients (Mendes, 2009; Wilson et al, 2013). Thus by 2011, all three countries had adopted a kind of hybrid discourse that during the first phase of reform had only been evident in Australia.

Conclusion: the coherence and diversity of neoliberalism

This chapter has provided a comprehensive background to the empirical study of public attitudes to social citizenship in New Zealand by exploring how the policy and politics that constitute the process of neoliberalisation varied across three phases. Given the evidence presented here and in Chapter Two, it seems likely the New Zealand public's policy mood will have turned against the first phase of radical and rapid reform in the 1980s and 1990s. But did the opposite occur when the Labour-coalition government reversed some neoliberal policies during the 2000s? Or, as Sefton (2003, 2009) and Curtice (2010) found in the UK, did the Third Way simply legitimise the retrenchment of social rights? To answer these questions, the next four chapters track New Zealand attitudes not only across these two phases but into a third period dominated by the return of a conservative

National government. The public's response to this unique, hybrid discourse will inform arguments about the long-term impact of neoliberalism on public attitudes towards social citizenship.

These arguments will be further supported by analysing key differences in the policy and discourses found in the two other case study countries. Table 3.1 summarises this chapter's finding that the three phases of neoliberalism brought sharper policy shifts in New Zealand and the UK when compared to Australia; a far stronger public opinion reaction might therefore be expected in the first two countries, particularly in the early period of radical and rapid reform in the 1980s and 1990s but potentially into the 2000s.

This chapter has further indicated that neoliberal reforms diminished social citizenship rights overall but were implemented with differing degrees of success across the four policy areas discussed. In all three countries, economic policy was implemented with the fewest policy reversals, even if Australia was slower in completing this process and New Zealand Labour-coalition governments renationalised some assets and both it and Australian Labor modified neoliberal changes in industrial relations. The greatest shift in public attitudes might therefore be expected to be seen regarding the right to employment, which is most heavily affected by economic policy.

Table 3.1: Neoliberalism three ways

	New Zealand	United Kingdom	Australia
Roll-back phase			
Nature of reform	Rapid and radical	Rapid and radical	Incremental and constrained by Senate
Communicative discourse	Largely ineffective	Largely effective	Effective
Social rights	Significantly retrenched	Significantly retrenched	Some retrenchment but also some expansion (health)
Key differences	Electoral reform 1993 + Healthcare significantly marketised with some reversals 1996 + Universal superannuation restored	Universal healthcare maintained	Greater consensus about need for reform

Industrial relations reform not completed

Focus on obligations *and* rights of unemployed |

(continued)

Table 3.1: Neoliberalism three ways (continued)

	New Zealand	United Kingdom	Australia
	Roll-out phase		
Nature of reform	Moderate policy reversals	Mild policy reversals	Incremental extension (industrial relations, privatisation) but reform constrained by Senate
Communicative discourse	Largely effective	Effective	Effective
Social rights	Strengthened in some areas (health, education, industrial relations) but weakened in social security	Strengthened in some areas (health, education) but weakened in social security	Mostly maintained but weakened in health, education and social security
Key differences	MMP Renationalisation of key assets Universal superannuation Interest-free tertiary loans Primary Care Organisations system established Employment services not privatised	Minimum wage introduced Child poverty reduction targets established	Industrial relations reforms completed in 2005 Work for the dole consistently maintained
	Roll-over phase		
Nature of reform	Incremental (privatisation, industrial relations)	Rapid and radical (education) or moderate (health and pensions)	Minimal
Communicative discourse	Effective	Effective	Mixed
Social rights	Retrenched (social security)	Heavily retrenched (education, health, social security)	Largely stable
Key differences		Economic crisis greater impact Large tertiary education and NHS cuts	Reversed industrial relations reforms

In social policy, New Zealand's reforms overall were some the most radical found in the three countries but New Zealand also saw significant policy reversals (notably in healthcare, superannuation and, to a lesser extent, education) from the mid-1990s (see Table 3.1). New Zealand attitudes towards the right to health, education and pensions might thus be expected to fluctuate more than those of their British and Australian counterparts. With the exception of minor changes in the Labour-coalition's first term in government, there were virtually no policy reversals in social security in any of the three countries. Although a distinction between the deserving and undeserving poor was not new, it is likely that attitudes towards social security hardened as 'welfare' became less proximate to members of the public due to increased targeting and conditionality. Similarly, it seems likely that New Zealanders will have come to accept neoliberal arguments that need and inequality are inevitable, given weakening policy interest in redistribution and the greater use of the tax system (through tax credits and cuts) makes redistribution less visible and less traceable as a form of government income assistance (Rankin, 1997).

However, New Zealand views about poverty and inequality may be mediated by an awareness that income inequality and poverty grew faster over the past three decades in New Zealand than in the UK and Australia (OECD, 2011). Certainly, this chapter has illustrated that policy and politics are dynamic, with alternative public discourses and economic conditions mediating the process of neoliberalisation and its likely impact on public beliefs about social citizenship. Both will be discussed further in the following four chapters, which explore shifts in New Zealand attitudes towards social citizenship since the 1980s.

FOUR

Employment and decent wages in a neoliberal economy

The most fundamental and enduring aspect of neoliberalisation is its economic agenda, predicated on low inflation, globalised free trade, support for business and a rebalancing of the worker–employer relationship. This chapter uses New Zealand Election Survey (NZES) and other relevant data to consider how public attitudes towards employment shifted in line with this economic transformation, which was facilitated by a fragile economic context in the 1970s and 1980s. A breakdown of the compulsory conciliation and arbitration system increased industrial conflict but trade union bargaining power weakened as unemployment grew significantly for the first time in decades and international trade was threatened by the oil shocks and the United Kingdom's (UK) 1973 admission to the European Community. The economy was left weak by Prime Minister Robert Muldoon's answer: abolish compulsory unionism and allow limited financial and trade deregulation while increasing export subsidies, freezing wages, prices and rents and embarking on a massive infrastructure investment programme. Moreover, Muldoon's refusal to devalue the New Zealand dollar after notification of an early election led to a foreign currency crisis, allowing the new Labour administration to frame 'government intervention' as part of the problem it needed to fix (Walsh and Brosnan, 1999; Roper, 2005; Starke, 2008).

Chapter Three provided an overview of the rapid, radical neoliberal reforms that transformed New Zealand's economy from 1984, diminishing the social right to employment and decent wages in visible and traceable ways. No longer considering job supply a government responsibility, the 4th Labour government abandoned the goal of full employment, cut import controls and agricultural subsidies and privatised many public sector assets. The NZES does not include questions on every aspect of social citizenship affected by such reforms, but the first section of this chapter uses those available to explore how such changes interacted with New Zealand views on the government's responsibility to provide jobs and on import and wage controls.

The National government's 1991 Employment Contracts Act completed the economic reforms and risked the very existence of unions as effective organisations promoting decent wages and conditions (Vowles and Aimer, 1993). Responding to public concern about the low wages that resulted, the Labour-coalition government's focus on 'making work pay' from 1999 brought regular minimum wage increases and the Working for Families In-Work Tax Credit for low and middle income earners from 2005 (Roper, 2005; Cotterell, 2009). Despite coming to power in 2008 as the country headed into another recession, National continued both policies and retained the Labour-coalition's 2000 Employment Relations Act, which softened some of the restrictions on union membership but arguably helped make a neoliberal labour market more palatable for workers and their union representatives. National certainly did not find it difficult incrementally to extend further 'business friendly' industrial relations policies after 2008. The second section of this chapter is thus concerned with how New Zealanders view unions, while a third considers whether a more 'business friendly' economy and the privatisation of many state-owned assets changed New Zealand attitudes towards big business and public ownership, despite the Labour-led government's renationalisation of some state assets in the 2000s.

Analysis is mainly focused on the covariance between policy and attitudes – both overall and across differing phases of neoliberalism – but the chapter also examines whether the unemployment rate may influence responses regarding employment issues. The assessment in this chapter of whether New Zealanders have rolled over and endorsed a neoliberal economic agenda is supported by consideration of how ideological affiliation and age shape attitudes. Qualitative data from 2007–08 are used to flesh out my analysis, although to a lesser extent than in the chapters that follow, given that economic issues were not a key focus on the qualitative study.

Each section ends by considering how the New Zealand findings compare with the available data on attitudinal change in the UK and Australia. There are important cases of coherence in both policy and attitudes but the variegated nature of neoliberalism is reflected in differing attitudes across time and space. Overall, the chapter illustrates that support for employment-related aspects of social citizenship has in many cases diminished, providing some evidence that citizens have rolled over. But in order to understand neoliberalism's mixed influence in the economic arena, the three key issues discussed must first be unpacked.

Government responsibility for employment

Considering public opinion about government responsibility for employment is the most direct way to assess attitudes towards the right to employment and decent wages. In 2011, 57.2% of NZES respondents still believed 'government should take responsibility to provide jobs for everyone', less than 3 percentage points lower than in 1990. As Figure 4.1 indicates, a majority supported this proposition in all years, suggesting little change in attitudes over time.

Other survey data, however, indicate far stronger support for similar propositions prior to 1990. In 1963, 90% of a voting study's respondents agreed 'government has a responsibility to see that anyone who wanted a job could get one' (Cleveland, 1986), while 86% of New Zealand Attitudes and Values Survey (NZAVS) respondents still agreed 'all should have a job who wants one' in 1987. The latter question does not ask whether the *government* should take responsibility for achieving this outcome but submissions to the Royal Commission on Social Policy (RCSP, 1988a: 235), which prompted the survey, commonly articulated that '[a] basic human right is the right to work and there should be observation of both moral law as well as economic law' to ensure this was achieved. This explains why 60% of NZAVS respondents wanted more spent on 'creating jobs', while 93% thought that the 'effect on jobs available' should be an important consideration for the government when making

Figure 4.1: 'Government should take responsibility to provide jobs for everyone' (LH) by unemployment rate (RH), percentage

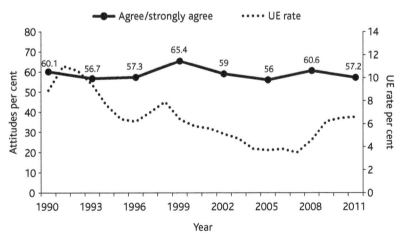

Sources: New Zealand Election Study; Reserve Bank

an economic decision (RCSP, 1988a). This evidence suggests that economic reforms affecting job supply, such as the tariffs and subsidies abolished prior to 1990, contributed to the New Zealand public becoming less likely to believe that the government could or should ensure jobs for everyone by 1990.

Although a majority of NZES respondents agreed that the government was responsible for providing jobs in each year, attitudes also fluctuated over time. Economic conditions affect the availability of employment and Figure 4.1's secondary axis shows some covariance between decreasing support for the proposition that the government should take responsibility for jobs and improved employment opportunities in the early 2000s. But earlier and later trends make it difficult to argue that there is a clear-cut relationship whereby support for government responsibility for jobs decreased with the unemployment rate. Support declined both when the 1991 Employment Contracts Act dismantled the wage earners' welfare state *and* when the Labour-coalition's 2000 Employment Relations Act *reversed* some of the harshest reforms introduced by National. It is therefore also hard to argue that attitudes towards government responsibility for jobs were closely linked to industrial relations changes.

Public anticipation of a change in government may explain the growth in support for government responsibility for providing jobs (and, as later discussion highlights, import controls) in the late 1990s and mid-2000s. Not only did National try to ward off criticism by making a long overdue minimum wage increase in 1997 but political rhetoric suggested a future Labour-led government would 'make work pay' (Department of Labour, 2013). The moderate increase in support for government responsibility for jobs between 2005 and 2008 may be similarly associated with the Labour-coalition's single biggest increase in the minimum wage in 2006 and the introduction/expansion of Working for Families tax credits between 2005 and 2007 as an alternative to the opposition's promised tax cuts. Even if these moves did not specifically address the *supply* of jobs, they had real (and visible) effects for low and middle income earners and may have diminished concern that the government was not taking sufficient responsibility for employment matters. Nonetheless, the overall evidence indicates a decline in the number of NZES respondents agreeing that jobs were the government's responsibility across the 2000s as a whole. After the minor increase noted between 2005 and 2008, support then fell by another 3.4 percentage points[1] when National was re-elected (see Figure 4.1).

A first indicator that the New Zealand public had come to accept a key tenet of neoliberalism is found in the fact that support for government responsibility for providing jobs declined from 76.8% to 66.4% over 21 years among NZES respondents self-identifying with the ideological Left. In contrast, support barely moved among the Centre and the Right, 55.1% and 49.4% of whom respectively supported this proposition in 2011. Moreover, the *Labour-coalition's* policies and rhetoric appeared to have the greatest impact upon the Left, who reported a 19.6 percentage point fall in support for government responsibility for providing jobs between 1999 and 2008. The Left's agreement with this proposition then increased by 8.2 percentage points once National returned to power, but it did not recover sufficiently to counter arguments that the roll-out phase of neoliberal governance was crucial for legitimating neoliberal economic agendas among the Left.

A second indicator is that support for government responsibility for providing jobs among the youngest respondents (aged <30) fell from 66.8% in 1990 to 60.9% in 2011. This suggests growing up under neoliberalism had a negative impact on attitudes, especially since the oldest group (aged >61) *increased* their overall level of support by almost 3 percentage points. Thus, by 2011 around 61% of both groups believed that the government had such a responsibility. That the oldest group's experiences of neoliberalism *strengthened* their views about government responsibility for providing jobs is supported by a middle-aged participant taking part in the qualitative study in 2007. His comments suggest that attitudes towards jobs being provided by the government can be shaped by personal memories of the individual and societal benefit gained from state sector employment prior to deregulation and privatisation:

> "I'm a person who believes that in the days when New Zealand Railway was over-staffed and Mr Smith or Mr Jones got up every morning and they went down and did their eight hours at New Zealand Rail, they probably drank a lot of tea and coffee and stood on a lot of brooms. But they come home at the end of the day, those people put their kids through the education system and they had a reason for life. I think that is a much better way of structuring our society than having Mr Smith and Mr Jones' modern equivalent not have a job to go to, so their day starts at four in the afternoon with a visit to the video shop and they still probably get a similar level of return but they haven't

> got any equity in the prioritisation of their time and their self esteem and self worth just drops. And I think that we have to have a recognition in our society that you will see people perhaps brushing the same piece of metal on the side of the road eight hours a day or something, but at least they're tired at the end of the day having done something that in their eyes is constructive and meaningful."

This participant acknowledged we could not turn back the clock but favoured financial incentives for employers to train an unemployed person for a permanent job and recognising child care as a valued form of work. In this way, his ideas about *how* the government might ensure jobs had changed but the basic belief that this was a government responsibility had not diminished.

It is therefore useful to consider public views on a major policy lever controlling the demand for employment in the Keynesian era: import tariffs and controls protecting domestic industries. The 4th Labour government completely removed quantitative import controls and left only low, steadily reducing tariffs. These reductions slowed after National took power in 1990 (Vowles et al, 1995) but the changed wording of the NZES question presented in Figure 4.2 highlights how such policy levers were virtually redundant by the mid-1990s.

There is no doubt that few New Zealanders believed import controls were an appropriate means for 'solving New Zealand's economic problems' by 2011, with support for this policy mechanism declining from 50.4% in 1990 to only 31.5%. A high income, middle-aged participant in the qualitative study articulated the apparently dominant view that import controls are no longer relevant:

> "I do think the government has a responsibility to encourage productivity, you know, and to basically make sure we can do the best we can given our productivity. But to me the solution is not by putting tariffs on stuff, it's actually to step out the way and let that happen and I think that is a responsibility that the government should have."

As with attitudes towards government responsibility for providing jobs, however, NZES responses fluctuated, with a sharp rise between 1996 and 1999 and a weaker increase between 2005 and 2008 suggesting the public was more willing to support import controls when a change of government was likely. Although several free trade agreements negotiated under the Labour-coalition may have

Figure 4.2: Attitudes towards government controls to help solve New Zealand's economic problems (agree/strongly agree only, LH) by unemployment rate (RH), percentage

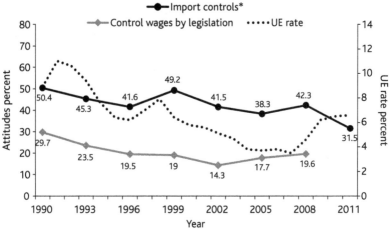

*1990 and 1993 'increasing import controls', 1996 'import controls', 1999 + 'introduce import controls'

Sources: New Zealand Election Study; Reserve Bank

influenced attitudes towards import controls during the 2000s, these provoked only relatively minor public debate and no agreements were made prior to the rise in support during the late 1990s (Ministry of Foreign Affairs and Trade – MFAT, 2013). There is also no clear pattern of covariance between support for import controls and the unemployment rate.

The greatest overall declines in support for import controls occurred under the Labour-coalition and between 2008 and 2011. This suggests public views on this issue had rolled over, as do significant falls in support across the ideological spectrum over 21 years. Left attitudes also fell most quickly in the 2000s, while this was true of the Right in the 1990s and Centre only after 2008. But the absolute percentage point fall in support between 1990 and 2011 was only slightly greater among the Left (from 51.2% to 29.1%) than among the Right (50.2% to 30.7%) and Centre (50.4% to 32.5%), leaving attitudes across all groups remarkably similar. Import controls also lost favour across all age groups, although particularly among those aged 46 to 60 and particularly during the 2000s. The level of support for import controls offered by the youngest respondents fell from 42.3% to 21.3% between 1990 and 2011, meaning the oldest group (whose support fell from 56.2% to 39.4%) continued to offer the highest level of support. Here having an historical reference point may have played some role in shaping attitudes regarding this issue.

Given that most New Zealanders did not view import controls as a viable policy lever in 2011, did they endorse government wage interventions in the neoliberal labour market? Between 1990 and 2008, the NZES asked respondents about wage controls, which can range from voluntary guidelines to a mandatory wage freeze but generally involve setting upper wage limits in an attempt to reduce inflation (Roper, 2005). NZES respondents participating in earlier surveys probably associated this question with National's controversial 1982–84 wage and price freeze, which 50% of Heylen poll respondents supported in conjunction with tax relief for low income earners in 1983 (Crothers, 1988). When Labour ended the wage freeze in 1984, industrial unrest saw many awards settled around 15.5% to compensate for it, so most workers did not experience significant wage cuts during Labour's first term (Vowles and Aimer, 1993; Roper, 2005).

Figure 4.2 shows that only 29.7% of NZES respondents agreed that the government should 'control wages by legislation to help solve New Zealand's economic problems' by 1990 and support fell by another 10.1 percentage points over 18 years. This shift reflects policy; the National government formed in 1990 had no need to reinstate wage controls because abandoning wage arbitration kept wages low and, by offering only four minimum wage increases in its nine years of office, the minimum wage represented only 41% of the average wage by 1999 (Vowles et al, 1995; Cotterell, 2009). However, there was a rise in support from 2002 that continued after National won the 2008 election. This rise cannot be explained by changing unemployment levels and is unlikely to be associated with industrial relations changes, given that support for wage controls declined following the enactment of both the Employment Contracts Act *and* the Employment Relations Act.

Attitudes might be expected to have been influenced by the visibility of New Zealand's growing levels of poverty and income inequality, along with media attention about the relatively low level of New Zealand wages and salaries compared to Australia, during both the 2002 and 2005 elections. But the Left, whose support for wage controls fell from 40.3% to 22.8% between 1990 and 2008, reported the largest decline across the 2000s, suggesting that those traditionally most concerned with poverty and inequality did not consider wage controls to be the answer. The Centre (whose support fell from 28.2% to 19.4%) and the Right (32.5% to 16.8%) still offered less support than the Left on this issue but attitudes converged considerably. Even if past social policy concessions had been gained through union-negotiated wage constraint, the Left may have negatively associated wage controls with the unpopular National government wage and price freeze in 1982–84 or accepted that opportunities for government wage interventions are limited in a neoliberal economy.

In fact, the timing of rising overall support for wage controls from the early 2000s suggests that recent NZES respondents may have associated wage controls with the Labour-coalition's nine minimum wage increases in eight years and Working for Families tax credits aiming to raise the incomes of low and middle income earners (Cotterell, 2009). Although National was ideologically opposed to the introduction of Working for Families, the use of tax credits rather than a social security payment to redistribute income may explain why respondents on the Right as well as the Left increased their support for wage controls by 5 percentage points under the Labour-coalition (the Centre stayed steady). Interpreting wage controls in this way may also explain why the youngest age group offered the highest level of support for wage controls (around 24% in both 1990 and 2011, reporting the largest increase of 4.8 percentage points under the Labour-coalition). In contrast, support among the oldest respondents (who probably interpreted wage controls in regards to historical wage freezes) fell from 46.9% to 21.4% across 18 years.

The argument that some NZES respondents may have conflated wage controls with other means of regulating or supplementing wages is supported by the fact that a significant minority (43–47%) of NZES respondents *disagreed* with the neoliberal argument that 'minimum wages reduce the creation of new jobs' between 1999 and 2005. 'Neutral' and 'cannot say' answers were also surprisingly frequent suggesting many New Zealanders found it difficult to respond to this question, due to inadequate knowledge or because other factors can also affect job creation. Indeed, even during a period of low employment, the qualitative study's participants felt something was wrong but could not identify policy mechanisms that might address it. When participants were asked to name government responsibilities some thought this should include ensuring decent work and wages but a young, middle income earner said:

> "I'm not really sure how it all works, but I would like to see someone be able to take control over it, because it is – in relation to what you get paid and what you've got to buy – it doesn't seem to be much of ... a nice relationship ... Buying a house, for example, around here, there's sort

> of like $450,000, and even on $50,000 a year wage, it's
> nowhere near what you're going to get for a mortgage and
> things like that ... So I think there's all those sorts of things
> which I don't know if the government could control. If the
> government could control it, then I think, yeah, perhaps
> they should ... Either lift the wages a bit or try and bring
> prices of things down ..."

While many participants were uncertain whether the government
could control factors shaping their employment experiences, if
anything, minimum wage mechanisms were the most salient in their
minds. An older, high income earner noted:

> "I don't think the government should go about creating
> extra work through government departments, like they
> may have done in '50s, '60s, '70s ... [but] I do think the
> government needs to take responsibility for things like the
> minimum wage, $12 an hour is not really a minimum wage
> ... people are working 40 hours on that, they're not going
> to survive. So, I think they have a responsibility in ensuring
> that the minimum standards are set at a level where people
> can actually afford to live."

Only 24% of the participants in the qualitative study, however, believed
government should ensure that basics are affordable by controlling
wages or prices, despite expressing considerable concern about the
food, petrol and housing increases faced by New Zealanders in the
months preceding the focus groups and interviews. More broadly, 34%
thought having their basic needs met was a right of citizenship; 30%
explicitly named decent work/wages as a government responsibility
but few (7%) considered this a social right.

The tension between a public desire for the government to take
responsibility for employment yet a lack of support for the policy
levers adopted by governments during the post-war period is the
dominant finding of this section. While a majority of New Zealanders
still believed that the government should provide jobs in 2011 and
support remained relatively steady across the previous 21 years, only
a significant minority agreed that import and wage controls were
an appropriate way of solving the country's economic problems and
support for both fell dramatically between 1990 and 2008–11. It is
perhaps more surprising that support remained as high as it did and,
in the case of wage controls, rose between 2002 and 2008, given that

neither form of control have been part of the policy lexicon since the 1980s. But the evidence suggests that support for wage controls grew when it did because recent respondents viewed minimum wage legislation and tax credits as a form of wage control.

Tax credits are not be widely understood as part of the 'welfare state' in New Zealand (Rankin, 1997) and, along with minimum wage increases, they represent government acceptance of the neoliberal view that employers are no longer responsible for providing a living wage. It is also notable that, aside from the covariance between Working for Families and increased support for wage controls and government responsibility for providing jobs, the policy direction offered by Labour-coalition governments during the 2000s had a more negative impact upon attitudes than the roll-back phase, particularly among the Left. That support for all propositions declined further after 2008 supports an argument that the New Zealand public have rolled over and struggle to believe it possible or advisable for government to intervene in most aspects of employment, with the important exception of wage protections – the only policy lever recent governments have been willing to utilise.

A matter of degree?

This section assesses whether the New Zealand findings regarding employment and wages are typical of other countries that have undergone the process of neoliberalisation. Table 4.1 shows support for the proposition that the government should take responsibility for providing jobs for everyone initially decreased then began to rise again in the late 1990s in the UK and Australia, as it did in New Zealand. British support for government responsibility for providing jobs then continued to grow until the early 2000s under the Labour government (1997–2010), before declining to an all-time low in 2006, then increasing again. Although New Zealand support declined between 1999 and 2005, before rising slightly by 2008, Labour governments in both countries had the overall effect of reducing support for this proposition. However, support continued to *increase* after the election of the British Conservative-Liberal Democrat government in 2010, while there was a rapid decline in support after 2008 in New Zealand. Support for the same proposition appears to have remained steady in Australia under the Liberal-National Coalition but no Australian data is available after 2007. The available data thus suggests that New Zealand attitudes have rolled to a greater degree than in the other countries.

Table 4.1: 'Government should take responsibility to provide a job for everyone who wants one' (agree only*), percentage

	1985	1987	1990	1992	1996	2000	2006	2007	2010	2012
United Kingdom	72	–	63	–	69	81	56	–	64	67
Australia	53	40	42	39	44	–	–	42	–	–

Note: * Australian 1987 and 1992 data combine 'agree' and 'strongly agree'; no weights provided. Remaining years and UK data combine 'definitely should be' and 'probably should be'.

Sources: British Social Attitudes Survey; International Social Survey Programme; Australian Survey of Social Attitudes.

Nonetheless, a majority of respondents believed that the government should provide jobs in New Zealand and the UK in the late 2000s while only a significant minority of Australians have done so since 1987, even though a Labor government was still at that time articulating a limited role for itself in ensuring employment opportunities. Wilson et al's (2012: 121) analysis suggests that Australians in the late 2000s were, on balance, opposed to the government taking responsibility for providing jobs and tended to 'frame the operation of the labour market, and a person's success or failure in it, in individualistic/market rather than social/government terms'. They similarly found Australians to be less supportive of such intervention than New Zealanders or Britons.

This finding sits in tension with evidence that Australians remained more open to import controls than their British or New Zealand counterparts. In 2003, 58.1% of British Social Attitudes (BSA) survey respondents believed 'Britain should limit the import of foreign products in order to protect its national economy', while 66% agreed with a similar question in the Australian Survey of Social Attitudes (AuSSA) in the same year. Indeed, when Marsh et al (2005) compared attitudes in 14 countries, New Zealanders were *least* likely to support limitations on the import of foreign goods to protect the economy and Australians were most likely. Notably, although Australia's trade exposure rose as a result of neoliberal reforms, support remained among the lowest of the countries they studied, while levels of support in the UK and New Zealand were far higher. New Zealand's particularly rapid and radical reforms therefore appear to have had the greatest impact on public attitudes in this realm, while Pusey and Turnbull (2005) note how Australian views reflected the free market model moderated by state regulation found in Australia.

Comparative data on wage controls is limited but BSA data suggests British support for wage controls 'as something the government might do for the economy', *grew* from 32.5% in 1985 to 37.2% in 1996.

This might have been a reaction to the abolition of wage councils during the roll-back period but notably the abandonment of New Zealand's more extensive wage arbitration system saw support for wage controls *decline* significantly across the 1990s in New Zealand. That 89.3% of BSA respondents agreed that 'the law should set a minimum wage so that no employer can pay their workers too little' suggests there was overwhelming support for British Labour's minimum wage legislation but the evidence is insufficient to argue that wage controls were similarly associated with government intervention to improve wages. There is no comparable Australian data but 73% of AuSSA respondents disagreed that 'a lower minimum wage is the best way to solve unemployment' in 2005, indicating that Australians also believe that the government should intervene to ensure decent wages (van Wanrooy, 2007). This is not surprising given the minimum wage had slowly declined through the 1980s and 1990s but unemployment peaked in the early 1990s (Wilson et al, 2013). It is also possible that Australia's relatively weak interest in the government providing jobs is linked to the greater level of redistribution to low income workers found there, meaning respondents did not feel *more* responsibility was needed. Although support for the same proposition fell slightly between 1996 and 2007, despite the highly visible WorkChoices debate capturing public attention, this trend might also be associated with the greater strength and visibility of unions in Australia compared to New Zealand and the UK, as discussed in the next section. Overall, the evidence suggests some coherence in the declining support for propositions relating to employment in all three countries but only in New Zealand do attitudes appear to have accepted 'there is no alternative' to neoliberal deregulation.

Trade unions

Whether New Zealanders still believe decent employment and wages should be a right of social citizenship can also be evaluated by considering public attitudes towards the trade unions which have historically played a strong role in protecting wages and conditions. Figure 4.3 indicates neoliberal policy did *not* radically shift the attitudes of New Zealanders towards unions in the long term, as around 66% of NZES respondents agreed that 'trade unions are necessary to protect workers' in both 1990 and 2011.

This overall finding again masks some important shifts over time. Agreement that unions are necessary grew by a surprisingly small amount (3.1 percentage points) between 1990 and 1993, when support

Figure 4.3: Attitudes towards trade unions (agree/strongly agree only, LH) by unemployment rate (RH), percentage

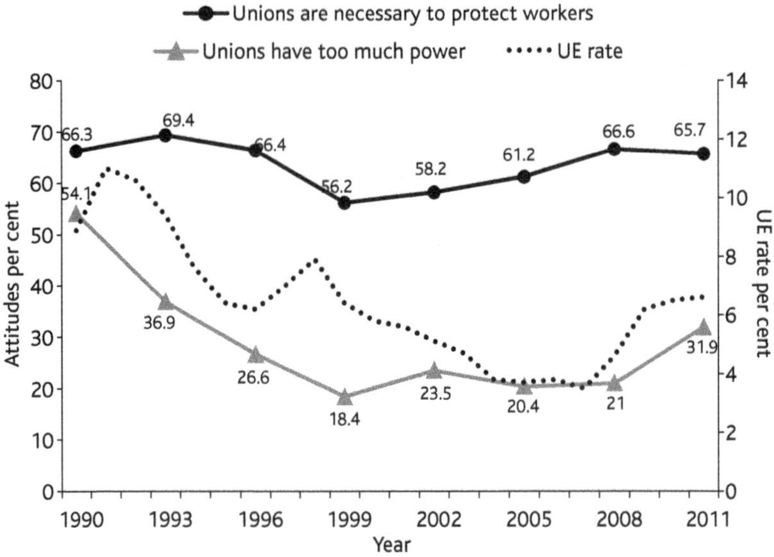

Sources: New Zealand Election Study; Reserve Bank

peaked at 69.4%, given the significant public dissent against the new law in 1991. However, that 51% of New Zealand Values Study (NZVS) respondents wanted to *abolish* compulsory unionism in 1989 suggests that attitudes may have started to shift in *anticipation* of the Employment Contracts Act (Crothers, 1988; Gold and Webster, 1990). This saw strike activity fall to its lowest level since the 1930s, while an already weakening union membership declined from almost 50% to 24% of the total employed labour force between 1990 and 1996 (Roper, 2005; Blumenfeld, 2010). The Act was further associated with slow wage growth and unsatisfied demand for longer hours of work (Waldegrave et al, 2003; Harré, 2010). But the proportion of NZES respondents who believed 'unions are necessary' fell from 1996 to an all-time low in 1999.

Other NZES data show that New Zealanders also became disinclined to agree that 'the Employment Contracts Act should be repealed', with support for this proposition falling from 53.4% to 38.5% between 1993 and 1999. Labour's very visible campaign promise to abandon the legislation had little impact on such views and trade union support for the Employment Relations Act suggests a significant lock-in effect had already occurred (Levine and Roberts, 2000; Vowles, 2002). Notably, support for a repeal of the Employment Contracts Act fell from 86.6%

to 65.9% among Left respondents between 1993 and 1999, compared to much smaller declines among the Centre (from 51.7% to 42.6%) and Right (21.6% to 16.6%). Although a clear majority still wanted a repeal, some members of the Left appear to have been swayed by National's view that the proposed repeal reflected Labour's 'ideological' approach and would contribute to a crisis of business confidence (Vowles 2002; Roper, 2005).

Nonetheless, once the Employment Relations Act was in place, agreement that unions are necessary grew through the 2000s to around 66.6% in 2008, with support staying fairly steady following National's return to power. Responses to this proposition did not therefore move in opposition to policy. Support grew as economic conditions improved through the 2000s but Figure 4.3's secondary axis shows no overall pattern of covariance between attitudes towards the idea that trade unions are necessary and the unemployment rate.

The nature of the Employment Relations Act itself may thus explain the growth in agreement that unions are necessary during the 2000s. First, the Act's changes may not have been sufficiently visible or proximate to the public. Industrial relations were far less divisive during the 1999 election than during the early 1990s (Rudman, 1999). It also took two years before amendments clarified minimum requirements consistent with good faith bargaining and addressed 'free-riding' by restricting collective agreement coverage to union members. In this time, the Employment Relations Act's minor improvements were overshadowed by substantial gains for worker conditions and wages delivered through government policy. These government-led initiatives may have mediated public views about unions (Rasmussen and Lamm, 2005; Rasmussen et al, 2006; Burton, 2010). Significant growth in self-employment arrangements also meant that many workers were not covered by the Employment Relations Act, while unions had fewer resources to promote themselves and their services (Harré, 2010).

Second, it is also possible that the public's initial hopes for the Employment Relations Act were only partly met. Employer groups complained and the National Party predicted the Employment Relations Act would have a strong and lasting detrimental effect on the economy (Roper, 2005). But individual agreements were maintained for employees whose job could be covered by a collective agreement and there was an initial drop in collective bargaining, although coverage steadied after 2001 and was around 15% in 2008. Union membership did increase slightly under the Employment Relations Act, but the *proportion* of the population who were union members stayed static at around 17% and membership remained concentrated in the public sector. Thus, despite National Party and business sector concerns, the Employment Relations Act did *not* stimulate rapid union growth (Waldegrave et al, 2003; Walker, 2007; Blumenfeld, 2010). This may explain the increased proportion of NZES respondents agreeing that 'unions are necessary' during the 2000s.

If this were true, we would expect the largest growth in support during the Labour-coalition's time in government to have occurred among the Left but, although Left support for the idea that unions are necessary did grow by 7.8 percentage points between 1999 and 2008, this was minimal compared to the 13 and 19 percentage point increases among Centre and Right respondents respectively. The Employment Relations Act thus encouraged *all* groups to believe that unions played an important role in protecting workers. However, the Left not only continued to report the highest level of support for the idea that unions are necessary in 2011 but agreement *increased* (from 81.2% to 86.4%) over 21 years. The levels of support reported in 1990 and 2011 stayed steadier among the Centre (65–67%) and Right (55%) in the long term. Yet both group's responses fluctuated considerably, suggesting they were most sensitive to perceived shifts in union power.

To understand these trends further, Figure 4.3 also shows NZES responses to a question about the power of trade unions. Wilson et al (2012) hypothesise that attitudes towards union power are 'mood' variables, fluctuating as the public moves through more progressive and more conservative moods, because the public registers periods of union power and influence, as well as weakness and marginalisation. This appears to be the case in New Zealand; the level of covariance between unemployment (when union negotiating power is reduced) and support for 'trade unions in New Zealand have too much power' is greater than for the other propositions discussed although support continued declining even when unemployment rose in the early and late 1990s.

Indeed, Figure 4.3 shows concern about unions having too much power fell from 54.1% to 31.9% between 1990 and 2011. This decline occurred most quickly during the 1990s (particularly between 1990 and 1993) when agreement fell by 35.7 percentage points. The proportion of respondents agreeing that 'unions have too much power', however, increased during the Labour-coalition's first term, settling around 20–21% for the remainder of its time in government. This represented less than half of those who thought unions had too much power in 1990, prior to the Employment Contracts Act, but the increase in support suggests some New Zealanders thought the Employment Relations Act inappropriately strengthened the position of unions. Concern that 'unions have too much power' continued to *increase* significantly (by 10.9 percentage points) between 2008 and 2011.

This is surprising given that by 2008 the National Party had publicly moved away from earlier promises to repeal the Employment Relations Act and it took an incremental approach to change once it formed a government (Rasmussen and Anderson, 2010). Several policies were detrimental to the right to decent employment, including: alterations to the personal grievance system; the introduction and extension of 90-day trial employment periods; restrictions on unions' workplace access; a cash option for one week of annual leave; and the disestablishment of the Pay and Employment Equity Unit and pay equity reviews. But the Labour-coalition's flexible work hours legislation and regular minimum wage increases were maintained and National waited until 2012 to reintroduce the youth wage, veto legislation extending paid parental leave based on financial grounds, and inhibit union activities (Burton, 2010; Wilkinson, 2010, 2012). It is possible rising concern about union power may have been influenced by a highly visible international union boycott in 2010 over New Zealand actors' wishes to negotiate a collective contract with Warner Brothers for work on *The Hobbit* series to be filmed in New Zealand (Davison et al, 2010; Key, 2010). Some members of the public, however, may simply have expected National to do more to restrict unions than it achieved during its first term.

Respondents associating with the Right and Centre certainly offered the largest increases in concern that 'unions have too much power' (by 15.8 and 12 percentage points respectively) between 2008 and 2011. But even the Left increased its support for this proposition by 6.1%, which suggests a lock-in effect for the softer, but still fundamentally neoliberal, industrial regime the Employment Relations Act represented. Overall, however, the Left was rather less concerned that 'unions have too much power', with agreement falling significantly from 34.2% to 11.7% between 1990 and 2011 but support also declined among the Centre (from 56% to 33.8%) and the Right (72.5% to 48.4%). In contrast to the Left and Centre, whose support fell most quickly between 1990 and 1993, the Right were slower to be convinced that union power had been broken by the Employment Contracts Act or was more responsive to the business community's alarm at the stalling of neoliberal reforms under the National-New Zealand First coalition (Roper, 2005). However, after initial concern when the Labour-coalition government was first elected, agreement that 'unions have too much power' among the latter group increased only by 5.4 percentage points across the 2000s. The Employment Relations Act thus came to be tolerated or was not as bad as expected.

But it remains that it only made minor modifications to the neoliberal industrial relations regime introduced in 1991.

Further evidence that the New Zealand public came to accept a neoliberal industrial relations regime lies in the fact that 65.1% of the youngest NZES respondents agreed that 'unions are necessary' in 1990 but only 58.6% did so in 1990. However, the oldest group *increased* their support from 63.3% to 69.6%. The youngest respondents were aware of the relatively weak power of unions, with only 27.6% in 2011 believing 'unions have too much power' compared to 46.8% saying the same in 1990. In fact, this awareness appeared to be stronger than among the oldest group, of whom 42.9% were still concerned that 'unions have too much power' in 2011 (down from 67.9% in 1990). The relative insecurity that young people face in the labour market may explain this finding, although the oldest group still reported greater levels of agreement that 'unions are necessary'. The Labour-coalition also did more to woo the business sector than unions during its time in government, and its focus on 'making work pay' through the minimum wage and tax credits offered younger workers little reason to believe unions were necessary to protect wages and conditions.

This section has argued that the Employment Contracts Act contributed to an initial growth in support for the idea that unions are necessary but, by 1999, feedback effects had diminished significantly and the number of NZES respondents agreeing that 'trade unions have too much power' had fallen. The Employment Relations Act coincided with an initial reversal in declining support for both propositions, suggesting many New Zealanders endorsed the Labour-coalition's attempts to weaken the harshest impacts of the earlier legislation. Although satisfaction with the levels of power held by unions peaked in the immediate aftermath of the Employment Relations Act, this legislation did not completely appease New Zealanders. This makes it so surprising that concern about trade union power increased between 2008 and 2011, a time when policy actually had the reverse effect. National's strategically incremental approach to industrial reforms in the late 2000s – along with improvements like paid parental leave and increased annual leave – appears to have successfully kept this issue *off* the public radar, thus calming potential concerns about the impact National might have on union power.

A continuing (if more confined) role for unions

As in New Zealand, the UK's initial industrial relations reforms were radical and rapid but do not appear to have had a permanent, regressive impact upon public attitudes towards unions, even if many citizens similarly accept that unions should play a less extensive role than in the past. Ipsos MORI (2013) poll data suggests agreement for 'trade unions are essential to protect workers' interests' *increased* (to around 80%) in the early 1990s before declining only slightly, a trend similar to that found in New Zealand. Table 4.2 also shows the proportion of British respondents agreeing that 'unions have too much power' dropped significantly during the early roll-back phase of neoliberalism, leaving only minority support for this proposition in both countries.

Chapter Three highlighted how Australia's industrial relations reforms were comparatively incremental and remained incomplete until 2005. This may explain why a higher proportion of Australians still agreed that 'trade unions have too much power' during the early 1990s than New Zealanders or Britons, with support dropping by only 6 percentage points between 1987 and 1996. However, it fell 28 percentage points across the Liberal-National coalition government's term when Australian labour relations moved into line with those already in place in the UK and New Zealand (Meagher and Wilson, 2007; McAllister and Pietsch, 2011). The number of Australians concerned with unions having too much power then rose by 12 percentage points over a three-year period following the Australian Council of Trade Unions' (ACTU) highly visible campaign against WorkChoices and the new Labor government's modification of this legislation (van Wanrooy, 2007; Goot and Watson, 2012). More favourable conditions for unions thus saw the public respond with greater concern about their level of power.

This kind of mood response was not evident in either New Zealand or the UK in the 2010s, when concern about union power *increased* at a time when industrial relations were again under threat. This suggests the public had rolled over and accepted the confines of the neoliberal labour market. However, Ipsos MORI (2013) poll data reports that 35% of respondents supported a similar question – 'trade unions have too much power in Britain today' – in both 2011 and 2013. Support may thus have fallen since the Conservative-Liberal Democrat

Table 4.2: 'Unions have too much power' (agree only*), percentage

	1983	1987	1992	1996	1997	2005	2007	2010
United Kingdom	74	–	34	–	24	25	–	41
Australia	–	71	–	65	–	–	37	49

Note: * Australia data combine 'strongly agree' and 'agree'; UK data represent just 'too much power'.

Sources: British Election Study; Australian Election Study.

government was formed in 2010, given a sharp rise in working days lost to industrial stoppages from large public sector strikes against austerity measures, particularly cuts to government funding and pensions reforms (Wilson, 2013). Both British (Edwards and Sayers Bain, 1988) and Australian (Meagher and Wilson, 2007) evidence suggests there may be covariance between public attitudes and strike activity. New Zealand had no comparable activity to provoke a public reaction because industrial relations policy changes were extremely cautious and incremental in National's first term; things may change once planned reforms are implemented. Van Wanrooy (2007) certainly argues that the visibility of WorkChoices and the ACTU's campaign helped increase support for 'employees cannot protect their working conditions and wages without strong unions' by 4 percentage points between 2003 and 2005.

The shifting nature of attitudes towards union power challenges the view that the erosion of long-term employment contracts permanently undermines loyalty, trust and a sense of belonging to a larger collectivity (Sennett, 1998; Bauman, 2001). Meagher and Wilson (2007) also found qualified but widespread support for unions even among Australian workers who did not belong to them. Notably, the young were least likely to belong but just as likely as older workers to *want to join a union*. This supports the earlier New Zealand finding that the decline in support for the idea that unions are necessary was smallest (although still significant) among the youngest group of NZES respondents. Dekker (2012: 83) argues that 'the changing nature of work shapes workers' perceptions of risks, fostering a need for risk reduction through social policy' and it is possible that the insecurity and low wages inherent in the neoliberal labour market encourages even young workers to conceive unions as useful and necessary.

Big business and privatisation

This final section considers New Zealand attitudes towards big business and privatisation, because both 'business friendly' neoliberal policies and the sale of state-owned assets had a negative impact upon both employment and worker conditions and thus may influence attitudes towards them. Figure 4.4 certainly suggests that New Zealanders became more tolerant of big business over time, with overall support for 'big business has too much power in New Zealand' falling from 69.3% to 53.6% between 1990 and 2011. The proportion of NZES respondents supporting this view fell by 6.7 percentage points during the 1990s but then diminished by 14.2 percentage points under the

Figure 4.4: 'Big business has too much power in New Zealand' (LH) by unemployment rate (RH), percentage

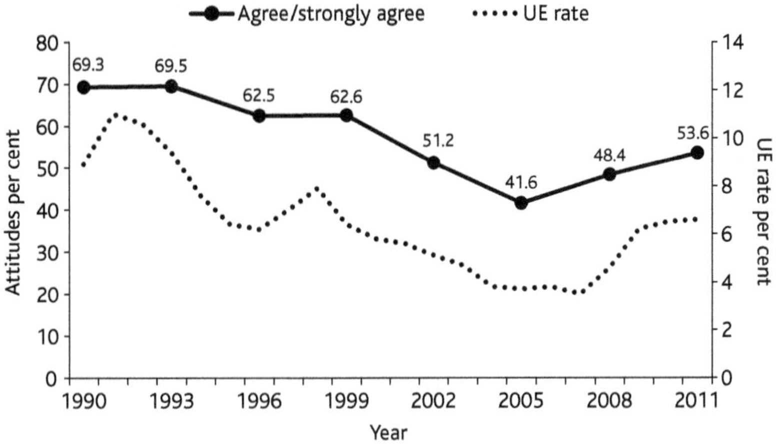

Sources: New Zealand Election Study; Reserve Bank

Labour-coalition government, mostly during its first term. If there were interpretative effects associated with Labour's framing of big business as necessary to New Zealand's success yet harnessed to ensure broader social needs are met, these diminished after 2005. Concern that 'big business has too much power' increased by 6.8 percentage points in the three years prior to 2008 and then by another 5.2 percentage points by 2011. This left over half the NZES respondents once again agreeing with the proposition.

The greatest overall decline (from 72.1% to 53%) in concern about big business power was found among Centre respondents and this occurred most quickly under the Labour-coalition government. Greater acceptance of a neoliberal economic agenda among this group makes it less likely a future government will see the need to harness the priority neoliberalism places on big business. However, while Left support also declined quickly under the Labour-led government, this fell only from 72.7% to 69.4% across the 21-year period, challenging the argument that Left attitudes had completely rolled over on this issue. In comparison, Right support declined from 57.7% to 39.9% but this occurred most quickly during the 1990s. Both the Left and Centre thus appear to have been swayed by the Labour-coalition's communicative discourse which aimed to keep both employers and workers happy, promising '[i]ntelligent regulation which shapes the market to meet the social and economic needs' and full employment, but in the context of 'constant innovation to drive a niche-oriented, skills-based, high technology knowledge economy' (Maharey, 1999b: A17). It is also possible that public attitudes were influenced by the Labour-coalition's activity in developing free trade agreements late in its term (MFAT, 2013). However, we would expect the Left to more strongly oppose free trade, yet respondents from across the ideological spectrum became concerned about the power of big business through the 2000s, even if ideological divisions remained. Surprisingly, the Right reported the largest increase (4.2 percentage points) in support between 2008 and 2011, suggesting this group were wary of National's future plans. This does not compare, however, with the significant 15.2 percentage point fall in Right support during the 1990s.

Concern about the power of big business also fell across all age groups, again mostly under the Labour-coalition. Between 1990 and 2011, the *smallest* declines in support were reported by the oldest (from 75.4% to 61%) and youngest age groups (58.5% to 42.5%). But only a significant minority of young NZES respondents (that is, people who were registered electors *and* took part in the survey) were concerned about the power of big business in 2011. This suggests that the many young people involved in the Occupy movement opposing corporate greed were *not* representative of young adult views and that there is considerable tolerance of big business dominance in New Zealand.

It is important to note that Figure 4.4's right-hand axis suggests concern about big business power tends to increase as unemployment grows and decrease when it diminishes. There are exceptions that make it difficult to be certain unemployment, rather than policy, matters here but the qualitative study data supports an argument that the broader economic context influences attitudes towards big business. In 2008, some participants were reassessing their attitudes towards deregulation as New Zealand followed other countries into a global recession. A businessman, for instance, was warming to the idea that some regulations on business were needed to avoid the kind of financial crisis emerging in the United States: "there's a fine balance, I think, between the ... free market and ... you know, government taking care ... that it's not so free, that it's [not] a free-for-all".

There was also little favour among the qualitative participants for more active forms of support for business and industry as the economy weakened; only 6% of participants considered this a government responsibility. In a globalised context, a young, high income earner sensed that: "if you want to be a big company and make your stamp on the world then you're going to have to be a lot more proactive than relying on a few government grants or a bit of funding". Importantly, declining concern with big business power among NZES respondents between 1990 and 2011 does not mean New Zealanders *trust* the business sector more. Although not a question asked specifically of the qualitative participants, a noteworthy minority (24%) mentioned the need for businesses to take more responsibility in society to help build public trust; for example, banks should not encourage people to get into debt when they cannot afford to pay loans back and corporations should care about keeping jobs in New Zealand. One middle-aged, high income participant saw business, alongside the government, as liable for decent wages:

> "I think the government needs to take responsibility for the minimum wage and minimum conditions. I think businesses need to take responsibility in that they take practices that encourage labour productivity and when labour productivity occurs to actually reward their workers by increasing their pay."

Although some of the interviews and focus groups were conducted following the global financial crisis, others were not. The qualitative data therefore suggest that many New Zealanders came to *tolerate*, rather than actively endorse, a more business–friendly economic environment.

This argument is buoyed by NZES data showing growing support for public ownership of key assets, even as concern about big business power declined. Table 4.3 shows public support for full or partial state ownership was higher in 2011 than in the early 1990s for all key assets for which 2011 data is available. Support for full or partial state ownership of electricity, Telecom, Bank of New Zealand, Air

Table 4.3: Agreement that government should fully or partially own* named assets, percentage

	1990	1993	1996	1999	2002	2005	2008	2011
Electricity	38.8	69.3	60	48.3	59.2	56.4	–	76.8
Tranzrail	–	55.1	47	–	56.7	–	72.2	78.6
Television NZ	–	47.3	45	43.5	46.8	43.1	60.6	71.3
Telecom	40.9	60.2	51.8	40.7	–	–	–	–
Bank of NZ	31.8	52.3	46.2	42.5	–	–	–	–
Air New Zealand	27.4	48.3	41.1	–	–	–	68.1	79.5
Kiwibank	–	–	–	–	–	55.7	73.4	81.5
NZ Post	47.7	67.5	–	–	–	–	–	79.5

Note: * In 1990, no distinction was made between partial or full ownership.

Source: New Zealand Election Study.

New Zealand and New Zealand Post increased rapidly in the early 1990s. Earlier survey data suggest the public were particularly worried about government organisations being sold to foreign investors and the privatisation of public services like education, healthcare and local government (Heylen, 1988, 1991; Perry and Webster, 1994). In popular discourse, privatisation was also associated with prominent local businessmen earning huge profits while 'average' New Zealanders lost their jobs and faced escalating prices for commodities such as telecommunications and power (Collins, 1990; Vowles and Aimer, 1993; Vowles et al, 1995).

As the public feared, most state assets passed into foreign ownership, perhaps explaining why NZVS data shows that public support for 'tighter government regulation of big companies and multinationals' grew from 55.1% in 1989 to 63.6% in 1993 (Perry and Webster, 1994). This aligns with the finding that more NZES respondents thought that 'big business has too much power' after 1993 (see Figure 4.4). By 1998, however, 50% of NZVS respondents believed 'private ownership of business and industry should be increased' and only 14% thought the same of government ownership (Perry and Webster, 1999). These results marry with the slight decline in support for full or partial ownership for the former state assets reported in Table 4.3 where we have data for the remainder of the 1990s. Focusing on this period alone thus suggests a lock-in effect where New Zealanders began to accept privatisation (even if reluctantly) once assets were sold.

However, support for public ownership grew significantly in the 2000s. The timing of this growth suggests the public were persuaded by the actual *implementation* of these policy promises rather than Labour's election rhetoric about maintaining key industries in New Zealand ownership to secure profits and keep jobs in the country in 1999. Privatisation was not a specific focus of the qualitative study but 28% of the participants in the qualitative study named 'infrastructure' as a government responsibility and a small number explicitly stated their support for the Labour-led government's recent decision to buy back the nation's rail network because they believed investment in infrastructure was lacking. Indeed, the two assets – Air New Zealand and Tranzrail – renationalised in the 2000s reported the greatest growth in support for public ownership between 1996 and 2008 (by 27 and 25.2 percentage points respectively). Support for state ownership of Kiwibank, established only in 2002, grew by 17.7 percentage points between 2005 and 2008, while the restructuring of Television New Zealand (TVNZ) as a Crown Entity in 2003 initially saw support decrease then grow by 28.2 percentage points between 2005 and 2011.

The election debate emerging from National's plans for further partial privatisation in 2011 appears to have had the biggest impact on attitudes. As noted in Chapter Three, Labour made 'no asset sales' a major part of its election campaign, rightly assessing New Zealand concern about this issue (Key, 2012). No such sales had been made by the end of 2011 but where we have 2008 and 2011 data there is evidence that support rose by a significant number of percentage points for the following assets: Tranzrail (6.4); Kiwibank (8.1); TVNZ (10.7); and Air New Zealand (11.4). Support for public ownership had been growing prior to National's election in 2008 but Labour's extremely visible and traceable election campaign likely turned more New Zealanders against privatisation. This issue did not decide the 2011 election, which National won, but its continued importance to the public was evident when more than two thirds of the 43.9% registered voters who took part in a 2013 citizen-initiated referendum rejected the partial asset sales (Bennett, 2013).

As might be expected, Left respondents offered the greatest level of support for state ownership across both decades (with only two minor exceptions). But Left support appears to have been less sensitive than the Right and Centre to the specific policies promoted by either National-led or Labour-led governments. The latter groups reported the largest increases in support for state ownership of state assets for electricity, TVNZ, Tranzrail and Air New Zealand, narrowing the ideological gap on privatisation over time. In contrast, NZES respondents of differing ages responded quite similarly to policy changes, leaving significant gaps in attitudes. For instance, only 64.3% of the youngest group supported full or partial ownership of electricity generation and distribution in 2011, compared to 80.2% of the oldest group, despite National's plans for partial privatisation being widely debated. Nonetheless, in the latest year for which data is available, the youngest group offered greater support for all the state assets discussed in Table 4.3 than the same age cohort did in the 1990s. Notably, the percentage gap between the youngest and oldest age group was narrowest regarding Kiwibank, which garnered the highest level of support for public ownership among the youngest respondents in 2011. This was the only new public asset created during this group's adulthood, indicating that we should not assume young people's attitudes are impermeable to progressive policy change.

Overall, New Zealanders were less likely to believe that 'big business has too much power' in 2011 than in 1990 but they strongly supported public ownership of key assets. While both policy *and* economic conditions likely shape responses to the former proposition, the qualitative data indicates that acceptance or tolerance of a 'business friendly' environment does not mean New Zealanders trust big business, and negative perceptions of the outcomes of privatisation likely contributed to increasing support for state control of key industries. Moreover, the Labour-coalition's renationalisation policy encouraged NZES support for public ownership, countering other findings that the roll-out period of neoliberalism had a negative impact upon attitudes regarding economic policy.

New Zealand's contradictory views?

There is, however, evidence that New Zealand's greater economic vulnerability may have led its citizens to accept big business to a greater extent than their UK or Australian counterparts. Concern about big business power generally fell in New Zealand until 2005 and overall, while it *increased* in the UK and Australia (see Table 4.4). There is no UK data for the period since the Conservative-Liberal Democrat coalition took power in 2010, but the proportion of both Australians and New Zealanders believing 'big business has too much power' increased in the late 2000s. However, in 2011 only 54% of the New Zealand public thought that 'big business has too much power' compared to 69% in 1990, while concern *increased* from 51% to 72% in Australia between 1985 and 2010. Given New Zealand attitudes prior to NZES data becoming available in 1990, these findings suggest that New Zealand's rapid and radical deregulation – and the resulting dominance of multinationals – normalised the role of big business more than it did in the other countries, leading to a 16 percentage point decrease in support for the idea that 'big business has too much power' since 1993.

In tension with this finding is New Zealand's increased support for public ownership of state assets. Based on questions about the privatisation of telecommunications and postal services between 1987 and 2003, there is evidence that Australians also came to

Table 4.4: 'Big business has too much power' (agree only*), percentage

	1985	1987	1990	1996	2001	2007	2010
United Kingdom	26	–	–	37	–	51	–
Australia	–	51	65	65	72	69	72

Note: * UK question was 'Do business and industry have too much power or too little power?', data combine 'too much' and 'far too much'; Australian data combine 'agree' and 'strongly agree'.

Sources: British Social Attitudes Survey; Australian Election Study.

disagree with privatisation in the long term but their support for full privatisation remained higher (around double that found in New Zealand) during the roll-out phase of neoliberalism, possibly because Australia's privatisation process was less radical and rapid (Pusey and Turnbull, 2005). In both countries, findings suggest that the experience of privatisation *diminished* support for this policy across the ideological spectrum, with no lock-in effect evident. Even *political rhetoric* about asset sales provoked a negative reaction from the public, as demonstrated by both National's election campaign in 2011 and the Howard government's plans to extend the private share of ownership in Telstra in 2004 (Quiggin, 2004).

In the UK, BSA respondents were asked a more general question about state ownership of public services and industries. Support for state ownership fell from 46% to 39% between 1994 and 1997 under the Conservative government, indicating that the public were similarly convinced by a free market communicative discourse at this time. Support for public ownership then rose to 42% in 2009 but responses were steadier under a British Labour government promoting public-private partnerships than in the other two countries, despite several private companies involved in such partnerships needing financial assistance from the government (Parker, 2004). A YouGov survey suggests a majority of the British public supported renationalisation of energy and rail companies by 2013 (Dahlgreen, 2013). There is, however no comparable data available regarding state ownership and privatisation for the latest phase of neoliberalism in either the UK or Australia. Given that Chapter Three noted a high level of protest in response to government spending cuts and other changes under the Liberal-Conservative coalition government in the UK, it seems likely support for state ownership would have increased if there is coherence on this issue across all three countries.

Conclusion: the (incomplete) normalising of neoliberal economics

This chapter has examined New Zealand attitudes towards government responsibility for providing jobs, import and wage controls, unions, big business and privatisation as a way of exploring if and how public opinion about the social right to work has changed over time. Analysing public attitudes over 21 years and across three countries has highlighted how differences in the implementation of 'actually existing' neoliberalism brought about some variance in public attitudes. Table 4.5 summarises the direction of attitudinal responses to the

Table 4.5: Attitudinal trends in economic policy across three phases of neoliberalism in New Zealand, the United Kingdom and Australia

	New Zealand	United Kingdom	Australia
Reforms	**1984–1990: Labour** Radical and rapid deregulation/privatisation of state assets Mild industrial relations reform **1990–1999: National** Radical and rapid industrial relations reform Completed privatisation of state assets	**1979–1997: Conservative** Radical and rapid deregulation/privatisation of state assets Radical and rapid industrial relations reform	**1983–1996: Labor** Radical but incremental deregulation/privatisation of state assets Moderate and incremental industrial relations reform
Government responsible for jobs	↑	↓	↓
Unions too much power	↓	↓	↓
Big business too much power	↓	↑	↑
	1999–2008: Labour Renationalised Air New Zealand and Tranzrail Repealed most extreme industrial relations reforms	**1997–2010: Labour** Introduced public-private partnerships for major infrastructure Introduced national minimum wage	**1996–2007: Liberal-National Coalition** Completed privatisation of state assets Moderate, incremental industrial relations reforms till 2005 then radical change
Government responsible for jobs	↓	↓	↔*
Unions too much power	↑	↔	↓
Big business too much power	↓	↑	↑
	2008+: National Incremental industrial relations reforms	**2010+: Conservative-Liberal Democrat Coalition** Incremental industrial relations reforms	**2007+: Labor** Repealed most extreme industrial relations reforms
Government responsible for jobs	↓	–	–
Unions too much power	↑		↑
Big business too much power	↑	–	↑

Note: * This represents 'steady' support, as defined in Table 1.1.

three questions discussed earlier in the chapter where similar survey questions have been asked in all three countries. It highlights important fluctuations in attitudes that make it difficult to argue that public views have been changed permanently and irrevocably. The evidence that neoliberal economic policy has become normalised in New Zealand and elsewhere is thus rather mixed, even if some worrying trends are apparent.

In the early 2010s, a majority of both New Zealanders and Britons still believed that the government had a responsibility to provide jobs for everyone, although only a significant minority did so in Australia in 2007. The early wave of neoliberal reform saw support for this proposition diminish in both New Zealand and the UK, but it had begun to increase again by the time Labour-led governments came to power and further increases were evident across their time in government. However, support for jobs being provided by the government was lower in both countries by the end of this roll-out phase of neoliberalism and it seems likely that citizen views about government responsibility in this area were shaped by attempts to 'make work pay' through minimum wages and tax credits. But did roll-out neoliberalism permanently change public views on this issue?

An increase in British support for government responsibility for jobs after 2010 suggests attitudes moved in opposition to the Conservative-Liberal Democratic coalition's radical reforms while the New Zealand public appears to have rolled over and accepted National's minor changes in economic policy. Australian support for the same proposition fell when the Labor government articulated its responsibility for employment then stayed relatively steady during the period the Liberal-National government was in power. This suggests that Australia's early, incremental approach to economic reform had the same regressive impact, although a lack of recent data makes it difficult to be certain. Hybrid discourses acknowledging neoliberalism's impact on workers without challenging employer needs for 'flexibility' thus appeared to convince citizens that more government responsibility for jobs is *un*necessary. The British data offers some hope that a more radical neoliberal agenda would still provoke the opposite reaction but significant shifts in the attitudes of the ideological Left and young adults do not encourage such optimism in New Zealand.

New Zealand support for government responsibility for providing jobs sits in tension with diminishing interest in policy mechanisms used to protect domestic employment during the Keynesian period. This tension was less evident in the other countries. Import controls also fell out of favour in the UK and, although the evidence is limited and New Zealand attitudes fluctuated more than might be expected given the lack of political interest in such controls, this was most notable under Labour-led governments. In contrast, Australia's more incremental approach to trade deregulation saw higher levels of support for import controls maintained. When it comes to wage controls, the early reforms had a negative impact in both New Zealand and the UK, but support grew through the 2000s in the former. Overwhelming British support for minimum wages in 1999 and earlier discussion highlighting that many New Zealanders associated wage controls with minimum wages and tax credits suggests British respondents may have done the same. This is particularly the case given that protections for workers also came increasingly about through legislative initiatives rather than industrial action in the UK.

Although many Australians benefited from tax credits under the Liberal-National coalition government, their views on employment and wages were likely mediated by their stronger support for unions. Analysis is limited by a lack of data about views on unions as necessary to protect workers but support for this proposition increased during the roll-back reform period in New Zealand and the UK as unions were decimated. Support continued to grow under the New Zealand Labour-coalition government during the 2000s, likely due to both the poor visibility of the Employment Relations Act and dissatisfaction that it did not go far enough, but support steadied after 2008 despite minor regressive changes. Australian evidence suggests that the visibility of the union movement's campaign against WorkChoices played a role in ensuring stronger and increasing support for unions there. Public concern about union power appeared to shift in opposition to changes in industrial relations , suggesting that citizens are aware of their policy context, even if fewer people belong to a union than prior to neoliberal deregulation of the labour market. Both the Left and younger people in New Zealand offered lower agreement that 'unions are necessary' in 2011 than they did in 1990. Importantly, support for unions indicates that Australians still believed that employers hold some responsibility for ensuring decent wages and conditions, while the default position in the other two countries was to appease voters by meeting some of the shortfall associated with low wages.

Finally, there is some evidence that New Zealanders became more tolerant of big business than their counterparts in the UK and Australia. The economy had surprisingly little impact on attitudes towards employment, controls and unions but the unemployment rate did appear to influence attitudes towards big business. Concern about big business power began to fall during neoliberalism's initial phase and continued under the Labour-coalition until 2005. It is unclear why support began to increase at this point or exactly what reference points respondents use when agreeing big business has 'too much' power. But in the context of this chapter's other findings, a continuing rise in concern after National returned to power in 2008 suggests that New Zealanders had not rolled over and simply accepted corporate dominance, even if only just over half of the NZES respondents considered big business as having too much power in 2011. The UK reported a similar level of support in 2007 but the limited evidence suggests support there had been growing since the 1980s. The same trend saw Australians become far more likely to be concerned about the power of big business than their counterparts in the two other countries. This is again likely tied to the more incremental implementation of neoliberal policies and the greater balancing of redistributive policies for low income earners in Australia. Attitudes towards big business may be linked to public resistance against privatisation both there and in New Zealand, although this trend was more apparent in the latter during the 2000s when a small number of assets were renationalised. Initial acceptance and then growing resistance was also apparent in the UK where public-private partnerships were promoted by Labour but support for public ownership was relatively weak compared to the other two countries by the late 2000s.

A process of neoliberalisation across three decades thus saw the public come to accept *some but not all* neoliberal arguments about the need for economic reform. Citizens in the three countries still perceived some kind of role for both government and unions in ensuring decent employment and wages, even if they were confused as to *how* this should happen. New Zealand data suggesting that support for the right to decent employment and wages diminished more significantly among the Left and younger people raises concern about the ongoing sustainability of the social right to work, but notably this trend was not apparent for every proposition. Moreover, roll-back neoliberalism may have had a significant impact on public attitudes, but significant reversals of neoliberal policies – notably regarding industrial relations and privatisation – appeared to trigger a turnaround in attitudes. That 'policy matters' in the area of economic policy offers some hope that the articulation and implementation of alternatives to neoliberalism could strengthen the discursive and practical value of the right to work for many citizens. In particular, with traditional policy mechanisms – such as import and wage controls – no longer considered feasible by most citizens, there is a need to rethink the means by which government can meet an enduring desire that it should ensure decent employment and wages.

Note

[1] As indicated in the discussion of Table 1.1, all percentage point shifts in support for a particular proposition represent an absolute change in the percentage of agreement reported. For brevity's sake, I have not provided figures depicting the shifting attitudes within sub-groups of the NZES sample but have simply highlighted relevant findings.

FIVE

Normalising neoliberal social security reforms

Social security reform is a second key aspect of neoliberalisation. This chapter considers whether the shift from 'welfare' to 'workfare' made New Zealanders less likely to support the social right to economic and social security. Central to New Zealand's comprehensive social security system established in 1938, this right was further endorsed by the Royal Commission on Social Security's (RCSS, 1972) recommendation that benefit recipients enjoy a sense of belonging and participation, irrespective of the cause of their dependency. It reflected growing concern about the inadequacy of benefits and poverty among those living on low incomes during the 1970s and 1980s. In this context, Muldoon's National government resisted cutting social spending, instead funding an increased range of work and wage subsidy schemes (Wright, 1981; Higgins, 1997; Roper, 2005).

By the early 1980s, however, the political opposition increasingly framed formal work testing as necessary for ameliorating the negative and potentially intergenerational social and psychological effects of unemployment (Adcock, 1981). Chapter Three indicated how the 4th Labour government abandoned work creation schemes and introduced work expectations to encourage the 'right' skills and behaviours among the unemployed, opening the way for National's benefit cuts in the early 1990s and for conditionality to be applied to all means-tested benefits by the end of the decade. The Labour-coalition government relaxed conditionality in the early 2000s but it had strengthened again by 2008, when National regained power and implemented further social security reforms. Given this context, the first section of this chapter explores whether the New Zealand public still believed that the government had a responsibility for assisting the unemployed and should spend more government funds on this group by 2011. It also considers whether New Zealanders believed the unemployed have a responsibility to work in return for their benefits.

A second section examines public support for broader neoliberal discourses around individual responsibility, welfare dependency and individualist causes of need. National governments in the 1990s were strongly influenced by American neopaternalist views that the welfare system creates dependency, leading to an intergenerational culture of worklessness (Murray, 1984; Mead, 1997). These views were reflected in the government-sponsored Beyond Dependency conference and the proposed Code of Family and Social Responsibility but were challenged by alternative public discourses in the late 1990s. The Labour-coalition preferred to focus on improving social inclusion and active citizenship but by 2007 its 'work-first' approach laid the groundwork for National to return with a more effective welfare dependency discourse after 2008. Did New Zealanders roll-over and accept the arguments many had rejected in the late 1990s?

In answering this and other questions, the chapter uses New Zealand Election Study (NZES) and other relevant data to explore trends in New Zealand attitudes over time. Where possible and relevant, changes in the unemployment rate, spending on unemployment and general social expenditure are analysed to assess their role in shaping attitudes. In supporting arguments about whether the New Zealand public have rolled over and accepted the neoliberal workfare state, this chapter considers not only ideological affiliation and age but also whether greater proximity to social security reform impacted upon attitudes. The views of 'benefit recipients', who receive the Unemployment, Domestic Purposes, Invalids' or Sickness benefit and are subject to work-related and other conditions, are compared with a 'superannuitant/student' group whose New Zealand Superannuation or Student Allowance is not subject to the same level of conditionality. This chapter also considers the attitudes of 'wage/salary earners' (including those working part time but not receiving a benefit and the self-employed). The qualitative data highlights both complexity and ambiguity in attitudes towards the unemployed but this chapter, nonetheless, argues that New Zealanders came to accept neoliberal social security reforms and their rationales. Assessing the relevant attitudinal data from the United Kingdom (UK) and Australia at the end of each section finds a high level of coherence in public views towards social security after three decades of neoliberalisation.

Responsibility for the unemployed

To determine whether New Zealanders still believed they have a right to basic economic and social security, this section considers their views about the government's responsibility towards the unemployed, government spending on this group and the unemployed working in return for their benefits. Figure 5.1 shows the proportion of NZES respondents who agreed 'government should be responsible to ensure a

Figure 5.1: 'Government should be responsible to ensure a decent standard of living for the unemployed' (LH) by unemployment rate and unemployment/total social expenditure (% GDP, RH), percentage

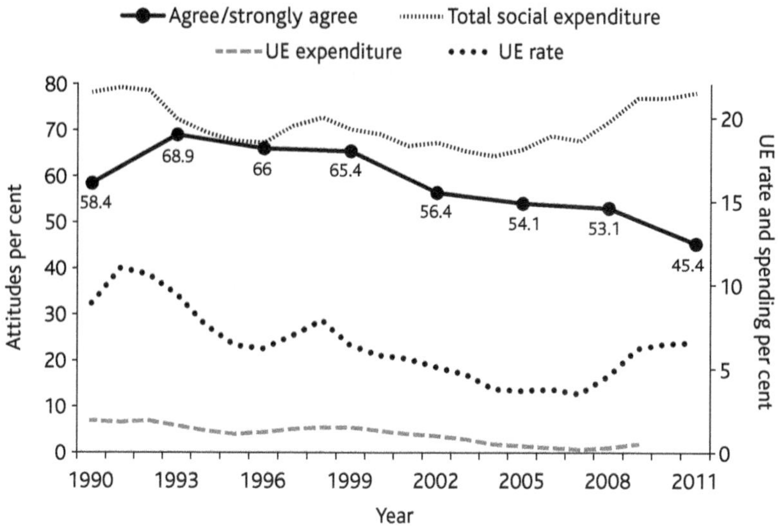

Sources: New Zealand Election Study; OECD; Reserve Bank

decent standard of living for the unemployed' fell from 58.4% to 45.4% between 1990 and 2011. The secondary axis suggests support declined as unemployment diminished and spending in this area as a percentage of Gross Domestic Product (GDP) decreased (there is no relationship with social spending more generally). But support did not increase between 2008 and 2011, when the economy weakened significantly, indicating a permanent weakening of the belief that the government should ensure a decent standard of living for the unemployed.

A more detailed analysis across the differing phases of neoliberalism identifies that support for this proposition did not decline until after 1993. Indeed, support *grew* by 10.5 percentage points between 1990 and 1993. The level of support in 1993 was similar to the proportion of New Zealand Values and Attitudes Study (NZVAS) respondents who agreed that 'government should use taxes to make sure people who cannot get a job have enough to live on' in 1988 (Royal Commission on Social Policy – RCSP, 1988a). Although the latter proposition suggests that structural rather than just personal factors may be behind unemployment, a similar level of agreement suggests that support for the proposition that the government should ensure a decent standard of living for the unemployed may thus have fallen temporarily in 1990 before rising in response to the significant benefit cuts and abolition of the Family Benefit announced in the 1991 'mother of all budgets'.

Many New Zealanders certainly felt betrayed by such moves. National's 1990 election campaign *did* criticise the cost of the welfare state and promised to get tough on 'welfare spongers', even mooting the idea of time limits on benefits (New Zealand Herald – NZH, 1990a, 1990b; Tattersfield, 1990). But the RCSP (1988b) had only recently reported that New Zealanders still saw the government as being responsible for social security, even if they wanted greater participation and involvement in deciding what it might look like and who might provide it. National leader, Jim Bolger (cited in Stone, 1990, p 8) also claimed that people in genuine need 'will be provided for generously if that is required' while Finance Minister, Ruth Richardson, spoke of a *higher* universal child benefit to facilitate the move of sole parents into part-time work (Tattersfield, 1990). Instead, all families with children lost the universal Family Benefit and the core benefit income for a sole parent with two children fell from 92% of the average wage in 1986 to just 65% in 1991 (Cotterell, 2009).

Despite the highly visible and proximate impact of social security changes and Labour's election promises to 'rebuild the sacred social contract between the people and their government' (cited in Vowles et al, 1995, p 83), National regained power in 1993. Support for the proposition that the government should ensure a decent standard of living for the unemployed fell slightly then remained around 65–66% for the remainder of the 1990s. National's communicative discourse around welfare dependency strengthened significantly as it extended its 'workfare' programme after 1997 but its attempt to extend the personal responsibility debate beyond benefit recipients through the proposed Code for Social and Family Responsibility provoked public resistance (Boston and McLeay, 1997). Larner (2000, pp 244–5) argues that the Code represented 'an explicit attempt to generate a post-welfare state consensus around social issues' that incorporated 'a hybrid assemblage of neoliberal and neoconservative rationalities and techniques' to attract support from differing social groups. Yet it was heavily criticised by welfare organisations, Māori and Pasifika[1] communities, feminist groups and even the right-wing New Zealand Business Roundtable. The effectiveness of National's welfare dependency discourse was also mediated by a Beyond Poverty conference organised by academics and non-governmental organisations in 1997 and thousands of protestors marching upon Parliament to demand fairer policies for disadvantaged New Zealanders a year later (St John, 1999c; O'Brien, 2008).

Not only did public resistance diminish once the Labour-coalition was formed but support for the proposition that the government should ensure a decent standard of living for the unemployed fell sharply (by 9 percentage points) among NZES respondents between 1999 and 2002, then diminished more slowly for the remainder of the government's term. Overall, support declined more during this roll-out phase of neoliberalism than any other. Figure 5.1 shows no increase in spending on unemployment but improving economic conditions and increased *total* social expenditure may have played a role in diminishing support for this proposition up until the mid-2000s, reducing public concern about the unemployed. However, the proportion of NZES respondents agreeing that 'government should ensure a decent standard of living for the unemployed' decreased by a further 7.7 percentage points between 2008 and 2011, meaning the same proportion of respondents disagreed as agreed. This suggests that the New Zealand public instead *supported* the Labour-coalition's increased conditionality requirements and 'work-first' approach in the late 2000s and National's extension of these policies. A focus on 'making work pay' may have helped to galvanise support around the working rather than workless poor, while the case management approach offering active training and support situated unemployment as a supply-side rather than demand-side issue.

National's communicative discourse focused on welfare dependency and 'welfare cheating' from 2008 certainly appears to have deflected much potential concern about greater conditions and obligations being placed on sole parents, young people and the sick. As Espiner (2010, p 94) noted, these reforms were 'about politics, plain and simple. The Government knows voters hate the idea that others might be ripping them off and few will have a clear idea of whether that is actually true or whether the solutions put forward will actually work'. The government-commissioned Welfare Working Group (WWG, 2011), which examined and offered recommendations on the issue of welfare dependency, provided weight to National's arguments. Given that by 2011 fewer than half of NZES respondents thought that the unemployed were the government's responsibility, it is no surprise that the alternative recommendations of The Alternative Welfare Working Group (Welfare Justice, 2010a, 2010b) had little impact on public debate. That there was a real change in opinion regarding a decent standard of living for the unemployed being ensured by the government is strongly supported by International Social Survey Programme (ISSP) data, which offers no evidence that the recession encouraged more empathy towards the unemployed (Gendall and Murray, 2010).

A significant decline in support for the same proposition among the Left (from 89.6% to 70.7%) across 21 years suggests that even traditional advocates of the social right to economic and social security had rolled over on this issue. Moderate falls in support were also found among the Centre (58.8% to 44.1%) and the Right (48.6% to 33.6%) but notably Left support for the proposition that the government should ensure the unemployed a decent standard of living began falling in the 1990s, when Centre and Right support *increased*. However, agreement with the proposition fell by the largest amount (around 14 percentage points) among the Left and Centre under the Labour-coalition. The Left's decline slowed to 4.5 percentage points between 2008 and 2011, comparing favourably with the 7.9 and 13.1 percentage point falls in support reported among the Right and Centre when National returned to power. But the Left's acquiescence, along with the significant hardening of Centre support, suggests National's explicit welfare dependency discourse reinforced a shift in attitudes that began in the mid-1990s and was enhanced during the roll-out phase of neoliberalism. Many on the Left may have simply followed the Labour-coalition's lead in viewing unemployment as a problem of undeserving individuals, particularly given the improved economic conditions.

While 50.7% of the youngest (<30) NZES respondents supported the proposition that the government should ensure a decent standard of living for the unemployed in 1990, only 41.9% did so by 2011 and this again supports the view that attitudes towards the unemployed had hardened beyond the point of return. But this was the *smallest* absolute decline across all age groups, with support among the oldest (>61) age group falling by from 71.3% to 52.8%. The youngest group also reported the smallest decrease (5.4 percentage points) in agreement with the proposition between 2008 and 2011, when the oldest age group again reported the largest decline (11.8 percentage points). Greater fluctuations in support among the youngest group overall also suggest that the vulnerability that young people face in the labour market continues to mediate National's message about welfare dependency.

Similarly, being subjected to work-related conditions did not harden benefit recipients' attitudes towards the standard of living for the unemployed being ensured by the government more than other groups; their support fell from 79.8% to 68.7% between 1990 and 2011, about the same absolute percentage point difference as found among wage-salary earners (from 48.6% to 38.6%). The biggest percentage point decline, however, was reported by the superannuitant/student group (from 70.6% to 52.6%). This group's support declined far more quickly than other groups during both the Labour-coalition's time in government and between 2008 and 2011. This suggests benefit recipients *not* subject to conditionality themselves were particularly attentive and/or receptive to the communicative discourses around social security offered by both the Labour-coalition and National.

Indeed, the qualitative study suggests that, despite an awareness of differences in perceptions and treatment, the relatively favourable experience of benefit receipt among superannuitants and students may make them unsympathetic towards the unemployed. A middle income wage/salary earner stated: "The students I think are valued a lot higher ... than people on the Unemployment Benefit, so even though they might get less [money], there's a sense of that they're actually achieving something ... So, students aren't second class citizens in the same way [as the unemployed]". Similarly, a retired participant said of New Zealand Superannuation: "I've earned it ... it's a different benefit than ... a thirty-five year old getting the dole ... it's a different benefit, I don't even class it as a benefit in many ways. It's [as] of right". Thus, superannuitants are perceived as having *earned* the right to government assistance, while financial support for students is seen as an *investment* in the future. Such perceptions of the deservingness may explain differences in the responses of the superannuitant/student group to questions about the government's responsibility for the unemployed when compared to those receiving other benefits.

Although young citizens and benefit recipients may not have hardened their attitudes more than other groups, the overall trends reported thus far do not bode well for social citizenship in the 21st century. Even lower support might be expected to be seen for government *spending* on the unemployed because principles (such as the government taking responsibility for the unemployed) often garner greater support than questions relating to specific expenditure (Vowles and Aimer, 1993). Chapter Two also highlighted how public support for social spending can be thermostatic, increasing when government spending is considered low and decreasing once governments have increased expenditure.

There is, however, no evidence that either trend is true in New Zealand. Unexpectedly, Table 5.1 indicates that support for increased 'spending on jobs and training assistance for the unemployed' reported in the NZVS data was *higher* than the level of NZES support for the proposition that the government should ensure a decent standard of living for the unemployment in the 1990s and into the early 2000s. Support for more spending also rose by 12.9 percentage points between

Table 5.1: Attitudes towards government spending on benefits (greatly increase/some increase only), percentage

'Government should increase spending, even though it might mean higher taxes ...'	1989	1993	1998	2004
On jobs assistance and training for the unemployed	60.9	73.8	62	57.2
On Domestic Purposes benefit	13.4	23.8	17.9	17

Sources: New Zealand Values Survey (cited in Perry & Webster, 1994; 1999; Gendall et al, 2000; Perry, unpublished data – unweighted). 1993 data comes from a partial replication of the NZVS in the International Social Survey Programme.

1989 and 1993, despite government expenditure on unemployment as a percentage of Gross Domestic Product (GDP) increasing slightly during the early 1990s (that spent on active labour market programmes stayed relatively steady). However, the highly visible benefit cuts and abolition of the Family Benefit in 1991 meant that benefit generosity decreased significantly during this period and public opinion is likely to have responded to this more obvious shift in the policy context. After peaking at 62% in 1999, support for more spending on job training and assistance for the unemployed had declined by almost 5 percentage points by 2004. Total social expenditure and spending on unemployment as a percentage of GDP (including active labour market programmes) also fell, but this response coincided with improved economic conditions and Labour-coalition's strong focus on education and training for the unemployed in the early 2000s.

However, it is possible that New Zealanders favour spending on active labour market policies more than cash benefit payments. When the ISSP asked about government spending on 'unemployment benefits' instead of jobs assistance and training, support was much lower, declining from 13% in 1997 to 6% in 2006 (Gendall et al, 1997, 2007). When NZES respondents were asked the same question about spending on unemployment benefits in 2011, 9.7% of participants wanted more spending. Methodological differences in the surveys may explain the small shift between 2006 and 2011; so might changed economic conditions. The 2011 survey also asked about spending on 'welfare benefits' and only a slightly higher percentage of respondents (13.9%) wanted more spending on these, indicating that New Zealanders largely correlate 'welfare' spending with the 'unemployed'.

This is not surprising because international studies of deservingness suggest that sole parents and the sick/disabled are often perceived as more deserving than other types of unemployed people (Larsen, 2006; van Oorschot, 2006; Orton and Rowlingson, 2007). Although van Oorschot (2008) notes five central deservingness criteria, control over neediness has been found to be the most important determinant of attitudes towards the poor. Benefit recipients with children or who are sick/disabled are usually regarded as less in control of their circumstances. However, Table 5.1 shows NZVS respondents offered even *lower* levels of support for increased government spending on the Domestic Purposes benefit, which is mainly used by sole parents, across the 1989–2004 period, than they did for spending on jobs assistance and training. Agreement that the government should spend more on the Domestic Purposes benefit was at its lowest in 1989, indicating negative perceptions of this group were not associated with *neoliberal* policy shifts framing sole parents as 'undeserving'; indeed, hostility towards Domestic Purposes benefit recipients had been long standing (Paske and Ray, 1981a; RCSP, 1988b; Campbell, 1990). There was also a 3.6 percentage point *increase* in the proportion of respondents who supported more spending on this benefit across the 1989–2008 period and support grew more rapidly (by 10.4 percentage points) between 1989 and 1993 in the wake of the 1991 benefit cuts and abolition of the Family Benefit which harshly affected sole parents. Support for more spending then fell again when the Labour-coalition was formed and stayed steady, despite work testing being removed from the Domestic Purposes benefit. These findings again suggest attitudes moved in line with government policy, rather than economic conditions.

A third way of assessing public beliefs about the right to economic and social security is to explore responses to an NZES question about whether 'people who are unemployed should have to work for their benefits'. Figure 5.2 indicates that support for this proposition increased from 68.1% to 85.9% across a 12-year period but a majority already agreed in 1999, just one year after National's Community Wage programme was introduced. Earlier data suggests even higher support for work for the dole activities in the 1980s (Crothers, 1988; RCSP, 1988a). However, the RCSP (1988a, p 339) noted that '[t]he physical and social wellbeing of unemployed people was of considerable concern and probably behind the most commonly expressed idea that unemployed people should do some sort of community work' and it stressed that many New Zealanders considered (rightly, in the RCSP's view) a job to be a *right* rather than an *obligation*.

The number of NZES respondents agreeing that the unemployed should work for their benefits nonetheless rose steadily across the Labour-coalition's term in government but most quickly in its first term when work for the dole was abolished. Support

Figure 5.2: 'People who are unemployed should have to work for their benefits' (LH) by unemployment rate and unemployment/total social expenditure (% GDP, RH), percentage

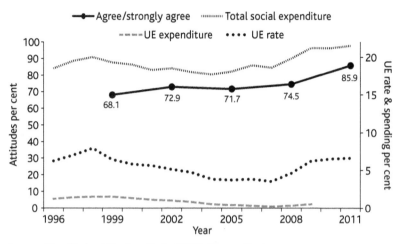

Sources: New Zealand Election Study; OECD; Reserve Bank

increased by the largest amount (11.4 percentage points) across the 12 years between 2008 and 2011, when welfare issues were highly visible at the 2011 election. Thus, 85.9% of NZES 2011 respondents favoured a policy ruled out by all political parties, with the exception of ACT and New Zealand First. The Labour, Green and Mana parties had, however, called for voluntary work with a recognised non-governmental organisation (NGO) to count as meeting work-related obligations (Barron, 2011; 3 News, 2011). Some respondents may have conflated this proposal with the work for the dole scheme implemented between 1998 and 2001, which required the unemployed to undertake work with NGOs in return for their benefit. But the next section highlights that 56.7% of NZES respondents agreed 'around here, most unemployed people could find a job if they really wanted one' in 2011, suggesting that many New Zealanders believe unemployed people have a poor work ethic, potentially justifying *coercion* into work. Figure 5.2's secondary axis shows little evidence of covariance between the unemployment rate and unemployment/total social expenditure, even though it shows these for three years before the NZES question was asked.

Although not *necessarily* influenced by neoliberal policy and politics, New Zealand attitudes towards the unemployed working for their benefits do seem well-entrenched. The Left reported the greatest absolute percentage point increase in agreement over 12 years (from

46% to 69.2%), although significant increases were also evident among both the Centre (66.5% to 87.6%) and the Right (80% to 96%). Notably, support among all groups grew fastest between 2008 and 2011 but the Left appear to have been particularly influenced by National's policy and politics during this period. However, it is also possible that Third Way politics have changed what being 'Left' means and this may now include a focus on work obligations. All age groups of NZES respondents also increased their support for the unemployed working for their benefits between 2008 and 2011 by 15–18 percentage points. It is notable that, although the youngest group's support grew from 64.6% to 83.2% between 1990 and 2011, its agreement remained the lowest of all age groups. The oldest age group offered the highest level of support in both 1990 and 2011, increasing from 71% to 89.3%. This seems surprising given its members had lived through a period of time when social security policy did not place a strong emphasis on work-related obligations given near full (male) employment. Benefit recipients also continued to offer lower levels of support for the unemployed working for their benefits than other respondents, although agreement grew from 43.5% to 66.8%. But, having stayed steady in the 2000s, when superannuitant/ student and wage/salary earner support increased their support by the greatest amount, agreement among benefit recipients rapidly increased by 21.6 percentage points after National returned to power. As a consequence, benefit recipients reported the largest (23.3 percentage points) increase in agreement over 12 years. The growth in support was still significant, however, among superannuitants/students (from 67.1% to 86.7%) and wage/salary earners (73.1% to 88.7%) and both groups offered higher levels of agreement that the unemployed should work for their benefits overall.

These massive increases in support for enhancing the work obligations among New Zealanders, no matter what their income source, indicate a point of no return in the hardening of attitudes towards the unemployed, but the qualitative data does temper this view somewhat. Although the NZES data suggests support for the unemployed working for their benefits hardened by the greatest degree between 2008 and 2011, National maintained the improved case management introduced by Labour from the early 2000s. The qualitative data indicates how some benefit recipients appreciated this individualised approach when compared to the 1990s, potentially shaping attitudes among this group. One of the younger qualitative participants was happy with the level of conditionality placed upon him as an Unemployment benefit recipient:

"…. I've actually found that it's been a good thing for me going in twice a week because it is about getting a job, it's about getting a job that's going to suit you … I'm really surprised cos I had heard horror stories from other people but it worked for me in that I was actually able to talk to them and tell them where my situation was and they didn't just try and throw me into some job that I'm going to pop out of, you know, down the track. Cos, you know, when I was on the benefit years and years ago, you know, you could just disappear off the radar and you'd just be paid and no one would do anything … But now they're actually actively trying to get you into work and those two appointments that you have a week, they bring people in from different places – whether it be like Aviemore College or something like that – and that's actually really good."

Although using the 'self-development' language of modern unemployment programmes, this participant might be less enthused about the unemployed working for their benefits if case management was less individually tailored and less focused on education and training. Certainly, when qualitative participants in my study were asked 'how might we encourage greater individual responsibility?' *prior* to specific discussion about conditionality, they were more likely to name education (45%), incentives (31%) and the role-modelling of values (21%) than sanctions (18%). This suggests that there was no majority support for coercive or punitive means for encouraging 'responsible' behaviour when participants were asked about this in a way not specifying work-related obligations.

A clear majority of the qualitative participants *did* nonetheless support work for the dole, work tests or other conditions in some way and their responses often reflected the Labour-coalition government's focus on 'no responsibilities without obligations'. When rationalising why he supported work for the dole, a former Unemployment benefit recipient said:

"… I think all citizens are subject to some form of obligation or another. I mean if you agree to go to work for [the name of his employer] then you agree that you're going to be there on time and you're going to adhere to a certain standard of, well, you're going to wear their uniform, you're going to adhere to a certain form of conduct that if for any reason you are asked to take a drug test that you'd do it or whatever. It's like, I mean, for someone on the Unemployment benefit, you know, to say 'okay, well if you want to be on the Unemployment benefit here are the terms. You have to turn up every second [day], you know, you have to do this that and the next thing', I mean everyone's got obligations of some sort on them."

It seems less likely that a reduction in the level of individualised service to benefit recipients would shift this kind of belief. Nonetheless, many participants did *not* consider work-related conditions appropriate for sole parents and sick or disabled benefit recipients. In addition, many were insufficiently proximate or otherwise knowledgeable about work conditions to offer a clear-cut answer. Unaware of how New Zealand's work for the dole programme had been implemented in the late 1990s, some supported the unemployed being asked to undertake work in the community. Those aware of New Zealand's failed attempt to implement such a programme through voluntary organisations tended to be less supportive. The broad, abstract questions asked in the NZES and other public opinion surveys may thus tap into the *principles* New Zealanders hold, but miss the pragmatism they demonstrate when faced with policy reality.

Overall, this section has found that New Zealand public attitudes towards the unemployed hardened significantly over time but this followed an *increase* in support for the propositions that the government should ensure a decent standard of living for the unemployed and spend more on job training/assistance and the Domestic Purposes benefit as New Zealanders responded to the roll-back reforms of the early 1990s. The evidence suggests attitudes towards both types of spending fluctuated in response to government policy, but this was not the case for the unemployed working for their benefits, where support increased steadily from 1999. National's welfare dependency rhetoric between 2008 and 2011 had the greatest impact on such attitudes, despite a rapid rise in unemployment, but a lack of empathy for the unemployed was well-entrenched before this time. The qualitative data indicates that such majority support for the unemployed working for their benefits may obscure considerable ambivalent and multiple interpretations of what this might or should mean and whether it is feasible in practice. Nonetheless, all signs point to a significant and permanent hardening of attitudes towards the unemployed, offering another indicator that the post-2008 period represents a form of roll-over neoliberalism.

A coherent turn against the unemployed

This hardening of attitudes towards the unemployed is not unique to New Zealand. Table 5.2 shows that support for the proposition that the government should ensure a decent standard of living for the unemployed also fell in the UK and Australia over time. However, although slight differences in the questions asked in different surveys must be noted, this shift was not as dramatic in Australia because the level of support offered in 1985 was considerably lower than that found in the UK and, to a lesser degree, New Zealand at that time.

Support for the proposition that the government should ensure a decent standard of living for the unemployed fell in both countries during the initial period of reforms, while earlier discussion highlighted that it *rose* moderately in New Zealand. This suggests the early and harsh benefit cuts and abandonment of universal family assistance provoked New Zealand concern about the unemployed in a way not apparent in the UK, where social security reforms were significant but incremental and the Child Benefit (although frozen in value) was retained, or Australia where more moderate reforms explicitly attempted to compensate for the abolition of the Child Benefit. The differing pace of policy change may therefore be a factor behind this difference in attitudes during this period. Although Australian support for the government ensuring a decent standard of living for the unemployed appears to have increased by 1996,[2] it had begun to diminish in all three countries by the mid-to-late 2000s.

Australian and New Zealand support continued to decline but it increased between 2011 and 2012 in the UK. This may have been a delayed thermostatic response to the recession, which was felt more strongly in the UK than in the two Antipodean countries, but it is yet to be seen whether the overall downward trend was reversed in the long term. Pearce and Taylor (2013, p 44) do indicate that, although the British public viewed unemployment benefit recipients as less

Table 5.2: 'Government should provide a decent standard of living for the unemployed' (agree only*), percentage

	1985	1990	1996	2006	2007	2009	2012
United Kingdom	85	81	78	55	–	–	65
Australia	55	51	65	–	57	51	–

Note: * All UK data and 1985,1990,1996 and 2007 Australian data combine 'definitely should' and 'probably should'; 2009 data combine 'strongly agree' and 'disagree'.

Sources: Australian Survey of Social Attitudes; British Social Attitudes Survey; International Social Survey Programme (1985 and 1990 Australian data cited in Bean & Papadakis, 1998).

deserving of support than three decades ago, 'this perception does not appear to have influenced views on the deservingness of welfare recipients as a whole'. The hardening of British attitudes towards the unemployed, however, was most pronounced among Labour Party supporters and the young (Sefton, 2009; Curtice, 2010; Clery, 2012a).

There are no directly comparable data on public views about spending on the unemployed. Table 5.3, however, indicates that when asked to prioritise extra government spending, the proportion of British Social Attitudes respondents naming 'benefits for the unemployed' as their first priority declined steadily between the 1980s and 2007, then recovered slightly by 2012. Once again, this may indicate a break in the long term trend of decline, but Pearce and Taylor (2013) note that similar fluctuations have been apparent in recent years. The increase in New Zealand support for more spending on unemployment benefits between 2006 and 2011 began *before* the downturn in the economy but given that the data for each year came from a different survey, it is difficult to ascertain whether this was also a temporary shift. Australian support for increased spending on unemployment benefits started from a much lower level but, after falling slightly between 1987 and 1990, it then stayed *steady* on 12% between the mid-1990s to the mid-2000s. This suggests that increased levels of conditionality – including the introduction of work for the dole in 1998 – had comparatively little impact upon attitudes.

Comparative analysis is also inhibited by a lack of data about public attitudes towards work obligations. In 2009, 86.5% of BSA respondents thought that unemployment benefit recipients who are fit and able to work should be 'required to do some work in the community' in return for their benefit. This stayed fairly steady in 2012, despite continuing poor economic conditions. Of course, New Zealand reported a similar level of support for the unemployed working for their benefits, even though the recession it faced was not as severe.

Table 5.3: Attitudes towards spending on the unemployed (agree only), percentage

	1987	1990	1991	1996	2000	2007	2010	2012
1st priority for extra spending on welfare – benefits for the unemployed								
United Kingdom	16	–	10	11	6	2	4	5
	1985	1990	1991	1996	2000	2007	2010	2012
Spend more or much more on unemployment benefits								
Australia	13	10	–	12	–	12	–	–

Sources: Australian Survey of Social Attitudes and International Social Survey Programme (both cited in Wilson et al, 2012a); British Social Attitudes Survey.

The number of AuSSA respondents agreeing 'benefit recipients should have more obligations to look for work' stayed fairly steady (ranging between 71–75%) between 2003 and 2009, contrasting with the 17.8% increase in support for the unemployed working for their benefits between 1999 and 2011 found in New Zealand.

Work for the dole is already a policy reality in Australia, so that around three quarters of respondents wanted *more* obligations during this period reinforces other evidence suggesting that Australians generally regard benefit recipients as undeserving of government assistance and are comparatively hard on the unemployed when compared to other countries (Eardley et al, 2000). Wilson and Meagher (2007) note that attempts by the Australian government to introduce time limits or directly cut benefits would provoke resistance but the number of respondents agreeing that 'the government should limit the length of time that people can get welfare benefits even if they end up without an income' did increase by 3 percentage points (to 28%) between 2005 and 2009 following Labor's election win. Although making some effort to avoid its predecessor's welfare dependency rhetoric, Labor did not focus stimulus spending on the unemployed and did not soften work obligations (Wilson et al, 2012). The public may have picked up on this continuation of Liberal-National coalition policy.

In conclusion, there is little doubt that the process of neoliberalisation had a coherent, negative effect on public attitudes towards the unemployed over three decades. Despite New Zealand's early benefit cuts and abolition of the Family benefit, policy there arguably did not harden as much as in the UK and Australia given that work for the dole was implemented only for three years. There has been no serious discussion of introducing benefit time limits and non-government agencies have played a lesser role in administering conditionality measures because employment-related services have not been contracted out to the same degree. New Zealand, however, offers the strongest evidence that public attitudes towards the unemployed have irrevocably hardened.

Neoliberal welfare discourses

The fact that economic conditions continue to shape some attitudes towards the unemployed suggests that the public do not necessarily endorse the broader discourses of individual responsibility, welfare dependency and individualist causes of need that have been central to neoliberal social security reform. The first discourse challenges social citizenship by encouraging citizens to be 'self reliant' and thus not expect the state to provide for all their social and economic needs. Individualism and hard work have long been valued in New Zealand, given its colonial history and experience as a liberal welfare state (Humpage and Craig, 2008). But the 1978 Commission for the Future reported that most references to individual responsibility were associated with individuals developing useful skills and knowledge and preventing illness through exercise and healthy eating (Zepke and Robinson, 1979). In 1987, 68% of NZVS respondents agreed 'people should be more self reliant' when asked about their attitudes towards things that 'some people would like to see happen in New Zealand' (RCSP, 1988a). But this may have been a response to New Zealand's highly regulated society, which many young people taking part in the 1989 NZVS survey considered to be unresponsive to individual enterprise and hard work (Gold and Webster, 1990).

The 1998 and 2004 NZVS surveys also asked respondents to indicate where their views regarding individual and government responsibility sat on a 10-point scale. This question was replicated in the 2008 NZES, allowing us to consider responses over a 10 year period. For ease of presentation, these data have been converted to the 5-point scale found in Figure 5.3. Although the differing data sources require some caution in interpretation, this shows the proportion of respondents positioning themselves at the at the far end of the scale, 'people should take more responsibility to provide for themselves', increased by 9.9 percentage points between 1998 and 2008, particularly during the last four years

Figure 5.3: 'People should take more responsibility for themselves' or 'government should take more responsibility to ensure everyone is provided for', 5-point scale, percentage*

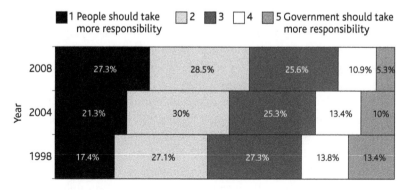

Note: *Does not add up to 100% because 'don't know' responses excluded from figure. Converted from 10-pt scale. 2004 data unweighted

Sources: New Zealand Election Study; New Zealand Values Study (cited in Perry & Webster, 1999 and Perry, unpublished data)

of that period. In contrast, the proportion who sat at the 'government should take responsibility to ensure that everyone is provided for' end declined by 8.1 percentage points over the same period, also mostly between 2004 and 2008. More generally, there has been a definite shift in attitudes across the 10-year period towards the idea that people should take responsibility for themselves, although the proportion of respondents who gave neutral responses stayed fairly steady. Given it was clear by the 2008 election that New Zealand was heading into a recession, economic conditions do not appear to have shaped attitudes.

Disaggregated responses for the individual–government responsibility scale discussed in Figure 5.3 are available only for 2008 and responses for the two points have been combined at the end of the same 5-point scale to get a sense of the general positioning of each group. The Left were, as expected, far less likely to situate themselves towards the individual responsibility (33%) end of the scale than respondents from the Centre (59.7%) or Right (72.6%). In addition, only Left respondents offered more support for government responsibility (34.3%) than the individual responsibility or neutral position. Although only a third of them did so, this suggests ideological distinctions remained important. The youngest age group were also *least* likely to position themselves at the 'individual responsibility' end of the continuum (48.2%) and most likely to sit at the 'government responsibility' end (19.2%). In contrast, around 60% of those aged over 45 favoured individual responsibility, while only around 14% thought that the government needs to take more responsibility. These findings are rather unexpected because older people were more likely to agree that the government should take responsibility to ensure a decent standard of living than the young. Around one third of benefit recipients positioned themselves across all three responses, challenging the view that their proximity to a neoliberal individual responsibility discourse shaped their attitudes more heavily than the superannuitant/student group and wage/salary earners, around 60% of whom believed people should take more responsibility for themselves.

At first glance, the qualitative study appears to contradict this finding, as participants receiving a benefit were slightly *more* likely than other groups to agree when asked to respond to the 'people should take more responsibility for themselves' proposition used in Figure 5.3's scale. However, when participants were asked to indicate activities that they considered to be an individual responsibility, paying tax was the only one named more often by benefit recipients than other groups and they were least likely to name work. In addition, benefit recipients were twice as likely as wage/salary earners to fully agree with the 'government should ensure everyone is provided for' statement and they most commonly named government responsibilities associated with social citizenship (health, education, housing, decent work/wages, ensuring basics are affordable and childcare/children). Participants receiving benefits were also most likely to believe that having their basic needs met and welfare entitlement were rights of citizenship. It is interesting that they were *most* likely to believe New Zealanders have more rights and *least* likely to think New Zealanders have more responsibilities today than in the past, given this group has been subject to a greater level of conditionality and surveillance than other New Zealanders. Work and Income New Zealand's attempts to emphasise *consumer* rights appear to have influenced this belief.

The qualitative study further highlights the difficulty respondents may have had in situating their views on the individual-government responsibility scale. Only about half the qualitative participants offered a clear 'yes' or 'no' response to the government responsibility statement. Of this group, 82% agreed in some way but 43% of those responding qualified their agreement, saying that the government should be responsible only for *some* groups of people *or some* activities. Notably, participants who expressed high levels of distrust in the government were usually *more* likely to support the government responsibility statement, confirming evidence discussed in Chapter Two that disenchantment with government services as a result of cutbacks, privatisation and user-pays *increases*, rather than diminishes, the expectations citizens have of government agencies and political representatives.

Similarly, 88% of the 67 participants responding to the statement about individual responsibility agreed in some way but only 46% did so categorically. Some saw themselves as *already* taking responsibility and thus felt affronted by any suggestion that they were not. Participants in a benefit recipient focus group, for instance, felt particularly aggrieved that Work and Income New Zealand does not recognise being a parent as important, instead regarding paid work as the main indicator of individual responsibility. A Māori benefit recipient also felt insulted by the individual responsibility statement because it suggested Māori had not been self-determining before colonisation: "I still don't understand why that question came out. 'People should take more responsibility to provide for themselves.' We've provided for ourselves since we were born". Only 12% of participants completely rejected the individual responsibility statement, however, while 42% offered ambivalent responses either because they thought *some* people should take more responsibility to provide for themselves or that *both* individuals and the government should share responsibility of provision.

Importantly, many participants did not directly respond to the individual statement at all. A middle income wage/salary earner rejected its premise outright because he did not trust the government: "Yeah, I think it's an easy way out for the government, you know, because it leaves them blameless". Further participants disputed the implicit focus on individuals, which ignores the societal context in which individuals live and leaves no room for a shared partnership between individuals, their families, communities *and* the government. A young, Pasifika wage/salary earner said:

> "... I was trying to work out how to address the question cos
> — but now I've figured out why, why it's a stumbling block.
> When you speak to, I guess, a lot of Pacific Islanders and,
> in particular Samoans, the question is very individualistic
> and so I'm thinking: 'by myself?' Or what are you trying
> to get out, because when you think of, you know, us, we
> think holistically. So 'people take more responsibility, should
> take more responsibility' — people equals communities, you
> know, and it's not just a one-person thing which I kind of,
> almost, the question almost kind of suggested that, that the
> person themselves takes ownership of themselves."

This resistance to the individual-centred emphasis of the proposition was especially notable in the focus groups held with Māori and Pasifika peoples but not exclusive to them. A European/Pākehā[3] wage/salary earner, for instance, unpacked different aspects of the statement:

> "... I just think stuff like that is actually quite ridiculous
> because, you know, the correct answer is 'of course, people
> should provide for themselves'. But, you know, what do we
> mean by 'provide for themselves', 'take more responsibility'?
> And, I mean, part of the taking more responsibility to
> provide for ourselves may, in fact, be to curb other peoples
> rapacious tendencies, you know."

Some participants went on to rephrase it to better reflect what they perceived to be an individual's role. A high income earner said: "I would rather say 'people should take more responsibility for helping provide for others'".

Commenting on 2004 NZVS data, Perry (cited in Collins, 2006) also stressed the long-running contradiction that New Zealanders appear to offer broad general endorsements of neoliberalism but more specific questions highlight ongoing support for the government continuing to be responsible for a wide range of social policy activities. This does not mean they are confused or ignorant about policy and its impacts, but rather public views on government and individual personal responsibility differ depending on the context and are shaped by both principle and pragmatism. Overall, New Zealanders may want to be self-reliant and they expect the same of others but they realise that total independence is impossible, making a balance between the two desirable.

This is especially the case given qualitative participants saw individuals and government as taking responsibility for quite different activities. There were 23 activities named as individual responsibilities, with children and family mentioned most frequently. Working and paying tax were the activities named third and fifth most often, appearing to endorse government rhetoric framing paid work as the most important way of demonstrating individual responsibility. However, these activities were less frequently mentioned when participants were asked how one might characterise a 'good citizen', suggesting paid work was important to many participants but there was no overwhelming belief that it constitutes a crucial aspect of *citizenship*. This may be because, as Dean (2012) found in his study of British Working Tax Credit recipients, views about the utility of paid work are more complex and varied than neoliberal discourses would suggest.

When asked specifically what activities they considered to be the *government's* responsibility, the most common responses were categorised as 'helping the needy' (66%). This included specific references to benefit payments, as well as more general comments about assisting those who cannot help themselves through sickness, injury or bad luck. Although only around a third of respondents thought having your basic needs met (34%) and welfare entitlement (31%) were *rights* of citizenship, it is notable that they were even *less* likely to name traditional political rights, such as freedom of speech (17%), voting (16%) or a passport or diplomatic protection (13%). Even if many New Zealanders were ambivalent when asked specifically about the unemployed, most therefore believed that the government should continue to help needy New Zealanders.

In continuing to try to understand why many NZES respondents favoured individual over government responsibility, it is also useful to consider public beliefs about the social security system, which may be conceived as encouraging dependency and discouraging self-reliance. Crothers (1988) argues that New Zealanders always favoured a largely residualist system, even during the 'golden weather' period of the welfare state, but the RCSS:

... found no public support for the view that the system has unduly affected initiative, sapped self-reliance, or restricted economic social or cultural growth and development. Rather, we found public opinion to be marked by the same humanitarian approach which has characterised New Zealanders from the earliest days of settlement, and generally in support of a system which redistributes income and reflects community responsibility for ensuring that no one fails to reach an adequate standard of living. (RCSS, 1972, p 6)

In 1987, the NZAVS certainly indicates that, when given several options as to 'why people are unemployed', more people named structural factors than personal reasons (RCSP, 1988a). However, NZVS 1993 findings led Perry and Webster (1994, pp xv–xvi) to argue that: 'Government welfare programmes are generally rated poorly as means of solving the problems of the needy in New Zealand. Furthermore, current government assistance programmes for disadvantaged social groups are judged to be neither well-targeted nor equitable'. While this suggests that the welfare system was not perceived as particularly effective at the time, it does not necessarily mean that New Zealanders believed it caused dependency.

Responses to NZES questions asked only in 2011 suggest a majority of New Zealanders *do* now see the social security system as part of the problem. Table 5.4 shows that roughly half the respondents agreed 'most people on the dole are fiddling in one way or another' and 'with lower benefits, people would learn to stand on their own two feet'. ISSP data suggests support for both propositions increased through the 2000s, as it did for 'most people who get welfare benefits don't really deserve any help' (Gendall et al, 2000; Gendall and Murray, 2010).

Table 5.4: Attitudes towards welfare (agree/strongly agree only), percentage

To what extent do you agree or disagree with the following statements ...	2011
With lower welfare benefits, people would learn to stand on their own two feet	56.0
Most people on the dole are fiddling in one way or another	50.8
Around here, most unemployed people could find a job if they really wanted one	56.7
Many people who get welfare benefits don't really deserve any help	38.8
Cutting welfare benefits would damage too many people's lives	50.3
The creation of the welfare state is one of NZ's proudest achievements	37.9
Welfare benefits make people lazy and dependent	62.5

Source: New Zealand Election Study.

Although half of the NZES respondents thought that 'cutting welfare benefits would damage too many people's lives' in 2011, indicating perhaps some awareness of the potential consequences of National's welfare reforms, only just over a third thought 'the creation of the welfare state is one of NZ's proudest achievements'. This implies that many New Zealanders may have a pragmatic rather than principled view about social security.

The NZES also asked respondents if they agreed that 'welfare benefits make people lazy and dependent' in 2005, 2008 and 2011 and around 62% did so in all years. In 2011, the lowest support for this proposition was found among the Left (40.8%) and benefit recipients (47.6%) but only they and respondents situated at the ideological Centre (62.3%) reported tiny increases in support over this six-year period. In contrast, support stayed steady among the Right (around 77%), the superannuitant/student group (around 62%) and wage/salary earners (64.8%). National's welfare dependency rhetoric seemed to have the strongest effect on benefit recipients, as well the youngest age group of respondents (whose growth in support from 64% to 66.7% between 2005 and 2011 occurred mostly after 2008). Interestingly, those aged 45 and under increased their support for the welfare benefits make people lazy and dependent proposition over time but it *decreased* among those over this age, with the oldest age group falling from 65.1% to 62.3%. These findings are clearly troubling, because they indicate the deserving/undeserving dichotomy is well-entrenched.

It is possible that those whom we might normally expect to support the welfare system were particularly influenced by National's framing of social security as the problem because they were aware of its potential negative impacts on the status and sense of belonging of benefit recipients. In 1999, 51% of ISSP respondents agreed 'people receiving social security are made to feel like second class citizens'. The New Zealand government has replaced the term 'social security' with 'income support' and this caused some confusion when participants in the qualitative study were asked to respond to the same proposition. The limitations of ISSP question were further revealed by their confusion regarding the term 'second class citizen'. However, when asked to interpret this as benefit recipients being devalued or treated unequally compared to other New Zealanders, 90% agreed in some way that people receiving social security benefits are made to feel like second class citizens.

Importantly, when asked *why* benefit recipients might feel 'second class', 48% of responses referred to the poor treatment of benefit recipients by Work and Income New Zealand or Accident

Corporation Compensation officials and policies while 33% of qualitative participants referred to the broader societal stigmatisation of benefit recipients. For instance, a benefit recipient said she felt 'second class' "[b]ecause I've been treated with suspicion or as if what I'm saying about my life isn't what my life is". Surprisingly few participants believed feeling 'second class' was associated with personal factors relating to benefit recipients themselves, such as being lazy or dependent. In addition, when participants were asked whether it was *appropriate* for benefit recipients to be treated like 'second class' citizens, only 3% agreed while 41% disagreed and 55% were ambivalent, usually because they said it depended on the circumstances or which groups of benefit recipients were being considered. Increasing perceptions of the social security system as part of the problem may, therefore, be partly driven by a concern that its policies and practices have a negative impact upon the sense of belonging found among benefit recipients. UMR Research (2009) certainly found that public trust and satisfaction with public services is linked to perceptions of confidence in public sector staff and a sense that citizens will be treated fairly.

Another way of understanding why New Zealanders endorse individual responsibility and believe welfare makes people lazy and dependent is to consider how they view the causes of need. Evidence suggests that in the 1980s New Zealanders viewed poverty, unemployment and other forms of need as shaped by structural more than individual factors (Heylen cited in Crothers, 1988; RCSP, 1988a). Table 5.5, however, indicates that when asked 'why people in this country live in need' over a third of NZVS respondents believed need was caused by individual behaviours such as 'laziness or a lack of willpower' between 1989 and 2011 and the proportion rose to almost

Table 5.5: Attitudes towards the causes of need (agree/strongly agree only), percentage

Why are there people in this country who live in need?	1989	1993	1998	2004	2008	2011
Laziness/lack of willpower	38	37	36.8	49.7	38.3	47.3
Bad luck	17	–	–	–	–	–
Unfair society*	30	37	36.2	18.8	21.7	21.5
Other reasons	15	–	–	–	–	–
Neither/don't know**	–	–	27	24.7	39.9	26.1

Note: * In 1989, worded 'unfairness & injustice in our society'. ** Respondents offered four options in 1989, later surveys only three plus 'neither/don't know'.

Sources: New Zealand Values Study 1989 (cited in Perry & Webster, 1994; 1999; Perry, unpublished data – unweighted). 1993 data from replication of same question in the International Survey Programme; 2008 data from replication in the New Zealand Election Study.

half in both 2004 and 2011. Responses may be steadier than they appear, given the 2008 data is drawn from the NZES which used a differing methodology than the other surveys, but these findings suggest a significant increase in this individualistic belief after 1998. Moreover, those who believe a 'lack of fairness in society' causes need also grew by 7 percentage points between 1989 and 1993 and, if this figure is combined with the 17% who said was need was caused by bad luck in 1989, this represents exactly the same amount of support (37%) offered for the latter proposition in 1993. It is also possible some 'other reasons' responses might have been captured by the unfair society category from 1993.

Weaknesses in the data require caution, but in the three years when a 'neither/don't know' option was given, at least a quarter of respondents opted for this, most notably in 2008 when 39.9% did so and the proportion supporting 'unfair society' hit an all-time low (21.7%). Thus more respondents gave an ambivalent answer than 'unfair society' from the mid-2000s, indicating a high degree of uncertainty or difficulty answering such a question. Increased government focus on meeting the needs of the 'socially excluded' at this time may have been influential here. Notably, when the ISSP included a similar question regarding the causes of need in 1999 but offered 'people are in need because it is an inevitable part of modern life' as an option, 54% of respondents agreed with it; 48% also agreed people are in need because 'they have been unlucky'. The number who thought such need was caused by an unfair society or laziness/lack of will power shrank when these options were offered, indicating that the more limited NZVS question fails to capture the complexity of their views on 'need'.

Nonetheless, a significant minority of New Zealanders believed need to be caused by individual behaviours and this belief grew significantly from the late 1990s. 77–78% of respondents in the 2004 NZVS and 2011 NZES surveys also thought 'most poor people in this country have a chance of escaping from living in need', suggesting entrenched structural problems are regarded to be a cause. Yet 59% of NZVS respondents thought 'government was doing too little for people living in need' in 1998; this had fallen to 34% by 2004, but it remains that many who thought poor personal actions created need still wanted the government to do something about the problem (Perry and Webster, 1999; Rose et al, 2005).

It might also be assumed that perceptions of any growth in the *level* of need in society would further shape public views about what causes need. In 2004, only 49.5% of NZVS respondents thought there was a larger share of people living in need than ten years ago (Perry, unpublished data), despite the fact that levels of income inequality, poverty and hardship increased significantly during the 1990s and minor improvements did not come until *after* 2004 (see Chapter Seven). When the NZES asked the same question in 2011, the proportion of respondents agreeing there was a larger share of people living in need had grown to 68.2%. Public perceptions of the growth of poverty in 2004 may have been mediated by the relatively buoyant economic conditions but it is also possible the Occupy movement and political discussion about inequality drew attention to growing poverty in the late 2000s.

Disaggregated data for 2008 shows, not surprisingly, that respondents from the Right (48.8%) were more likely to favour individual causes of need than the Left (17%), while 41.6% of the latter agreed 'unfair society' was the cause of need but only 16.3% of the Right did so. Importantly, the Centre's views were generally closer to those of the Right than the Left. Yet analysis of NZVS data by political party affiliation suggests the ideological divide *grew* rather than decreased over time (Gold and Webster, 1990; Perry and Webster, 1999). In addition, only 39.1% of the youngest NZES respondents believed that individual attitudes or behaviours shaped needs, while 23.9% said 'unfair society' in 2008, compared to 47.3% and 17.1% respectively reported among the oldest age group. Benefit recipient support for the idea that need is caused by laziness/lack of willpower (25.3%) was lower than among the superannuitant/student group (44.4%) and wage/salary earners (42.8%). Not surprisingly, more benefit recipients thought need was caused by a lack of fairness in society than the other two groups (around 17%). But it remains that less than half the benefit recipients saw societal factors as central, suggesting they may have come to endorse neoliberal welfare dependency rhetoric.

In conclusion, many New Zealanders appear to endorse the key discourses around individual responsibility and welfare dependency promoted (to varying degrees) under different phases of neoliberalism. More people believed people should take more responsibility for themselves in 2008 than in 1998, but the qualitative data suggests New Zealanders interpreted this statement variably and agreement does not *necessarily* provide evidence that neoliberal rhetoric has been internalised. Similarly, support for individual responsibility did not always exclude a belief that the government should take responsibility for key activities improving social wellbeing. The evidence does clearly indicate that many New Zealanders saw the welfare system as part of the problem by 2011, although half of the NZES respondents still thought cutting benefits would damage too many people's lives and the qualitative evidence suggests many New Zealanders believed the social security system stigmatises benefit recipients. This helps explain why many respondents, particularly those who were on the Left, young or receiving a benefit, still wanted the government to do something about reducing need supposedly caused by individual behaviours.

The uneven discursive power of neoliberalism

The limited evidence available suggests that Britons and Australians similarly endorsed neoliberal discourses about social security but not to the same degree as New Zealanders. The Australian Values Study included the same individual–government responsibility 10-point scale used in New Zealand. Not only did attitudes barely change between 2005 and 2012, but only around a third of Australians agreed people should take more responsibility for themselves compared to 45% who thought that the government should ensure that everyone is provided for. This indicates a stronger collective focus than found in New Zealand.

In addition, although BSA data shows increasing agreement that laziness/lack of willpower is the reason people live in need since 1989, only 23% did so in 2010 compared to 47.3% in New Zealand one year later. British respondents were offered a differing number of options, but a similar number (21%) believed an unfair/unjust society was the cause in both countries. BSA data also shows that the proportion of Britons who believed people receiving social security are made to feel like second class citizens fell by 10 percentage points to 43% between 1986 and 2000. This was considerably lower than the 90% of the participants in the qualitative study who agreed in 2007/08; however, differing methodologies were used to collect data. It is also possible that the varied impact of the global financial crisis may contribute to these differences.

Although these findings suggest most citizens in all three countries do not consider benefit recipients to be deserving, a significant minority of Britons and a majority of New Zealanders and Australians believed that 'cutting welfare benefits would damage too many people's lives'. Table 5.6 shows that, once again, British support reversed a clear trend of declining support for this proposition with a 5 percentage point increase in support between 2011 and 2012. Australian support also increased by 4 percentage points during the late 2000s but, as in New Zealand, there is insufficient data to indicate if this also reversed an established decline. Clearly, the public in all three countries recognised the cost of social security cuts but active resistance against actual policy changes seems unlikely.

Table 5.6: Attitudes towards the unemployed and welfare (agree/ strongly agree only), percentage

	1987	1991	1996	2000	2003	2005	2007	2009	2010	2011	2012
Cutting welfare benefits would damage too many people's lives											
United Kingdom	–	–	–	59	55	48	45	47	43	43	48
Australia	–	–	–	–	66	68	–	72	–	–	–
Around here most unemployed people could find a job if they really wanted to											
United Kingdom	42	39	40	61	67	71	69	56	55	58	56
Australia	–	–	–	–	59	64	–	61	–	–	–

Sources: Australian Survey of Social Attitudes; British Social Attitudes Survey.

New Zealanders may have endorsed neoliberal welfare discourses to a greater degree but the idea of welfare dependency appears to have become normalised in all three countries. Table 5.6 highlights that a growing proportion of both BSA and AuSSA respondents agree that 'around here most unemployed people could find a job if they really wanted to' over time, although the British data suggests that support for this proposition fell after 2007, presumably in response to the economic conditions. However, other BSA evidence indicates there was virtually no change in support for other statements tapping into beliefs about welfare dependency between 2010 and 2012 (Pearce and Taylor, 2013). In Australia, the number of AuSSA respondents who said 'welfare benefits make people lazy and dependent' fell slightly (from 56% to 53%) between 2005 and 2009, a somewhat lower level of agreement than the 62% of New Zealanders supporting this proposition across a similar period of time. The proportion of Australians agreeing that 'the government should limit the length of time that people can get welfare benefits even if they end up without an income' rose, however, by 3 percentage points to 28% between 2005 and 2009. Although Australia's economy did comparatively well, this suggests that weakening economic conditions had little effect on attitudes towards the unemployed.

Conclusion: the 'workfare' state endorsed

This chapter has demonstrated that significant reforms diminishing the right to economic and social security are likely to have influenced public beliefs about government assistance for the unemployed, hardening attitudes towards this group in all three case study countries. Although the public are far less empathetic towards the unemployed than three decades ago and there is some evidence that New Zealanders endorsed neoliberal welfare discourses around individual responsibility, welfare dependency and individualised causation of need to a greater extent than Britons or Australians, the New Zealand qualitative data suggests they have not been completely accepted. This presents an important, if rather small, window of opportunity for advocates of social citizenship.

Importantly, discussion highlighted how the highly proximate, visible and traceable benefit cuts and abolition of the Family Benefit in 1991 saw New Zealanders, with the notable exception of those on the Left, increase their support for the proposition that the government should take responsibility for ensuring a decent standard of living for the unemployed. This suggests that the communicative discourse focused on economic necessity and individual responsibility offered was largely ineffective at the time, as Schmidt (2002) has argued. Table 5.7's overall summary of trends across the three countries shows an increased proportion of NZES respondents agreeing that the government should ensure a decent standard of living and spend more on job assistance/ training for the unemployed across the 1990s overall. But support did decline after 1993, just as found in the UK and Australia. There is a lack of 1990s New Zealand and Australia data regarding the view that the unemployed could find a job if they really wanted one, but they likely followed the British pattern of hardening attitudes towards the unemployed over this period. The roll-back phase of neoliberalism thus had a generally negative impact on public beliefs about the social right to economic and social security.

Moreover, neoliberal social security policies and politics were normalised in all three countries during the 2000s, even in Australia where the Liberal-National coalition government offered an explicit welfare dependency discourse that contrasted with the 'no rights without responsibilities' and social inclusion rhetoric found in the UK and New Zealand. Table 5.7 highlights how support for government ensuring a decent standard of living for the unemployed, and for various propositions relating to spending on the unemployed, declined during this period in all three countries but more Britons believed that the unemployed could find a job if they wanted one. Earlier discussion also highlighted that more New Zealanders came to believe people should take more responsibility for themselves, that welfare benefits make people lazy and dependent, and that need is caused by individual behaviours.

Many indicators suggest the late 2010s represented a period where the public rolled over and accepted the need for further social security

Table 5.7: Attitudinal trends in social security across three phases of neoliberalism in New Zealand, the United Kingdom and Australia

	New Zealand	United Kingdom	Australia
	1984–1990: Labour Mild incremental increase in conditionality for unemployed Mild, increase in targeting **1990–1999: National** Significant benefit cuts Abolished universal family benefit Significant but incremental increase in conditionality	**1979–1997: Conservative** Significant, incremental increase in targeting but retained universal child benefit Moderate increase in conditionality	**1983–1996: Labor** Moderate, incremental increase in targeting Abolished universal child benefit but poorest compensated through taxes and benefits Moderate increase in conditionality but with job guarantee/ training
Government should ensure decent standard of living for unemployed	↑	↓	↑
Increase spending on unemployed*	↔**	↓	↓
Most unemployed could find a job if really wanted one	–	↑	–
	1999–2008: Labour Coalition Initially softened then significantly increased conditionality but with focus on training/education Moderate restructuring of social security	**1997–2010: Labour** Significant increase in targeting and conditionality but with focus on training/education Radical restructuring of social security and moderate privatisation of employment services	**1996–2007: Liberal-National Coalition** Significant increase in targeting and conditionality Radical restructuring of social security and significant privatisation of employment services
Government should ensure decent standard of living for unemployed	↓	↓	↓
Increase spending on unemployed	↓	↓	↓
Most unemployed could find a job if really wanted one	–	↓	↑
Cutting benefits would damage too many people's lives	–	↓	–

(continued)

Table 5.7: Attitudinal trends in social security across three phases of neoliberalism in New Zealand, the United Kingdom and Australia (continued)

	New Zealand	United Kingdom	Australia
	2008+: National Significant, incremental increase in targeting and conditionality	2010+: Conservative-Liberal Democrat Coalition Significant restructuring of social security Significant, incremental increase in targeting and conditionality Increased targeting of child benefit	2007+: Labor Some softening of conditionality with greater focusing on training but extended compulsory income management
Government responsible for ensuring decent standard of living for unemployed	↓	↑	↓
Increase spending on unemployed	↑	↔	–
Most unemployed could find a job if they really wanted one	–	↔	↓
Cutting benefits would damage too many people's lives	–	↑	↑

Notes: * See earlier discussion indicating that all three countries have asked about spending on the unemployed in different ways. ** This represents 'steady' support, as defined in Table 1.1.

reform but there are some glimmers of hope. Britons appear to have had a delayed reaction to poor economic conditions (and possibly also proposed radical reforms of social security), increasing agreement that the government has a responsibility to ensure a decent standard of living for the unemployed and to spend more on this group. There was also increased support in both the UK and Australia for the idea that cutting welfare benefits would damage too many lives. Although comparison with the UK and Australia suggests New Zealanders have hardened their attitudes to a greater degree than elsewhere, the New Zealand qualitative study found that some citizens may view the social security system as part of the problem more because of the way it stigmatises benefit recipients rather than because of 'dependency' among this group. They also considered individuals to be responsible for differing activities than the government, requiring a balance between the two. This chapter has told a largely negative story of the coherence and power of neoliberalisation across three decades, but these findings offer a limited basis from which to galvanise beliefs that all citizens should have a right to economic and social security.

Notes

[1] A term commonly used to refer to migrants from islands in the Pacific ocean or their descendants who live in New Zealand.

[2] There is some evidence that Bean and Papadakis' (1998) analysis of ISSP data in 1985 and 1990 was quite conservative, so this increase in 1996 must be treated with some caution.

[3] A Māori term commonly used to refer to New Zealanders of European descent.

SIX

The endurance of healthcare, education and superannuation

The last chapter found that neoliberal social security reforms and discourses around individual responsibility and welfare dependency strengthened institutionalised distinctions between the deserving and undeserving and were likely behind a hardening of attitudes towards the unemployed. The focus here is on the 'universal' programmes of healthcare, education and – in the New Zealand context – superannuation for the elderly. These have not only traditionally framed citizens as human beings of equal moral worth but have disproportionately benefited the middle classes. Chapter Two noted evidence suggesting such universalism may garner wider levels of support than targeted programmes. Universalism always represented more of an ideal than a reality in New Zealand but was nonetheless important to the national psyche (Boston and St John, 1999; Vowles and Aimer, 1993).

By the 1980s, however, New Zealand's worsening economic position saw the cost of universal programmes become increasingly politicised. The public were concerned about diminishing government subsidies for private General Practitioners (GPs), tertiary student living costs and the sustainability of 'New Zealand welfare's sacred cow', the universal, tax-funded state pension introduced by National in 1976 (Paske and Ray, 1981a, p 16; St John, 1999a; Cheyne et al, 2008). This chapter explores whether attempts to introduce neoliberal marketisation, targeting and/or privatisation into these three policy areas changed public views of their rights as citizens. Many writers to the Royal Commission on Social Policy (RCSP, 1988a) already felt the principle of universalism was under threat in the late 1980s. Chapter Three, however, highlighted that feminist, Māori and other critiques of universalism in healthcare and education may have made the public more receptive to neoliberal arguments about 'choice' and 'diversity' which appeared to overlap with a desire for greater particularity in the meeting human needs.

Nonetheless, the speed and extent of New Zealand's quasi-market health reforms from 1991 provoked a significant public reaction and important policy reversals, particularly after 1996. U-turns were less evident in education, although there was certainly public disquiet when compulsory education reforms aiming to improve community involvement led to experiments with bulk funding and zoning that increased inequalities in the resourcing and outcomes of schools and their students (Nash and Harker, 2005). Substantial tertiary fee increases in 1990, followed by the introduction of the Student Loan Scheme in 1992, represented an even more visible – and contested – shift of the responsibility for tertiary education costs on to individuals. Significant public resistance meant New Zealand attempts to privatise retirement income and target government-funded pensions were even less successful, with universal superannuation reinstated in full from 1998.

The failure of neoliberal reforms in these three policy areas is evident in the changes made after 1999. The Labour-coalition government's Primary Health Organisation (PHO) reforms significantly reduced the cost of, and improved accessibility to, community-based healthcare. School zoning was reintroduced, decile-funding increased and many tertiary students were shielded from interest on their student loans, while the Labour-coalition's New Zealand Superannuation Fund aimed to fund universal pensions into the future. The same government introduced the KiwiSaver private savings scheme but with extremely popular government-funded incentives in 2007. Notably, the National government formed in 2008 did little to radically undo the Labour-coalition's work in ameliorating some of the harshest outcomes of marketisation and targeting in the 1990s.

In considering how such shifts in policy shaped public views of healthcare, education and economic security in old age as rights of citizenship, this chapter follows the same methodology as the previous two, drawing upon data from the New Zealand Election Survey (NZES) and other relevant studies to illustrate how public attitudes have changed over time. In addition to considering how public opinion shifts over the three key phases of neoliberalism, it assesses whether attitudes are shaped by fluctuations in spending specific to health, education and old age pensions, as well as total social expenditure. Even when the impact of ideological affiliation and age on attitudes are examined, it is difficult to argue that the New Zealand public rolled over and accepted neoliberalisation in these three policy areas. Qualitative data once again flesh out these findings, which are compared with the United Kingdom (UK) and Australia after New Zealand discussion of each policy area. Importantly, the chapter highlights that in all three case study countries continuing public support placed similar limits on neoliberalisation, ensuring the roll-back neoliberalism's agenda to *permanently* cut social expenditure in these three policy areas were largely unachieved. This is despite significant policy differences, as exemplified by the UK's universal National Health Service (NHS) and New Zealand's universal superannuation.

Government responsibility for healthcare

Considering public views about government responsibility for free healthcare and for spending in this policy area makes it possible to assess New Zealand's support for health as a social right. Despite the multiple policy shifts described in Chapter Three, Figure 6.1 shows significant support for the statement 'government should be responsible to provide free healthcare for all', throughout the period 1993–2011. Overall, agreement did decline from 75.8% to 69.5% but, having diminished through the 1990s, it increased between 2002 and 2008, before falling once again by 2011. The secondary axis provides little evidence that attitudes fluctuated thermostatically with health spending as a percentage of Gross Domestic Product (GDP). If anything, there was a weathervane effect, as support for government responsibility for ensuring free healthcare mostly (but not always)

Figure 6.1: Attitudes towards health (agree only, LH) by health/total social expenditure (% GDP, RH), percentage

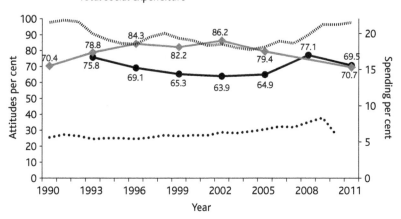

Sources: New Zealand Election Study; OECD

increased and decreased in line with both health spending and total social expenditure.

A lack of data for 1990 makes it difficult to assess whether the implementation of National's quasi-market reforms from 1993 is associated with the fall in support for free healthcare during the 1990s. However, the Royal Commission on Social Security (RCSS, 1972) and the RCSP (1988a) both drew upon consultations with the public to recommend the *continuation* of a universal, tax-funded healthcare system, suggesting strong support for it prior to the restructuring. The RCSP (1988c, p 8) specifically framed access to healthcare as a right and noted 'the capacity of the market to provide a just and socially acceptable allocation of health services is seriously limited'. Although National's leaked plans to further cut health spending and make health insurance compulsory did not stop it winning the 1990 election (New Zealand Herald – NZH, 1990c), they were controversial enough to ensure health was a major campaign issue. This further indicates the level of public support for free healthcare in the early 1990s.

Support for free healthcare did *fall*, slowly but steadily from 75.8% in 1993 to a low of 63.9% in 2002 (see Figure 6.1). But although New Zealanders may have regarded *free* healthcare as less viable given the political and economic context, considerable public resistance to the health reforms indicates they were unconvinced by neoliberal arguments about marketisation. There was a strong public perception that the restructuring from 1991 was destroying the health system (Heylen, 1991). Generalised underfunding forced Crown Health Enterprises (CHEs), the publicly-owned hospitals required to produce a profit, to borrow to keep operating and to increase surgical waiting lists (Roper, 2005; Duncan, 2007). Clinical professionals and health sector unions challenged the introduction of GP contracts, while large-scale street protests expressed disgruntlement with reductions to healthcare access and affordability (Glennie, 1990; Ashton, 1999). As indicated in Chapter Three, the scale of public opposition saw part charges for public hospital services removed and plans to fund provision through state subsidies for private health insurance cover dropped by 1993 (Roper, 2005; Cheyne et al, 2008).

An older participant in the qualitative study talked about his experience of the 1990s reforms, indicating how the general public associated them with declining quality and increase costs in healthcare:

> "... you just think of the hospital boards, the way they seem to always be working in the red and their budgets just stretched and yet and I think too often accountants run

these organisations instead of doctors and nurses ... And I think all that happened with Rogernomics,[1] I think there was probably a certain amount of pruning needed to be done. But I think his policies went overboard really and over the past years I think that the bottom line has been looked at, at the expense of the service that should be provided."

While poorer service initially encouraged many citizens to use the private health system, rising private insurance premiums made it inaccessible to those most in need. The number of New Zealanders holding private health insurance actually *fell* from around 50% in 1991 to 37% in 1998, not least because Regional Health Authorities (RHAs) did not allow individuals to transfer their share of state funding to the private sector, making those with insurance effectively pay twice (Roper, 2005; Duncan, 2007).

Given this context, New Zealand First made health central to its coalition agreement with National in 1996, negotiating free GP services for children under six, the removal of pharmaceutical, outpatient and day-stay hospital part charges and eventually income/asset testing for the elderly in long-stay public and private hospital care. The four RHAs were also merged into a single central funder in 1996 and the quasi-commercial profit motive was removed from management of hospitals (Kelsey, 1993; Ashton, 1999; Duncan, 2007). Notably, however, Figure 6.1 indicates that support for government responsibility for ensuring free healthcare continued to fall, even as a 1997 referendum petition requested increased spending on health services and numerous street protests highlighted continued public dissatisfaction with the public health system (Ashton, 1999). These facts suggest New Zealanders still saw the government as responsible for healthcare but simply could not conceive of *free* provision being possible at that particular time.

This argument is reinforced by attitudinal trends in the 2000s. Support for free healthcare stayed fairly steady in the early 2000s. Although the Alliance Party coalition partner promised universal free healthcare in the 1999 election, this finding suggests attitudes were unaffected by both the Labour-coalition government's win and early structural reforms abolishing the Health Funding Authority, re-establishing the Ministry of Health and replacing CHEs with District Health Boards that reinstated popular control over local provision of health services (NZH, 1999; Duncan, 2007; Cheyne et al, 2008). However, support for free healthcare rose substantially after 2005, peaking at 77.1% in 2008, when health spending rose significantly and brought substantive improvements in service. The new PHO system established in 2002 took some time to significantly impact upon peoples' lives in terms of improving access and affordability. Although healthcare costs remained a significant issue, the rapid enrolment of New Zealanders into PHOs suggests they appreciated their benefits (Schoen et al, 2007; Quin, 2009). The highly visible, proximate and popular PHO system thus likely had a positive effect on attitudes towards free healthcare.

This raises the question as to why Figure 6.1 shows a 7.6 percentage point fall in support for free healthcare between 2008 and 2011. Total social expenditure continued to rise and National maintained the PHO system. Health spending did drop significantly but, as earlier noted, there is no clear-cut covariance between this and attitudes towards free healthcare. It is possible National sufficiently reassured the public that it would not reintroduce the kind of restructuring vehemently opposed in the 1990s to avoid health being a major election issue in 2011. But its political rhetoric focused mainly on specialist/hospital access and waiting times, not the PHO system, and National did not replicate the social inclusion and equity discourses framing the Labour-coalition's promotion of PHO and other health promotion initiatives (National Party, 2011). Although potentially a case where attitudes have rolled over and endorsed neoliberal arguments that the country could not afford free healthcare, previous findings suggest New Zealanders may have pragmatically believed that free healthcare was not as achievable under a National-led government compared to when the Labour-coalition was in power.

In particular, support among NZES respondents affiliated with the ideological Centre diminished quickly (by 10.5 percentage points) between 2008 and 2011, even though this group reported the *largest* growth in support (12.4 percentage points) under the Labour-coalition government and stayed relatively steady during the 1990s when the Left and Right reported their largest overall falls in support for free healthcare. Given National did little to modify the Labour-coalition's health policies, the Centre's attitudes appear to have been influenced by the general political direction of the government, rather than the specific policies implemented. The strength of Centrist views during the 2000s helps explains why National was reluctant to implement further pro-market reforms; in 2011, 68.7% of the Centre still supported free healthcare (down from 75.5% in 1993). Moreover, Right support had *grown* from 56.5% in 1993 to 62.3%. Left agreement had decreased 92.2% to 84.4% across the same period, representing the largest absolute percentage decrease overall. But the continuing strength of support, along with continuing divisions and fluctuating responses over time, suggests the public did not simply roll-over and accept neoliberal arguments in this policy area.

The health system was similarly protected by strong support among citizens of all ages, including the young: although the oldest NZES respondents (>61) offered the highest level of support (81.6%) for free healthcare in 1993, this was no longer the case by 2011 when agreement sat at 68.2%. Instead, the *youngest* (<30) age group offered the highest level of support in 2011 (76.9%), agreement having *increased* from 69.1% in 1993. Younger people are likely to have greater interaction with the PHO system than hospitals and this new initiative may have fostered an appreciation for a good public health system. However, the youngest group's attitudes fluctuated little over time, declining by the smallest amount during the 1990s and increasing by the smallest degree under the Labour-coalition, even between 2005 and 2008. Their support also stayed steady once National was re-elected. This stability may stem from young adults being relatively healthy and thus needing little medical attention. Notably, however, the attitudes of those aged 31–45 stayed relatively steady over the 18-year period but saw the largest increase between 2005 and 2008 and the smallest fall after 2008. Differences were not huge but many in this age group have young families who would have immediately benefited from PHO subsidies, in contrast to their older counterparts for whom hospital waiting lists and waiting times were likely to be more important. That the greatest falls in support between 2008 and 2011 occurred among those aged over 46 suggests National's political rhetoric focused on these issues did not have the desired effect.

The qualitative data largely endorses the finding that a free public health system remains important to New Zealanders. Participants made clear distinctions between emergency care (which they thought should remain free for all citizens) and visits to the GP (where they displayed more ambivalence) that are impossible to discern from the NZES question on free healthcare, but only 25% of the participants thought it was an individual's responsibility to look after and/or pay for their own health. In most cases this referred to people eating responsibly, exercising and doing all they could to prevent costly health problems rather than shouldering the cost of healthcare services. Indeed, 61% of the participants in the qualitative study named health as a government responsibility (the second most commonly named activity after helping the needy) and 54% thought health was a right of New Zealand citizenship in 2007–08.

The participants also demonstrated some awareness that privatisation represented a threat to social rights. One middle-aged, high income earner said:

> "... that whole privatisation thing of social services, it's just crap. I mean it can't be, you can't make it into a money-making thing without screwing somebody which is what the private medical companies do, they charge huge medical insurances and they can afford to do it and they make money. And yeah, it's just ... that's the [point] of the government, that's what it's meant to be there for and old age and young and ... health and ensure that somebody has somewhere to live. You know, a safe warm place and ensure that they have enough to eat, that's what the government is there for. Otherwise it's pointless having a government."

By 2012, only 30% of New Zealanders held private health insurance, well below the Organisation of Economic Co-operation and Development (OECD) average (NZH, 2012). This probably contributes to the strong belief that the government has a responsibility for healthcare. Nonetheless, having private health insurance did not necessarily diminish this belief among some participants in the qualitative study because they felt it relieved the burden on the public health system for others who could not afford to pay. A middle income earner stated:

> "... we've got private health insurance, because I wanted to provide, you know, the level of healthcare for my family that I'm able to. Because if there isn't ... if we didn't then we'd be another person waiting for – if we needed healthcare – we'd have to wait, so to me that's adding to the woes of the healthcare."

The desire to ensure all were able to access decent healthcare was often articulated by contrasting this with overseas health systems. A benefit recipient said: "it's really shocking when you go to the [United] States and with the whole health insurance thing and ... the costs of medical care and people just not being able to receive it basically". Such comparisons indicate a fear of radical shifts towards a more insurance-based system.

While some participants believed the British NHS was a better model, not all those who had experienced it considered it better than the New Zealand system. A middle income earner said: "although it's free, you know, you wait two weeks to get into the doctor's and stuff like that, so whereas here you can ring up the doctor in the morning and go and see them straight away, pay for your $50 and it's done". Believing New Zealand did not have a population large enough to support an NHS-style system, the same participant was happy with a user-pays model: "but I think that it needs to be the same sort of quality for everybody, even if they can't afford it, they should be able to get the access to that good healthcare". This latter statement draws upon an egalitarian discourse common among participants who stated that user-pays might be necessary but those who could afford to pay should not receive any better service: this went against a New Zealand sense of 'fairness'. Such a view sits in tension with the inegalitarian attitudes towards the unemployed reported in the last chapter.

It was also earlier noted that support for a principle does not always translate into support for greater public expenditure in that policy area. Yet, as with spending on assistance/training for the unemployed, *more* NZES respondents thought that the government should increase health spending than supported the principle of free healthcare in all years except in 2011. Figure 6.1 indicates that the proportion of NZES respondents favouring increased government spending on health, even when reminded about the tax costs of such spending, rose by 13.9 percentage points between 1990 and 1996. Thus, the roll-back reforms of the 1990s *encouraged*, rather than stifled, a desire for health spending among the New Zealand public. This is not surprising given the public concerns discussed above. After a slight fall in the late 1990s, support for more spending peaked at 86.2% in 2002 before dropping steadily to 69.5% in 2011. This recent decline should not be read as a rapid loss of support for the health system because the number of respondents wanting to keep spending about the same rose during the same period to 25.4% in 2011, having diminished significantly through the 1990s as more respondents wanted increased spending. Except for the period between 2008 and 2011 when support for more spending continued declining despite a significant fall in health expenditure, public support for greater spending on health appears to have moved in the opposite direction to actual government spending on health as a percentage of GDP. That New Zealanders were more satisfied with the higher levels of spending of the 2000s than the lower levels of the 1990s is supported by data from both the New Zealand Values Study (NZVS – Perry and Webster, 1994; Perry, unpubl data) and the ISSP (Gendall et al, 1997, 2007).

Among the NZES respondents, those from the Right and Centre appeared to be more responsive to changes in health spending and policy than the Left. The latter group's support for more health spending grew only from 78.8% to 82.7% between 1990 and 2011, compared to from 61.3% to 66.6% among the Right and a decline from 69.5% to 65.7% among the Centre over the same period. This decline occurred mostly between 2005 and 2011 but the Centre had reported the greatest *increase* in support during the 1990s (by 15.9 percentage points), while the Right reported the *only* increase (by 4.4 percentage points) in support during the roll-out phase of neoliberalism under the Labour-coalition. The Left were still more likely than the Right and Centre to support more spending on health in 2011 and such fluctuations challenge the view that the public have rolled over and accepted a neoliberal view that healthcare is simply a market commodity. Furthermore, there was little difference in the levels of declining support for more health spending found among different age groups between 1990 and 2011. As with government responsibility for ensuring free healthcare, the oldest age group reported the largest decline in support after 2005, suggesting it was particularly sensitive to increased spending and improved primary healthcare, but its level of support was relatively stable between 1990 and 2011 (67–68%). Meanwhile, support for more spending among the youngest age group fell from 66.8% to 61.8%, the biggest decline in support over 21 years across all age groups. However, this was a relatively small shift and fluctuating responses among the youngest age cohort make it unlikely this represents a permanent hardening of attitudes among those who became adults during the neoliberal era.

In summary, a clear majority of NZES respondents still thought that the government should ensure free healthcare for all in 2011. New Zealanders remained pragmatic about the need for more spending in this policy area, with around 70% of respondents desiring this in both 1990 and 2011. Support for the principle of free healthcare in 2011 was 6.3 percentage points lower than in 1993 but it peaked in *2008*, not in the early 1990s. This suggests New Zealanders continued to regard health as a key social right. Later discussion illustrates a similar trend for free education but, given the different timing of the recovery in support, such attitudes appear to be shaped not by the election of a Labour-led government but the specific policies it implemented. Certainly the PHO system established in 2002 played a significant role in resurrecting support for free healthcare, particularly among the Centre, and diminishing a desire for spending in the late 2000s.

Healthcare's continuing significance

Were similar trends apparent in the differing policy contexts of the UK and Australia? It is necessary to compare New Zealand views about *free* healthcare with British and Australian responses to a question about 'government's responsibility to provide healthcare for the sick', an ISSP proposition that 97–98% of New Zealanders supported in 1996 and 2006 (Gendall et al, 1997, 2007). Although not addressing exactly the same issue as free healthcare, Table 6.1 shows that virtually all Britons also agreed that the government should be responsible for healthcare for the sick and attitudes also stayed steady over time. The UK's highly proximate, visible and symbolic NHS system is likely behind such high levels of support for the proposition around healthcare. New Zealanders offer a similar level of steady support to this proposition, despite the country's more chequered history with universalism in healthcare, but the New Zealand data for this proposition is extremely limited and discussion earlier found attitudes towards free healthcare to be more variable.

British support for government responsibility for ensuring healthcare for the sick *did* fall slightly in the early 2000s, then increased to previous levels following the Conservative-Liberal Democrat coalition's plans to offer no real increase in NHS funding until 2015 and to devolve management responsibility of the NHS (Appleby and Lee, 2012; Clery, 2012b). There is evidence that the government's austerity measures encouraged perceptions that the standard of healthcare had declined: in 2010, British Social Attitudes (BSA) survey respondents reported their highest ever level of satisfaction with the NHS (70%), after Labour nearly doubled NHS spending between 2000 and 2007 and

Table 6.1: Attitudes towards healthcare and health spending (agree only), percentage

	1985	1990	1996	2000	2006	2007	2012
*Should be government's responsibility to provide healthcare for the sick**							
United Kingdom	98	98	97	98	95	–	97
Australia	84	77	94	–	–	98	–
	1985	**1990**	**1996**	**2006**	**2007**		
Government should spend much more/more on health							
United Kingdom	88	90	91	81	–		
Australia	62	68	80	–	90		

Note: * Agree combines 'definitely should' and 'probably should'.

Sources: Australian Survey of Attitudes; British Social Attitudes Survey (cited in Pearce & Taylor, 2013); International Social Survey Programme (1985 and 1990 Australian data cited in Bean & Papadakis, 1998 – first proposition; Wilson et al, 2012 – second proposition).

waiting times fell to an historic low, but satisfaction had dropped by 12 percentage points by 2011, the biggest fall since 1983 (Appleby and Phillips, 2009; Appleby and Lee, 2012). While Table 6.1 shows that British support for more spending on health increased slightly in the late 1980s and stayed steady in the 1990s, it had also fallen by 2006. This suggests a desire for more spending moved in the opposite direction to actual spending levels (Pearce and Taylor, 2013). There is no data available for this same question in the 2010s but a similar proportion of BSA respondents (41–42%) named health as their first priority for government spending in 2010 and 2012. This challenges the idea that attitudes towards spending are thermostatic and could be read as a first sign of Britons rolling over and accepting less funding in this area. But this seems unlikely given the extremely high support; possibly the freeze on health spending over several years was simply not immediately visible or proximate enough to influence attitudes.

Table 6.1 indicates that an overwhelming majority of Australians also agreed that the government should ensure healthcare for the sick in all years but attitudes were more variable than in the UK. Support fell between 1985 and 1990, following the introduction of Labor's Medicare system in 1984, then increased through the 1990s and into the 2000s. The 1985 and 2007 data were collected from differing surveys, requiring cautious comparison, but Australian support appears to have increased by 14 percentage points in the latter year. Australian desires for more spending on health were also variable, declining through the late 1980s and early 1990s, then increasing through the 2000s, so that support for more spending increased overall by 28 percentage points between 1985 and 2007. The data were, once again, collected from different surveys but this suggests a growing dissatisfaction with health that was also evident in the trends reported for government responsibility for ensuring that healthcare is provided for the sick. Wilson and Meagher (2007) found, however, that increased spending after 2003 led to a fall in the proportion of Australians who thought 'the standard of health services including Medicare' had decreased in the late 2000s.

Overall, these findings suggest that citizens in all three countries continued to regard health as a social right that should be protected by the government. The New Zealand data suggests support for some parts of the health system being protected from market forces may be higher than others. But it remains that when governments were perceived as not fulfilling their responsibilities, support for increased expenditure rose while the opposite was true when governments made significant investments in healthcare. As a result, the roll-out phase of neoliberalism in New Zealand and the UK appeared to calm concerns about government responsibilities as Labour-led governments prioritised health funding and there is little evidence that this phase encouraged citizens to become more accepting of neoliberal arguments for less spending and greater marketisation and privatisation. Similarly, the conservative Liberal-National government in power in Australia during this period encouraged greater concern, despite various tax incentives to encourage private healthcare.

Government responsibility for education

New Zealand views about education as a right of citizenship can be assessed by considering NZES responses to questions about free education and spending on education. In contrast to the 6.3 percentage point fall in support for free healthcare across 21 years, Figure 6.2 indicates that support for 'government should be responsible to provide free education from preschool to tertiary/university levels' fell by *15.7* percentage points between 1990 and 2011. This implies that far

Figure 6.2: Attitudes towards education (agree only, LH) by education/ total social expenditure (% GDP, RH), percentage

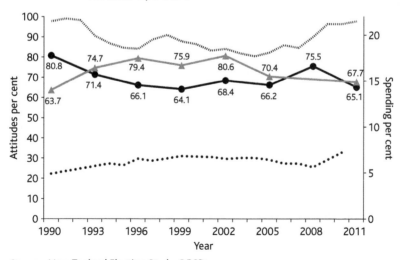

Sources: New Zealand Election Study; OECD

fewer New Zealanders saw education across these different stages as a right than prior to the neoliberal reforms in this policy area.

However, this overall trend hides a rapid decline in agreement in the early 1990s, after which support ranged from 64% to 68% between 1996 and 2011 with the exception of 2008 when support *increased* to 75.5%. There is a mildly thermostatic effect between falling support for free education and government expenditure on education, which increased through the 1990s. At both key points (1995–96 and 2007–08) when education spending increased most substantially, public support for free education fell. However, until 2008 there also appeared to be covariance between falling support for free education and total social expenditure, with support for free education usually *following* the level of government spending and thus suggesting a weathervane rather than a thermostatic response. This was not the case after 2008 when expenditure continued to increase, if more slowly than before, but support for free education declined by 10.4 percentage points. As with health, this weathervane response does not necessarily mean New Zealanders came to endorse neoliberal discourses promoting individual responsibility, choice and diversity in education; rather they changed their view of whether free education was feasible at that particular time.

This argument is supported by considerable evidence that the idea of free education remained important to New Zealanders during the 1990s, despite the reported decline in support for free education. Surveys in 1987 indicated little support for the marketisation of education through a voucher system or user-pays even at the tertiary level (Heylen cited in Crothers 1988; RCSP, 1988a). Noting the public's growing frustration with a highly centralised, bureaucratic approach to education, the RCSP (1988c, p 11) argued that: 'because of education's crucial role in enhancing life-chances, access to it should not be dependent on the ability to pay. The state has a clear duty to its citizens to ensure both access to education and a consistently high quality of education'. Given the highly visible negative social outcomes emerging in compulsory education in the 1990s, educational affordability and quality were unsurprisingly key election issues during the 1990s, leading New Zealand First to negotiate extra spending on education as part of its coalition agreement in 1996 (McQueen, 1990; Vowles et al, 1995; Peters and Olssen, 1999).

Protest marches and mass occupations of university campuses against rising fees and student debt also indicate a high level of public concern about the radical shift from virtually free tertiary education and relatively universal student allowances to substantial tuition fees and highly targeted student allowances (Roper, 2005). National pledged to scrap tertiary fees in the 1990 election but fudged the issue by abolishing Labour's tertiary fee in 1991 then allowing universities to set their own fees in response to reduced government funding per student (NZH, 1990c, 1990d). National also replaced the universal allowance with a tightly targeted 'Study Right' scheme in 1992, reducing eligibility by two thirds. Thus, many New Zealanders felt betrayed by the new government as public expenditure on tertiary education dropped and the number of student loans increased (Boston, 1999b). Such dissatisfaction makes it unlikely that declining public support for free education meant New Zealanders were actually convinced by arguments about individual responsibility and equity in this policy area.

This argument is further supported by attitudinal trends in the 2000s. Having remained stable through the late 1990s and into the 2000s, support for free education across the primary, secondary and tertiary levels rose by 9.3% between 2005 and 2008. The timing of this shift suggests the Labour-coalition's interest-free loans policy shaped attitudes. The underfunding and diminishing affordability of tertiary education became central election issues for the first time in 1999, encouraging Labour to promise a fairer loans system while its potential coalition partners, the Alliance and Green parties, vowed to reinstate the universal student allowance for full-time students and remove fees (NZH, 1999; Levine and Roberts, 2000; Vowles, 2002). After first freezing tertiary fees between 2000 and 2003, the Labour-coalition government removed interest from tertiary student loans for students still studying in 2001 and then extended this policy to all New Zealand residents from 2006 (Roper, 2005; St John and Rankin, 2009). Political opposition meant these policies were far more visible and traceable than the coalition government's earlier changes in compulsory education.

Support for free education decreased by 10.4 percentage points between 2008 and 2011, the largest fall in 21 years. However, this simply reset support at about the same level as reported before an increase of a similar percentage in the Labour-coalition's last term, suggesting the public's desire for free education was satiated by the 2006 extension of interest-free student loans. National was expected to revoke the interest-free loans policy once elected in 2008. As such, many New Zealanders may have regarded new time limits and grade-based performance conditions on borrowing as a reasonable exchange for the continuation of the interest-free policy. The Māori, New Zealand First and Green parties promoted universal student allowances, but there is little evidence the public perceived this as a realistic policy given the political and economic climate (Barron, 2011; 3 News, 2011).

The participants in the qualitative study were certainly much more ambivalent about free *tertiary* education than free compulsory education. Once again, the NZES cannot tap into such distinctions because it does not ask separate questions about compulsory and tertiary education, but a middle income earner who took part in the qualitative study is representative of the commonly articulated view that compulsory schooling should be free but: "[w]hen it comes to tertiary education, again, I think that's actually [a] personal responsibility ... and maybe we need a system that they have in the [United] States where when your child's born you set up a fund, an education fund for that child". Only 44% of the participants considered education to be a right of citizenship and pragmatism often outweighed principle when they discussed tertiary education. One participant, who was training to be a teacher, generally supported free education for all tertiary students but accepted this might only be practical for those studying for essential occupations. He said:

> "I don't feel that student[s] should have to pay the amount that they do to get their education. Particularly for really sort of upper-echelon jobs ... doctors, dentists, that sort of thing, healthcare professionals that we need in the community shouldn't have to pay ridiculous amounts of money, yeah, you know, it's just sick ... all education and all healthcare should be free and training to be those people should be free as well and I'd happily pay a lot more tax if that was the situation."

Some participants also indicated support for a right to *access* tertiary education (for instance, through the Student Loan Scheme), but did not necessarily believe that the government has a responsibility to fund it entirely for all students. A young participant who had recently left tertiary education stated:

> "... you have a right to education and I think it's good that we have a right to ... borrow money for education because not too many people have that much money sitting in their bottom drawer but, yeah, like I said, I think it's my responsibility to pay for part of it because I'll be getting such a benefit from it."

However, many participants supported tax breaks or targeted assistance towards low income earners to ensure access was maintained, a finding supported by ISSP data showing that 80% of respondents agreed the 'government should give financial assistance to university students from low income families' in 2006 (Gendall et al, 2007).

Only 18% of the participants in the qualitative study explicitly disagreed with the idea of free education across all levels. In particular, some believed that individuals should finance tertiary education because they receive the greatest benefits from it. A young, high income earner originally from the United States also said:

> "I'm fine with, I would pay $10,000 a year, I would, yeah, I just think it's — and especially cos it's interest-free, that is like 'holy moly, that's fantastic, they don't know how good they have it!' (laughter) — So I'm fine with that, yeah, student loans, pay some fees ... I think that ... in order to get that quality we need to be able to pay for it."

These ideas directly reflect neoliberal values but given such a small number disagreed with free education in both the qualitative and the NZES studies, this discourse does not appear to have been particularly persuasive in New Zealand. Although highlighting some differences in views about compulsory and tertiary education, the qualitative data therefore largely supports the NZES finding that a majority of New Zealanders continued to favour free education in the late 2000s.

Views around government responsibility for ensuring free education also remained ideologically divided. Left agreement was extremely high and declined by only a slight amount (from 85.1% to 81.7%) across the 21-year period. Right support fell from 77.6% to 56.7% between 1990 and 2011, while support among the Centre also fell significantly (from 81.1% to 62.3%), bringing this group's views closer to the Right on this issue. Nonetheless, Right and Centre attitudes were, once again, more sensitive to policy shifts than the Left, declining in the 1990s, increasing in the 2000s and then declining again after 2008. Notably, the *Right* increased its support by the greatest degree (14.9 percentage points) under the Labour-coalition government, with much of this change occurring between 2005 and 2008. This group thus appears to have endorsed, rather than rejected, the Labour-coalition's policy changes, including interest-free tertiary loans. While offering some hope for advocates of social citizenship, it remains troubling that the Centre's support fell so significantly (by 14.8 percentage points) when

National came to power, given few changes in education had been announced at this point in time.

Nonetheless, the principle of free education remained important to young adults in 2011. Their support fell from 79.4% in 1990 to 65.5% but this was a slightly smaller decline than that found among other age groups, notably the oldest (79.7% to 62.9%). Policy shifts appear to have acted as a weathervane for attitudes across the age groups, with decreased support for free education during the 1990s and increased support during the 2000s. This effect was weakest among the oldest group until 2008, perhaps suggesting that debate about the interest-free tertiary loan policy had an impact. But overall, there was little change in the level of support offered by the different age groups in the 1990s and 2011 and the gap between the oldest and youngest groups increased only marginally.

In addition to majority support for free education, most New Zealanders also continued to want more government spending in this policy area. Figure 6.2 shows that a significant majority of respondents supported more spending on education across the entire 21 years studied. Importantly, the devolution of compulsory education administration and the tertiary fees/loans systems implemented in neoliberalism's initial phase is *not* associated with New Zealanders reducing their support for more spending on education, even as their support for the government taking responsibility in this area fell. Expenditure data is incomplete but the secondary axis shows that, at least until the mid-2000s, support for more spending was generally higher when actual spending on education and total expenditure were relatively healthy. This mildly weathervane effect is confirmed by NZVS (Perry and Webster, 1994; Perry, unpubl data) and ISSP (Gendall et al, 1997, 2007) data but it is still not clear why support for more spending on education stayed static even as actual spending increased after 2005. Given discussion above, this may be further evidence that a public desire for spending on tertiary education had been more or less met. However, it is also possible that neoliberal discourses around the privatisation and marketisation of this policy area were tempered by growing tertiary participation rates, which made this form of education proximate to more people.

It is interesting that, although Right and Centre support for free education fluctuated more than the Left's over time, this was not the case for increased *spending* on education. Right support for more spending declined significantly in the early 1990s but grew by a slight amount over the 1990s as a whole while support grew significantly among the Left and Centre across the decade. The 2000s saw support for more spending on education fall across the ideological spectrum but by 13.5 percentage points among the Left, while Centre agreement declined by only 4.8 percentage points and the Right stayed relatively steady. Attitudes shifted in a similar way between 2005 and 2011. This meant that Left support for greater spending on education *grew* from 76.1% to 86.8% between 1990 and 2011 but it remained virtually static among the Centre (63%) and Right (62%). This is a sign that education remained a central issue for all New Zealanders but one where the ideological divide grew significantly.

It is more concerning that support for more spending on education fell from 79.4% to 66.1% among the youngest age group between 1990 and 2011; in comparison, those aged 31–45 remained static and citizens aged over 46 *increased* their support (for instance, from 54.2% to 62.5% among the oldest group). Nonetheless, between 2005 and 2011 both the youngest and oldest respondents reported a more significant decline (around 6 percentage points) than other age groups. This is most surprising among the youngest group given they are most proximate to education – and National only modified rather than radically reformed tertiary education policy. Both groups appear to have been particularly receptive to National's rhetoric around greater conditionality in return for maintaining interest-free loans.

In conclusion, a clear majority of NZES respondents still favoured the government taking responsibility for ensuring free education from preschool to tertiary/university levels in 2011 but support *was* 15.7 percentage points lower than that reported in the early 1990s. Support for more spending on education was steadier and this *grew* by 4 percentage points over 21 years. As with free healthcare, New Zealanders may have become more circumspect about a *totally* free education system (especially at the tertiary level), but worries about fair access and service quality meant that they remained pragmatic about the need for the government to invest in education. Notably, the Labour-coalition's policy of extending interest-free loans to all New Zealand residents appeared to provoke positive policy feedback towards free education, even if the evidence suggests the public would not necessarily expect (or want) tertiary education to become completely free. More generally, New Zealanders have largely followed the government's lead, being less supportive of progressive education policies when the government believes them to be unaffordable and inadvisable yet more sympathetic when they are actually implemented. Later discussion highlights that this weathervane effect was not evident when considering policies for the elderly, while the following indicates that it was also not apparent in the two other case study countries.

Differing responses to education policy

Citizens in the UK and Australia have not been consistently asked about free education or even government responsibility for providing education but Table 6.2 presents support for government spending on education over time. As with New Zealand, a clear majority of Britons and Australians wanted more spending across all years and support increased through the 1990s as governments placed greater responsibility upon individuals for the cost of education, especially at the tertiary level in New Zealand and Australia (Wilson et al, 2012). Later data is extremely limited but support for more spending declined in the 2000s in the UK, as it did in New Zealand (with fluctuations) while it increased in Australia. This makes sense given that Labour-led governments in the two former countries placed significant emphasis on education while the Australian Liberal-National coalition government reduced funding per tertiary student and introduced tuition fees, even if it subsidised them through the Higher Education Contributions Scheme (Bryson, 2001; Brennan, 2005). In this context, there was a rise in the proportion of Australian Survey of Social Attitudes respondents who thought the standard of public education had decreased from 42% to 51% between 2003 and 2005 (Wilson and Meagher, 2007).

Although there is no contemporary UK data for the question presented in Table 6.2, support for education as the *first priority* for more government spending rose from 28% in 2006 to 32% in 2010, before then falling to 30% by 2012. Britons did not, therefore, simply roll-over and accept the Conservative-Liberal coalition's tertiary funding cuts which led to massive tuition fee increases (Levitas, 2012; Zimdars et al, 2012). New Zealand support fell more significantly between 2008 and 2011 but, given National maintained a very generous interest-free loan policy and put funds into school infrastructure, this response also does not represent a roll-over of attitudes. Indeed, although a weathervane effect was apparent in New Zealand, attitudes in each

Table 6.2: Government should spend more/much more on education (agree only), percentage

	1985	1990	1991	1993	1996	2006	2007
United Kingdom	75	80	84	83	84	72	–
Australia	64	70	–	–	70	–	80

Sources: Australian Survey of Social Attitudes and International Social Survey Programme (cited in Wilson et al, 2012); British Social Attitudes Survey.

country have shifted in line with spending levels in ways that suggest education continues to be perceived as a right of citizenship.

Government responsibility for old people

This final section considers whether New Zealanders also believe they have a right to economic security in old age, which can be gauged by considering views on government responsibility and spending in this policy area. Figure 6.3 demonstrates that virtually all New Zealanders (93–94%) agreed 'government should take responsibility for ensuring a decent standard of living for old people' between 1990 and 2008. There was then a sudden – if not quite significant (4.2 percentage points) – drop in support but 90.1% still agreed with this proposition in 2011. In contrast to health and education, the history of significant policy change in superannuation discussed in Chapter Three appears to have had virtually *no* impact on public support across a 21-year period.

This is the case even though the 1990s represented a period of volatile policy change; National's attempt to turn superannuation

Figure 6.3: Attitudes towards superannuation (agree only, LH) by old age/total social expenditure (% GDP, RH), percentage

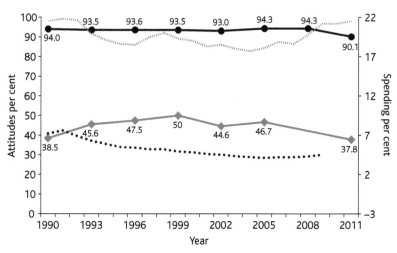

Sources: New Zealand Election Study; OECD

into a tightly targeted social welfare benefit was reversed in 1992 and universal New Zealand Superannuation fully reinstated in 1998 (Vowles et al 1995; St John, 1999a). Yet NZES support for the proposition that the government should ensure a decent standard of living for old people stayed steady during this time, a trend confirmed by ISSP data (Gendall et al, 1997, 2007). There is also no clear pattern of covariance between public expenditure on old age (including New Zealand Superannuation, the Veteran's Pension and KiwiSaver) or total social expenditure as a percentage of GDP; the former fell reasonably steadily between 1990 and 2009, while the latter fluctuated significantly across the entire 21-year period.

That New Zealanders share the same basic belief about government responsibility for old people is supported by the minimal impact ideological affiliation and age had on NZES respondent attitudes. The Right's support fell from 92.2% to 84.6% between 1990 and 2011 but there is no evidence to suggest this was a permanent shift because support fluctuated significantly across time, declining during the 1990s (especially in the first three years when the superannuation surcharge was applied), increasing through the 2000s as the Labour-coalition established the New Zealand Superannuation Fund and KiwiSaver, and declining again when National was re-elected in 2008. Falls in support were much smaller among the Left (from 100% to 97.7%) and Centre (from 93.5% to 89.3%). Support did fall across all age groups between 1990 and 2011 but this was only marginally greater among the youngest group (from 93.2% to 88%) than the oldest group (96.1% to 91.7%). As such, there were only minor variances in support between age groups, even across differing phases of neoliberalism.

The NZES data indicates that New Zealanders view the elderly as more deserving of government support than the unemployed (see Chapter Five) and there are several reasons why this might be the case. First, a retired participant in the qualitative study indicated that working and paying taxes throughout your life creates a sense of entitlement:

> "... it's funny when I signed up for the Super and I went into the Work and Income, I felt out of place ... But then when I stopped and thought about it I thought 'well, no, I am entitled to this'. I mean I was brought up with the ethic of work hard and get your independence and you don't want to be a burden to anybody so all those things are proud to be in a country that you are able to do that, I suppose."

Old age is also an experience that all citizens eventually share, no matter what their background. In contrast, not everyone will be unemployed and this circumstance can result from both structural and individual factors (van Oorschot, 2008). Furthermore, the elderly have not been targeted by the same individual responsibility and welfare dependency discourses as the unemployed, neither historically nor during the last three decades of neoliberalisation. A further participant noted how Work and Income New Zealand (WINZ) treated him differently when he retired compared to when he received a means-tested benefit: "I went into see WINZ, you know, when I turned 65 and ... they couldn't have been nicer really. I mean, it was such a contrast to having been there with other people, and myself, one period of my life when I was unemployed".

Such comments were commonplace and may explain why only 3% of the participants in the qualitative study mentioned the elderly when asked to name groups they thought might feel 'second class' in New Zealand. However, a mere 35% identified the elderly or superannuation when asked to identify government responsibilities. Even fewer participants named superannuation (5%) as a right they associated with New Zealand citizenship without prompting. These findings obviously sit in contrast with the NZES results but may have been influenced by recent debate about child poverty which highlighted New Zealand's comparably low rates of poverty among the elderly, potentially shaping views of the level of need among this group of New Zealanders (Perry, 2010).

The qualitative data nonetheless highlights how we should not take for granted the high levels of steady support for the proposition that the government should ensure a decent standard of living for old people reported in the NZES. Falling support for this proposition after 2008 suggests that 2011's election debate about superannuation influenced attitudes. As noted in Chapter Three, Labour announced it would retain universality but gradually lift the age of New Zealand Superannuation eligibility. Framed in terms of 'taking the hard decisions for future, not soft decisions for today' (Young, 2011, n.p.), this pledge targeted younger New Zealanders concerned about universal superannuation being abandoned or undermined in the future. National leader, John Key's determination to *retain* the current age of eligibility provoked much criticism because Labour's policy was in line with the Retirement Commissioner's recommendations and a general belief that the future cost of New Zealand Superannuation would inevitability require change. Only the conservative ACT party wanted to abolish New Zealand Superannuation but this proposal was never seriously debated during the election campaign (Barron, 2011; Hartevalt and Vance, 2011a, 2011b). The ideological Right may have responded to this debate, however, reducing its support for government responsibility for ensuring a decent standard of living for old people by 7.2 percentage points while Left and Centre responses stayed steady.

A further NZES question in 2011 specifically asked whether 'between 2020 and 2033, the age of eligibility for NZ superannuation should be gradually raised to 67'. Overall, 46.5% of respondents agreed the eligibility age should be increased, while 38.4% disagreed. Although responses swung in favour of Labour's proposal, the party polled more poorly than it had done for years. Labour leader, Phil Goff (cited in Hartevalt and Vance 2011b, n.p.) said 'I think that a lot of New Zealanders only got the message that the retirement age will go up, not the time frame and not the exclusion of people who physically just weren't capable of continuing to work' but the NZES evidence suggests many of them actually supported the policy, just not its implementation by Labour. There were only relatively small differences in support among the Left (98.9% of whom agreed with an increased eligibility age), the Centre (93.8%) and the Right (91.8%). Self-interest was more important for explaining responses, but not as much as we might expect: 40.4% of respondents who would definitely not receive New Zealand Superannuation (NZS) until age 67 (those aged >45) and 44.7% of those affected by transition arrangements (aged 46–55) agreed with Labour's proposed increase compared to 56.6% of respondents who would still receive NZS at 65 (aged <56).[2]

New Zealanders clearly endorsed the idea that the government should ensure a decent standard of living for old people and this view shifted little over the differing phases of neoliberalism, even if 2011 findings suggest this may be changing. However, Figure 6.3 shows agreement that 'government should spend more on superannuation' was lower and more volatile than that for ensuring a decent standard of living for old people. The proportion of respondents wanting more spending on superannuation was also well below those wanting the same in health and education in all years. This may be because of greater satisfaction with government spending on superannuation. Yet Figure 6.3's secondary axis provides only limited evidence that support for such spending was associated with changes in old–age expenditure as a percentage of GDP. Such support did grow as actual spending steadily declined during the 1990s but changes in spending were very small in the 2000s yet attitudes fluctuated significantly between 1999 and 2008.

There is good to reason to believe support for increased spending on superannuation was more closely linked with highly visible shifts in the policy context. NZVS data, for instance, suggests there was a significant drop in support for spending in this policy area prior to 1990; a similar question asked in 1989 found 53% of respondents wanted more 'spending on pensions', even if it meant higher taxes (Perry and Webster, 1994). Just over half of NZAVS respondents also thought that people should get a lower pension if they were 'well off' in 1987 (RCSP, 1988a), potentially indicating concern about spending at this time and reflecting the kinds of concern with 'fairness' expressed earlier by participants in the qualitative study. However, the largest *increase* in NZES support for more spending on pensions occurred between 1990 and 1993 when National failed to reverse Labour's surcharge and instead further targeted superannuation. Although New Zealand Superannuation was reinstated in 1992, the surcharge increased and it is possible NZES respondents in 1993 were somewhat sceptical about this relatively recent policy shift. Support for more spending then grew at a slower pace for the remainder of the 1990s as the Superannuation Accord was forged between the major parties to avoid significant policy lurches and New Zealand First negotiated a public referendum on compulsory superannuation, and the abolition of the surcharge in 1998. These may have reduced, but not completely assuaged, public concern about spending levels. This concern declined further only after the Labour-coalition government restored the link between wages and pensions and established the New Zealand Superannuation Fund in 2001 to help pay for future pensions (St John, 1999a; Davey, 2001; Roper, 2005).

There were no major policy changes between 2002 and 2005 but support for more spending increased slightly during this period, before falling by 8.9 percentage points to a low of 37.8% in 2011. The latter shift was likely associated with the introduction of KiwiSaver in 2007. Although extremely popular due to generous government subsidies, this ultimately represented a means for encouraging *individuals* to take greater responsibility for ensuring they have sufficient retirement savings. Without data for 2011, it cannot be gauged whether the significant election debate about superannuation in that year had an impact on support for spending in this area, as it did for the more principled statement, but clearly superannuation remains a sensitive policy topic for New Zealanders.

Indeed, although support for more government spending fell from 52.6% to 42.3% among the Left, it stayed steady among the Right (34–35%) and Centre (33–36%) across the 21-year period studied, different phases of neoliberalism provoked varied reactions among these groups. While Left and Centre support for government ensuring a decent standard of living for old people stayed relatively steady, both groups increased their support for more spending during the 1990s while Right support initially fell then steadied. Attitudes among both the Centre and Right also remained fairly stable through the roll-out phase of neoliberalism but support fell by 14.2 percentage points among the Left between 1999 and 2005. During the 2005–11 period which covers the Labour-coalition's last and National's first term government, support decreased by 5–7 percentage points among the Left and Right but the Centre's support fell dramatically by 16 percentage points. Left and Right concern about spending on superannuation thus diminished when a government of their own ideological flavour took power, while the Centre remained relatively steady until the debate about superannuation emerged as an election issue in 2011. The greater visibility of government spending in this area appears to have encouraged a decreased desire for spending among this group.

Despite unanimous agreement that the government should ensure a decent standard of living for old people across all age groups, the level of support for more spending on superannuation fell among the youngest group from 39.6% to 25.5% between 1990 and 2011, while growing marginally from 38% to 40% among the oldest group. However, the youngest group's attitudes on this issue were comparatively steady over time, possibly because superannuation is less immediately proximate to them than older New Zealanders and debates about superannuation tend to frame the baby boomer generation as reaping benefits that younger people will not enjoy. During the 2005 to 2011 period, when KiwiSaver was introduced in 2007 and 2011 election debate raised the visibility of this issue, the oldest and youngest groups did nonetheless report the largest falls in support for more spending across all age groups (17.3 and 14.9 percentage points respectively). Few of the former will belong to KiwiSaver and none will be affected by age of eligibility changes but they are likely most tuned into government policy in this area, while the youngest group will be most affected by any future cuts in government funding of superannuation.

This section has identified that New Zealanders still overwhelmingly supported the right to economic security in old age in 2011, even if there was a moderate drop in support after 2008. This fall was likely associated with the 2011 election debate about the age of entitlement for New Zealand Superannuation, raising concern that New Zealand attitudes had begun to roll-over and reflect debates about restrictions on superannuation in the future. But earlier policy volatility did *not* have a significant impact on attitudes towards this proposition and any chance of the superannuation surcharge and Guaranteed Retirement Income policies developing a lock-in effect was quashed by public protest and interest group lobbying. Similarly, although only around half of the New Zealand public offered support for more spending on superannuation at best, support *rose* through the 1990s as National failed to meet its election promise to fully restore universal superannuation. This bodes well for the future, indicating the New Zealand public may resist any significant weakening of their right to economic security in old age. Overall, this principle was more strongly supported than a more pragmatic interest in spending but this is not surprising given universalism frequently ensures relatively high levels of satisfaction with superannuation.

Coherence despite diversity

KiwiSaver's potential to build significant private savings may challenge the belief that the government should ensure a decent standard of living for old people over time but Table 6.3 indicates that the privatisation of retirement funds may have less impact upon attitudes about government responsibilities in this area than might be expected. With heavily privatised earnings-related superannuation programmes (alongside a basic means-tested pension), the UK's pension system ranks only fourth and Australia's eighth most progressive in the OECD, while New Zealand's universal superannuation means that it ranks first (Joumard et al, 2012). Despite these differences, British support for the proposition that the government should ensure a decent standard

Table 6.3: Attitudes towards the elderly and pensions (agree only), percentage

	1985	1990	1996	2000	2006	2007	2012
Should be government's responsibility to provide a decent standard of living for the old*							
United Kingdom	97	97	95	97	94	–	96
Australia	86	77	94	–	–	94	–
	1985	1990	1996	2006	2007		
Government should spend much more/more on old age pensions/retirement							
United Kingdom	75	82	78	72	–		
Australia	55	55	50	–	54		

Note: * Agree combines 'definitely should' and 'probably should'.

Sources: Australian Survey of Social Attitudes and International Social Survey Programme cited in Wilson et al, 2012).

of living for the old remained steady (declining only by 1 percentage point between 1985 and 2012 but by a greater degree in the early 2000s) and Britons offered slightly *higher* support than found in New Zealand. In contrast, Australian support declined by 9 percentage points between 1985 and 1990 but then rose quickly once Labor's 1992 Superannuation Guarantee made private saving mandatory and presumably assuaged concern about the government's responsibility in this area (Wilson et al, 2012). There was little change in spending but an increasing number of tax concessions for pensioners under the Liberal-National coalition, which may be why support shifted little during the 2000s (Harding et al, 2009).

Citizens in all three countries believe that the government has a responsibility to ensure an old-age pension, which is unsurprising given that international studies show that the elderly are usually considered to be highly deserving (Larsen, 2006; van Oorschot, 2008). Support for spending in this policy area *is* significantly lower in all years than that for the principle of the government ensuring a decent standard of living, but cuts to spending generally encouraged a demand for *more* resources and vice versa in at least New Zealand and Australia. Britons expressed the greatest desire for more spending across all years, with support increasing through the roll-back phase of neoliberalism and decreasing under Labour. Attitudes were comparatively steady in Australia but around half of all Australian respondents wanted more spending. New Zealand support for more spending in this area was relatively low, presumably because they were relatively happy with the status quo of a low, flat-rate but universal pension. Nonetheless, the overwhelming trend is the similarity in overall trends in the three countries, despite the differing levels of privatisation in this policy area.

Conclusion: support for core welfare state services lives on

In contrast to the previous chapter's finding that attitudes towards the unemployed have hardened over time, this chapter presented quite a different story. Neoliberalisation *has* had some impact on public opinion but the evidence suggests that a majority of New Zealanders, Britons and Australians still regard healthcare, education and economic security in old age as rights of citizenship. Table 6.4, which summarises key policy events and the direction of attitudinal responses to the propositions available across all three countries, further highlights considerable coherence in the responses of New Zealanders, Britons and Australians to policy trends, even if attitudes did not always shift at the same time in each country.

Instead of turning the public against the welfare state, the roll-back phase of neoliberalism generally had the opposite effect. Support for government spending on health and education *grew* in all three countries as governments attempted (often unsuccessfully) to trim social expenditure and privatise responsibility in these policy areas. New Zealand support for *free* healthcare and education did diminish during this period but this chapter has argued that this represents a pragmatic response to the political context rather than a irreversible shift away from the principle that the government should ensure healthcare is available; certainly support for this broader proposition

Table 6.4: Attitudinal trends in healthcare, education and superannuation across three phases of neoliberalism in New Zealand, the United Kingdom and Australia

	New Zealand	United Kingdom	Australia
	1984–1990: Labour Limited health reforms Decentralisation of school governance and funding, radical increase in tertiary fees Introduced super surcharge	**1979–1997: Conservative** Initial cuts to health and education spending/services Substantial privatisation of pensions	**1983–1996: Labor** Established universal Medicare health system Introduced tertiary fees Introduced mandatory private superannuation
	1990–1999: National Radical marketisation of health, weakening after 1996 Introduced student loan system, increased tertiary fees Means-testing of superannuation		
Government responsible for healthcare for sick (NZ: free healthcare)	↓	↔	↑
Spending on health	↑	↑	↑
Spending on education	↑	↑	↑
Government should ensure decent standard of living for old people	↔	↔	↑
Spending on pensions	↑	↑	↓

(continued)

Table 6.4: Attitudinal trends in healthcare, education and superannuation across three phases of neoliberalism in New Zealand, the United Kingdom and Australia (continued)

	New Zealand	United Kingdom	Australia
	1999–2008: Labour-coalition Introduced Primary Health Organisations Removed interest on student loans for NZ residents Introduced incentives for private retirement funds	**1997–2010: Labour** Increased marketisation/ privatisation of health and pensions Introduced tertiary tuition fees	**1996–2007: Liberal-National Coalition** Increased marketisation/ privatisation of health and superannuation, tertiary education
Government responsible for healthcare for sick (NZ: free healthcare)	↑	↓	↓
Spending on health	↓	↓	↑
Spending on education	↓	↓	↑
Government should ensure decent standard of living for old people	↔	↓	↔
Spending on pensions	↓	↓	↑
	2008+: National Maintained Primary Health Organisations Reduced tertiary funding but kept interest free loans Reduced incentives for private retirement funds	**2010+: Conservative-Liberal Democrat Coalition** Restored pensions-earnings link but increased pressure to reduce public pensions Radical increase in tertiary fees Significant devolution of responsibility for health	**2007+: Labor** Reduced incentives to take up private health insurance
Government responsible for healthcare for sick (NZ: free healthcare)	↓	↑	–
Spending on health	↓	–	–
Spending on education	↓	–	–
Government should ensure decent standard of living for old people	↓	–	–
Spending on pensions	↓	–	–

Note: *This represents 'steady' support, as defined in Table 1.1.

stayed steady in the UK and increased in Australia during this period. We also know that significant public resistance discouraged the UK's Conservative government from replacing universalism with private medical insurance in the 1990s and led to a reversal of the quasi-market reforms undertaken in New Zealand after 1996 (Hills, 1998; Cotterell, 2009). Australia stands out because universal access to low-cost healthcare was only introduced during the initial phase of neoliberal reforms but this appears to have encouraged greater support for the idea that the government should both ensure healthcare is available and spend more on it.

Similarly, while support for the idea that the government should ensure a decent standard of living for old people stayed steady in New Zealand and the UK, despite volatile policy reforms, this increased in Australia as the 1992 Superannuation Guarantee was implemented but support for spending declined while it increased in both other countries. Labor's mandatory private superannuation scheme thus appears to have helped ameliorate concerns about investment in this area while its interpretative effects may have encouraged a weathervane response in beliefs that superannuation was a government responsibility.

The public responded differently during the 2000s, when Labour-led governments continued rolling out neoliberalism but placed a greater focus on social policy and the conservative Liberal-National government in Australia also courted middle class electoral support with incentives for private health insurance and superannuation. Support for the idea of the government ensuring free healthcare increased in New Zealand during this period, a shift which this chapter has argued is associated with the implementation of the proximate, visible and popular PHO system. Agreement that the government should ensure healthcare declined in both the UK and Australia; in the former this trend is likely a thermostatic response associated with the Labour government's investment in the NHS. This shift is less clear in Australia but increased private health insurance incentives contributed to Australia having one of the highest levels of private social expenditure in the OECD (Bryson, 2001; Lewis et al, 2010). This may have discouraged a sense that healthcare was a government responsibility. A decline in this belief may also have been shaped by concerns about a diminishing rate of bulk billing, which enables Medicare to say it offers free services (Wilson and Meagher, 2007). Certainly, support for spending on health, education and pensions declined in the UK and New Zealand but not in Australia, where support for more spending increased in the same three areas. Meanwhile, support for the idea that the government should ensure a decent standard of living for old people stayed steady in New Zealand and Australia, it declined very slightly in the UK. There is thus little evidence overall that the roll-out phase of neoliberalism pacified the public, setting them up to adopt harsher reforms in the future.

The impact of the last phase of neoliberalism must be assessed largely from New Zealand data and this provides insufficient evidence to believe the public have come to accept a neoliberal market agenda in social policy. There *was* a decline in support for free healthcare and education and for the government ensuring a decent standard of living for old people, as well as for more spending on health, education and pensions, even though no major policy changes were implemented by National after 2008. It is possible that this shows that New Zealanders rolled over and accepted neoliberal ideas but earlier discussion has highlighted that most attitudes towards spending are thermostatic, so a public desire for greater investment support would increase if National attempted to roll-back core welfare services in any significant way. Indeed, Table 6.4 indicates that the British public responded to the Conservative-Liberal Democratic reforms of the NHS by increasing and maintaining their support for the government taking a responsibility for healthcare and spending. Given that Australia's stimulus package in response to the financial crisis included extra social spending (Starke, 2013), public support for health, education and pensions might be expected to decline if attitudes are indeed thermostatic.

Overall, this chapter's findings suggest that the public responded to perceived institutional failure by demanding more spending and perceived improvements in quality, accessibility and, in some cases, affordability by becoming less concerned about funding (Taylor-Gooby, 2008). But there was more of a weathervane response for broader principles regarding healthcare and education, with support following the general policy direction of the government and, in some cases, specific policies. Discussion about the interplay between tax and government spending in the next chapter also bolsters the argument in this chapter that the public were not 'brainwashed' by the political rhetoric of the time, but rather lowered and raised their expectations depending on the politics and policy efforts of the government.

It is notable that public support for core welfare state services tended to be lower in Australia than in the other two countries. Although such comparisons need to be cautious, this may be associated with the fact that churches, charitable organisations and informal support systems have traditionally played more of a role in service provision in Australia than in the UK (and New Zealand) where the state 'loomed large in the imaginations of its citizens' (Wright et al, 2011, p 299; Bryson, 2001; Davey, 2001). However, despite increased levels of privatisation and greater targeting, there is no doubt that the majority New Zealanders, like their British and Australian counterparts, still view the government as playing a key role in ensuring social rights in all three policy areas. Neoliberalism appears to have influenced attitudes but this effect was somewhat weaker regarding healthcare, education and superannuation when compared to employment or social security.

Notes

[1] This refers to the radical neoliberal reforms promoted by Minister of Finance, Roger Douglas, during the late 1980s.

[2] These age categories are based on Hartevalt and Robinson's (2011) calculations.

SEVEN

Equality with little tax or redistribution

Changes to taxation and other means of redistributing income are the final policy shift examined by this book. Based on the neoliberal premise that poverty is a problem of personal behaviour, rather than economic conditions, low tax has been reoriented as the best means for ensuring fair redistribution of income (Harvey, 2007). This sits in contrast with the emphasis placed on progressive, relatively high levels of taxation during the post-World War II period which was regarded as a trade-off for extensive welfare state services built around a general principle of equality (Boston and St John, 1999). In New Zealand, however, the weakening of the wage arbitration system, the wage freeze and high unemployment meant increasing numbers of low income families were facing financial difficulties by the early 1980s (New Zealand Herald – NZH, 1981a, 1981b). The universal Family Benefit had lost its purchasing power yet, at the same time, there was increasing tax avoidance among high income earners and companies (Roper, 2005; St John and Rankin, 2009). Income inequality remained low by Organisation for Economic Co-operation and Development (OECD, 2011) standards but the Labour Party opposition argued that the 'rich are getting the richer, the poor poorer and the people in the middle squeezed' under the Muldoon National government (Clark cited in NZH, 1981c, p 2).

Chapter Three highlighted how the 4th Labour government nonetheless radically reduced income and company tax rates from 1985, while also introducing a new comprehensive, uniform, value-added consumption Goods and Services Tax (GST). Roper (2005, p 186) believes these reforms 'constituted the single largest handout to the rich in New Zealand's political history, and did more than any other policy change from 1984 to 1999 to increase socio-economic inequality'. Labour offered some new benefits and taxation dispensations for low income earners but these were narrowly targeted and largely ineffective. National abolished the Family Benefit in 1991 by merging it with the income-tested, child-related tax rebate called Family Support, whose real value eroded over the 1990s even if some improvements were made to low income assistance and tax credits after 1996 (Vowles and Aimer, 1993; St John and Rankin, 2009). The Labour-coalition government made tax slightly more progressive in 1999 but New Zealand continued to have one of the lowest personal income tax burdens in the OECD (Joumard et al, 2012). During the roll-out neoliberalism phase, tax credits – such as those included as part of the Working for Families package from 2005 – became the means for 'making work pay' among low and middle income earners and National weakened but did not abolish this package when elected in 2008 (St John and Rankin, 2009).

To gain an understanding of whether the New Zealand public came to endorse neoliberal ideas around taxation, the first section of this chapter explores support for reduced tax when asked in relation to both the country's economic situation and social spending. A second section considers views on redistribution by investigating whether New Zealanders believe in progressive taxation and want more government spending on low income earners. Policy shifts in taxation and redistribution contributed to income inequality growing at a rate faster than found in either the United Kingdom (UK) or Australia between the mid-1980s and the late 2000s. Inequality did fall slightly under the Labour-coalition government in the mid-2000s, a shift thought to be linked to the redistributive impact of Working for Families. By the late 2000s, income inequality was, however, increasing again (Perry, 2010; OECD, 2011). The final section therefore analyses New Zealand beliefs about income inequality as a third means of assessing whether equality remains a key principle of citizenship in the 21st century.

As with the previous three chapters, attitudes towards tax, redistribution and inequality are analysed by drawing upon the New Zealand Election Study (NZES) and other relevant data. Given such views may be influenced by contextual factors, such as the levels of unemployment and inequality, these are considered while differences based on age, ideological affiliation and income level indicate the varied impact of the three phases of neoliberalism. Although to a lesser degree to than the two previous chapters, data from the qualitative study is used to supplement this analysis. Each section also ends by considering whether the New Zealand findings represent part of a coherent trend also found in the UK and Australia. Once again, the different timing and strength of Australian reforms made some difference but this fact reinforces the argument that attitudes are responsive to shifts in government activity.

Taxation

Two NZES questions allow us to tap into public views about taxation. The first asks whether 'government should reduce taxes to help solve New Zealand's economic problems'. Figure 7.1 indicates that 30.1% of NZES respondents agreed with this statement in 2011, down from 36.4% in 1993. But support almost doubled between 1993 and 2008 with the most significant growth (by 18.1 percentage points) occurring between 2002 and 2005. It is difficult to know how respondents interpreted 'economic problems' in this question. The secondary axis of Figure 7.1 shows no covariance between levels of total social expenditure and agreement that the government should reduce tax to help solve New Zealand's economic problems, suggesting responses were not associated with general welfare effort. Support for reduced tax did increase rapidly as unemployment, a particularly visible and increasingly proximate problem with the economy, dropped through the 1990s and 2000s. New Zealanders thus became more willing to endorse tax cuts when the economy improved and were less supportive of reduced tax when unemployment began to rise from 2008.

The sheer magnitude of the fall in support for reduced taxes, however, suggests that attitudes towards tax were also affected by income tax policy changes, with support rising in periods when tax cuts were not implemented and declining once the public desire

Figure 7.1: 'Government should reduce taxes to help solve New Zealand's economic problems' (LH) by unemployment rate (RH), percentage

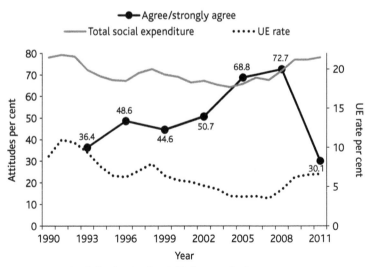

Sources: New Zealand Election Study; OECD; Reserve Bank

for them had been satiated. There are no NZES data for the period before the initial, radical tax changes of 1985 and 1987 but other survey evidence suggests the public went from being fairly neutral on tax issues during the early 1980s to a significant minority believing taxation was not progressive enough by 1987 (National Bureau of Research cited in Crothers, 1988; Royal Commission on Social Policy — RCSP, 1988a; Perry and Webster, 1994). Labour's regressive income tax changes, alongside the introduction of and subsequent increase in Goods and Services Tax (GST), thus appear to have encouraged New Zealanders to support more progressive taxation.

Only minor tax changes were made through the 1990s and National did not, as the next section highlights, try to offset the negative impact of the tax reforms by modifying family assistance until the mid-1990s. Tax was thus a significant election issue in 1993, by which time benefit cuts, the abolition of the Family Benefit in 1991 and increased user-charges in healthcare and education had also reduced family incomes. Church and voluntary service organisations articulated concern about growing inequality during the 1993 election campaign but only the Alliance Party proposed progressive tax reforms; National even talked of further institutionalising tax rates to make it harder for future governments to change them (Vowles et al, 1995). But with no major change in policy, NZES support for tax cuts to help solve economic problems rose by 12.2 percentage points between 1993 and 1996 (see Figure 7.1). It was not until after improvements to low income assistance and tax credits in 1994 and 1996 that there was a slight, 4 percentage point decrease in support for reducing tax between 1996 and 1999, a shift evident even though unemployment actually increased a little at this time.

Support for reduced tax rose again after 1999, most dramatically between 2002 and 2005. Tax had not been a highly significant issue during the 1999 election but Labour kept its promise to increase the top marginal tax rate from 33% to 39% in 2000 (Hayward and Rudd, 2000). By the mid-2000s, the Labour-coalition government was under pressure – given both a budget surplus and the National and ACT parties adopting an effective communicative discourse calling for tax cuts – to reverse this change (Levine and Roberts, 2003). The Labour-coalition attempted to defuse the issue by announcing the Working for Families package, aimed at low and middle income families with dependent children in 2004. Alongside a new In-Work Tax Credit, this included increases to Family Support, changes to abatement rates and thresholds for the Accommodation Supplement, and increased child care subsidies (St John and Rankin, 2009).

However, mounting political pressure around the 2005 election saw the Labour-coalition announce a significant extension of Working for Families to provide further 'tax relief' for low and middle income families in lieu of a general tax cut mostly benefiting high income earners (St John and Rankin, 2009). This improved the proximity of the policy by increasing the number of New Zealanders eligible, while the political opposition's reframing of Working for Families as 'middle class welfare' ensured the policy was highly visible and traceable. Other survey evidence suggests that there was a strong perception among New Zealanders in 2006 that New Zealanders were overtaxed, particularly low and middle income earners (Lawson et al, 2006; Gendall et al, 2007).

Figure 7.1 suggests that Working for Families slowed New Zealand desires for tax cuts, but did not quell them completely. The Labour-coalition finally relented to opposition pressure and implemented a small regressive tax change prior to the 2008 election (St John and Rankin, 2009). Once National was in power, further tax cuts were implemented over three consecutive years, GST was increased and the emerging economic recession was used as an excuse to reduce the income threshold and increasing abatement levels for Working for Families (St John and Rankin, 2009). Support for tax cuts dropped dramatically (by 42.6 percentage points) between 2008 and 2011 and tax was relatively uncontroversial in the 2011 election, suggesting that this tax strategy appeased many New Zealanders (Barron, 2011). This was, of course, in a context where unemployment had started rising, although by 2011 it was clear this was unlikely to increase to the levels seen during the 1990s.

This evidence suggests that low tax did not become normalised as a solution for solving the country's economic problems among New Zealanders in the long term. However, there was a greater absolute percentage point decrease among the Left (from 32.3% to a surprising low of 13.6%) than the Right (from 48.5% to 34.3%) between 1993 and 2011. Centre support stayed steady at around 31% across the whole period but it grew fastest under the Labour-coalition government, while the Right appears to have been most responsive to the actual tax changes after 2008. Moreover, although those aged 31–45 were *least* likely to support reduced tax in 2011 (25.2%), support among the youngest (<30) age group fell from 45.5% to 28.8%, declining once National had returned to power in 2008. The youngest group offered the highest level of support for reduced tax in 1993 but by 2011 the oldest group (>61) did so, with its support having grown from 33.2% to 35.6%. These shifts suggest a cohort effect whereby respondents who were young adults in the roll-back period continued to favour tax cuts as they aged, while those born later are less likely to do so. Finally, overall support for reduced taxes fell by the greatest degree among the groups whom they benefited the most, high income earners (whose support fell from 48.4% to 20.4%) and middle income earners (from 53% to 27.6%). In contrast, the attitudes of low income earners stayed relatively steady (increasing slightly from 34.8% to 37.9% between 1993 and 2011). This long-term picture, however, hides the fact that low income earners reported a 34.5 percentage point decline in support after 2008, compared to 29.5 and 15.5 percentage point falls among middle and high income earners respectively. This suggests the tax cuts finally started to have a visible impact on their lives. By 2011, low income earners nonetheless offered the highest level of support for reduced tax, while high income earners offered the lowest and middle income earners sat in between. Low income earners did not, therefore, simply accept their situation as the result of individual failings but they did appear to come to endorse tax cuts that benefited them far less than those on middle and high incomes.

The finding that New Zealanders became increasingly supportive of tax cuts through the 1990s and into the early 2000s challenges the last chapter's argument that there is continuing majority support for free healthcare and education and increased government spending in these social policy areas. This raises the question as to whether respondents really understand the relationship between tax and spending. An early Heylen (1991) poll suggests New Zealanders did in the early 1990s with 97% naming personal taxes when asked where the government gets money for social services. But has neoliberal rhetoric about individual responsibility and minimal government intervention reshaped New Zealanders' understanding of the relationship between key social services and tax? In 2007–08, only 22% of my qualitative participants referred to tax when asked what activities they considered to be an individual's responsibility, and some found it difficult to see the connection between tax and services. One high income participant had migrated to New Zealand on a student visa and had been unable to access many tax-funded services despite paying tax. Having recently gained New Zealand citizenship, she was now concerned about where her taxes went:

> "... taxes to me – and I'm really ignorant – but they seem very high for what I, it's like what am I going to get back? ... I want to see what my 39% on the dollar is going to and

I want to know how it's helping me and it doesn't feel like it is, and the whole wage thing is around that, yeah, you make, I feel like I work myself to the bone and, what are they doing with all my money?"

However, other participants made a direct connection between paying tax and public services provided by the government and were thus happy to fulfil their tax obligations. A middle income earner said:

"... I was discussing with someone the other day and they were saying 'oh, apparently there's some sort of loophole in the tax law where like legally you don't actually have to pay tax like' and they went on this whole spiel and I was like 'cool, so, you know, if I was the cops and those people rung me up it'll be "yeah, sorry, yeah, you haven't paid your tax, so we can't come to your aid"'. You know what I mean? ... I don't mind being charged tax because it pays for things like roads and police ..."

Further NZES evidence suggests that many New Zealanders also understand that core welfare state services are funded by tax. When explicitly asked whether the 'government should reduce taxes or increase taxes and spend more on health and education', tax cuts were less popular among respondents than when they were questioned about them in the context of improving New Zealand's economy. Figure 7.2 reports findings from a NZES question where respondents were asked to situate their views along a 5-point scale with 'government should reduce taxes' at one end and 'government should increase taxes and spend more on health and education' at the other end. Only a minority of respondents sat at either extreme between 1993 and 2008, so it is more meaningful to compare the combined percentage of those who situated themselves at the *two* points closest to each end of the continuum. Notably, more respondents wanted tax to *increase* rather than decrease overall, but by 2008 the proportion supporting increased tax had fallen from 44.4% in 1993 to 34.2%, while that desiring tax cuts had grown from 18.9% to 23.6%.

Focusing on this long-term trend once again ignores significant differences across the years, which suggest that policy and/or political discourse played a role in shaping attitudes. Although support for reduced tax increased steadily during the 1990s overall, it is also notable that support for *increased* tax grew, following a decline in support between 1993 and 1996. It is not clear why such a dip was

Figure 7.2: 'Government should reduce taxes' or 'government should increase taxes and spend more on health and education', 5-point scale, percentage*

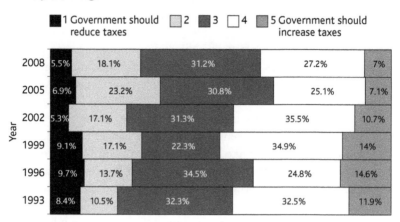

Note: *Does not add up to 100% because 'don't know' responses excluded from figure.
Source: New Zealand Election Study

apparent, given both economic conditions and social spending were still relatively poor, but by 1999, when both had improved, almost twice as many NZES respondents wanted to see more spending than wanted to reduce tax in 1999. Thus roll-back neoliberalism appears to have polarised attitudes but a greater number of New Zealanders still wanted increased taxes and spending rather than tax reductions.

When again combining the two responses at each end of Figure 7.2's scale, support for increased taxes dropped through the 2000s, at first slowly and then picking up speed after 2005. By 2008 only 34.2% of respondents sat at this end of the continuum. In contrast, support for reduced taxes fell slightly in the early 2000s, then grew between 2002 and 2005 before dropping to 23.6% by 2008. Without 2011 data the impact of National's multiple tax cuts made in the late 2000s cannot be assessed, but these findings suggest a thermostatic reaction to government spending. However, as with responses to the question about reduced tax to resolve New Zealand's economic problems, support for tax cuts was highest (30.1%) in 2005, having grown rather rapidly from only 22.4% in 2002. This suggests some New Zealanders were swayed by National and ACT's election rhetoric about tax cuts. Support for *increased* tax was highest between 1999 and 2002 (48.9%) in the Labour-coalition's first term, but support dropped steadily once the new government increased social spending, especially on health and education.

These findings challenge the view that the New Zealand public rolled over and strongly favoured low tax over core welfare state services in the 21st century. But National's proposed tax cuts were likely to have been central to winning Centre support and thus the 2008 election. When again calculating the two points at each end of the scale, Centre support for reduced taxes, even when this might mean less spending on health and education, increased from 16% to 39.4% between 1993 and 2008, most rapidly in the early 1990s but with a large fall in support between 2005 and 2008. Reduced taxes in the latter year was also supported by 39.4% of the Right, but support had grown only from 34.9% in 1993 and occurred most quickly under the Labour-coalition. Left support *fell* from 16.2% to 9.9% across 15 years, most notably during the early 1990s and the 2000s. Thus, the Centre appears to have come to endorse neoliberal ideas about low tax; however, this group's responses fluctuate across time more than the other groups, indicating it may have been particularly responsive to shifts in government spending.

In contrast, attitudes stayed fairly steady over 15 years among both the youngest NZES respondents (whose support for reduced tax fell only from 24.5% to 22.9%) and the oldest (whose agreement barely grew from 16.2% to 17.4%). Instead, middle-aged New Zealanders appear to have been most influenced by political rhetoric about tax cuts and/or the improved economic and social conditions of the 2000s. Moreover, there was little change in support for reduced tax when taking into account spending on health and education among low income earners (growing from 18.3% to 19.3%) and middle income earners (from 27.9% to 28.5%) between 1993 and 2008. In contrast, support from high income earners increased from 28.9% to 36.2% mainly during the 1990s, with significant declines during the 2000s. Yet, while this groups' support for *increased* tax and spending stayed steady, it fell among the other groups. This suggests relative satisfaction with the status quo regarding both tax and spending by 2008.

In summary, the year 2011 saw New Zealanders report their lowest level of support for reduced tax in 18 years when asked about this in the context of the economic situation, with fewer than a third supporting this proposition. Just less than a quarter of NZES respondents in 2008 also supported reduced tax when the trade-off of lower spending on health and education was brought into the picture. The wording of survey questions is thus very important on this issue, making interpretation of findings difficult. Nonetheless, responses to both questions relating to reduced tax fluctuated in ways that suggests a groundswell for tax cuts developed until the Labour-coalition felt compelled to implement them, after which support diminished. The evidence indicates that the political Opposition played a crucial role in provoking public demand for tax cuts in the mid-2000s, highlighting how an effective communicative discourse can shift opinion even by political parties not currently part of the government. But there is little evidence that the Left, young New Zealanders and low income earners have rolled over and endorsed low tax as a continuing policy solution. That support for tax cuts significantly diminished when social services were considered also indicates that New Zealanders are willing to pay for increased spending on health and education and are not confused about the use of tax revenue on these policy areas. A discourse of social citizenship rights thus still appears to play some role in shaping attitudes towards tax, even if attitudes fluctuate over time.

The ebb and flow of the tax-spending balance

The New Zealand findings are broadly supported by evidence from the UK and Australia. Table 7.1 shows responses to survey questions that are similar to – but not the same as – the NZES proposition presented in Figure 7.2, allowing us to consider how citizens in the other two countries weigh up the balance between tax and spending. Notably, only a tiny minority of British Social Attitudes (BSA) respondents supported reduced tax and spending less on health, education and social benefits while at least a third (but at times well over half) of

Table 7.1: Attitudes towards tax versus social spending (agree only*), percentage

	1985	1987	1990	1993	1996	1998	2001	2004	2007	2010	2012
Increase tax and spend more											
United Kingdom	47	51	56	65	60	64	60	50	42	31	35
Reduce tax and spend less on health, education and social benefits											
United Kingdom	6	3	3	5	4	3	5	6	7	9	7

	1987	1990	1993	1996	1998	2001	2004	2007	2010
Favour spending more on social services									
Australia	15	–	18	17	26	30	37	47	34
Favour less tax									
Australia	65	–	55	57	47	42	36	34	39

Note: * Australian data combine 'strongly favour' and 'mildly favour' and excludes 'it depends'; UK data exclude 'keep taxes & spending on these services at the same level as now'.

Sources: Australian Election Study (cited in McAllister & Pietsch, 2011); British Social Attitudes Survey.

Australian Election Study (AES) respondents favoured less tax. In contrast, British respondents were far more likely to express a desire for increased tax and more social spending than the proportion of Australians who favoured more spending on social services – except in 2010 when around a third of respondents in each country agreed with these propositions.

New Zealand levels of support for both reducing and increasing tax sat somewhere between these two extremes. It is important to acknowledge differences in the questions asked and the options that respondents were given (notably, the AES did *not* indicate that spending more on social services would require higher taxes) but this evidence suggests that Australians were more neoliberal in their thinking around tax, while the British held a far more collectivist ethos. Chapter Two noted that direct taxation and contributory programmes tend to encourage greater support for government intervention. It is possible that the UK's contributory social insurance programmes encourage citizen awareness of the link between tax and social spending to a greater degree than in New Zealand and especially Australia where such programmes are mostly funded through general taxation.

If responses over time are considered, however, more similarities emerge across the three countries. As in New Zealand, support for increased tax and social spending in the UK increased in the roll-back phase of neoliberalism of the late 1980s and early 1990s, then stayed relatively steady until it fell away in the mid-2000s. British support then diminished to an all-time low (31%) in 2010 before recovering slightly (to 35%) by 2012, a level similar to that reported in 1983 (Pearce and Taylor, 2013). Although changing economic conditions are likely to be important here, this suggests there is covariance between attitudes and government activity, with increases in public spending during the roll-out phase of neoliberalism apparently reducing a public desire for more spending, while spending cuts in the 1990s and after 2010 had the reverse response (Curtice, 2010; Pearce and Taylor, 2013). This is the case in the UK even though Sefton (2009) contends that New Labour successfully changed public perceptions of the Labour Party, with the number of British Election Study (BES) respondents believing that Labour favoured increasing taxes and spending more on health and social services falling from 59% to 5% between 1992 and 2005. Indeed, 49% of BES respondents in 2011 thought spending cuts were necessary due to mismanagement by the Labour party during its tenure (Clarke et al, 2012). Sefton (2003) believes attitudes around tax versus spending are probably linked to general perceptions about the quality of public services, given that British support for higher spending rose the most among those who were actually satisfied with healthcare services.

In Australia, a desire for more spending was extremely low in 1987 but grew steadily until 2007, then fell away by 2010, while a substantial desire for reduced tax followed the reverse trend. Having analysed the trade-offs between taxes and social spending throughout the mid-1980s and early 1990s, Grant (2004) and Wilson (2006) argue that early, consistent public support for *cutting* taxes made sense given the Australian Labor government did more than its contemporaries to counteract the negative impacts of economic and tax reforms at this time. However, Wilson (2006) believes tax resistance became institutionalised in Australia due to an 'anti-tax coalition' built on three diverse publics: high and middle income earners attuned to self-interest; those hostile to welfare beneficiaries; and those 'tuned out' of politics and willing to support *any* call for tax cuts. Although offering regular tax cuts, the Liberal-National government also adapted the welfare state to meet the needs of an 'aspirational' middle class, by using tax revenues to channel public funds to private education and to subsidise private health insurance and child care (Wilson and Meagher, 2007). This helps to explain why Table 7.1 shows support for increased tax and spending grew significantly under the Liberal-National coalition government (Wilson, 2006). A desire for more spending diminished when Labor returned to power in 2010 and increased spending, indicating a thermostatic effect similar to that found in New Zealand and the UK. Overall, attitudes regarding the balance between tax and social spending thus appear to shift with the ebbs and flows of public expenditure and – as the New Zealand and Australian cases show – political discourse about tax cuts.

Redistribution

Neoliberalisation has by no means eliminated redistribution from the policy lexicon, but it does sit in tension with the neoliberal view that individuals are in control of their own destiny and that poverty is an outcome of their poor choices or behaviours. Regressive income tax reforms do not necessitate less redistribution; nor does increased taxation ensure low income inequality (Joumard et al, 2012). But have public attitudes towards redistribution come to reflect neoliberal rhetoric about tax cuts? This question can be answered by considering where NZES respondents placed themselves on a 7-point scale when asked 'some people think that the government should redistribute income and wealth, others feel rich people should keep their income

– where do you see yourself on this point?'. Figure 7.3 shows that between 1990 and 2005 support for redistribution of income and wealth dropped significantly (by 21.6 percentage points when calculating the proportion of responses at the three points closest to this end of the scale). Meanwhile, a desire for rich people to keep more of their own income grew (by 17.4 percentage points, calculated by adding the three points at the other end of the continuum). Indeed, the positions of those wanting to redistribute versus those who believed that the rich should keep their income were reversed over the 15-year period; by 2005, 40.6% wanted the rich to keep income, which is close to the 48% who had favoured redistribution in 1990; similarly, only 26.4% wanted redistribution in 2005, around the same number (23.2%) who had wanted the rich to keep income in 1990. This suggests neoliberal policy and discourse significantly weakened support for redistribution overall.

No NZES data is available prior to the regressive tax reforms of 1985 and 1987 or for the period after 2008, when a fresh round of tax cuts began. But we can still assess whether this likely represents a permanent change in attitudes by analysing responses across the differing phases of neoliberalism. Using the same means of measurement as above, Figure 7.3 shows support for redistribution grew through the 1990s as public concern about the roll-back policies of Labour and National

Figure 7.3: 'Government should tax the rich more and redistribute income and wealth' or 'the rich should keep their income', 7-point scale, percentage*

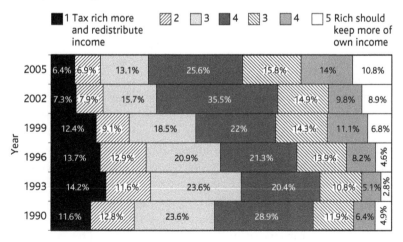

Note: *Does not add up to 100% because 'don't know' responses excluded from figure.
Source: New Zealand Election Study

and their social impacts grew, unemployment stayed at historically high levels and social expenditure was reduced. However, support for redistribution decreased from 1999 onwards as the public presumably became less concerned about these issues and their desire for the rich to keep their income grew, particularly between 1999 and 2002 when support increased by 7 percentage points. The announcement of Working for Families in 2004 did not stop the decline in support for redistribution that had been evident since 1993. The proportion of International Social Survey Programme (ISSP) respondents favouring the proposition 'people on high incomes should pay a larger share of their income in taxes than those on low incomes' also fell from 70% in 1992 to 50% in 2009, despite minor progressive tax changes in 1999 (Gendall and Murray, 2010). While a bare majority still favoured progressive taxation in the late 2000s, the differently framed question did not produce the same kind of fluctuations apparent in responses to the NZES proposition referring to the redistribution of income and wealth.

Despite these fluctuations and despite income inequality remaining a significant issue, evidence suggests that the roll-out phase of neoliberalism had a particularly regressive impact upon support for redistribution. Combining the three points at the end of the scale again, between 1990 and 2005 agreement that the government should redistribute income and wealth fell most significantly among the *Left* (from 70.8% to 47.7%) when compared to the Centre (47.5% to 25.3%) and Right (34.7% to 11.4%). The Left remained the most likely to support redistribution in 2005 but support fell steadily, having peaked at 85.3% in 1993, and this group did not appear to be receptive to the alternative discourses around poverty and inequality evident during the 2002 and 2005 elections. Nor was the Centre, whose support peaked in 1996, then declined steadily, while Right support fell in each and every election year.

Support for redistribution also declined from 51.4% to 27.4% among the youngest NZES respondents between 1990 and 2005, representing a fall only slightly larger than that among the oldest group (from 46.9% to 26.6%). The youngest group offered the highest level of support for redistribution across all age groups in 2005, but with agreement so low there is little reason to believe that attitudes could be easily reversed. Finally, low income earners were most likely to believe that the government should redistribute income and wealth in 1990 but middle income earners sat in this position by 2005. This is because low income earner support fell from 52% to 29.6%, particularly under Labour-led governments; Centre agreement decreased only from

46.8% to 38%, while Right support did so from 19.9% to 11.4% between 1990 and 2005. Notably the all-important Centre voters were the only group to increase their support (by 7.4 percentage points) between 2002 and 2005, a period when the Labour-coalition announced its Working for Families strategy benefiting both low and middle income earners.

The qualitative study was conducted during the roll-out phase but participants were not specifically asked about redistribution. Although 31% of them thought collecting taxes for social services was one of the government's key roles, only 10% spontaneously named redistribution when asked about government responsibilities. Some participants were wary about redistribution due to a perceived lack of clarity about where taxes go and for what purpose. A high income earner noted that taxes were lower in Victorian times but there was a greater level of charitable donations, allowing individuals direct control over redistribution. In contrast:

> "... these days the levels that tax is worth, it's sort of assumed that that money will be redeployed to those other good works and there's ... not a lot of decision making — it's probably the decision making power, isn't it? There's not a lot of decision making power left to the individual any more as to where the outputs of their labour are applied in the community. Those decisions are made by central administrators ... not at a local community, and, you know, council's a joke ..."

Another, younger high income earner was concerned about efficiency and transparency:

> "... I don't mind paying tax if I'm seeing that's it's improving ... Cos I've got that sense of wanting to help the wider community as well, cos it, it always comes back to you, it's always like, there's always a benefit for everyone ... if things are working the way they need to be working so, yeah, putting more money into that kind of stuff. Or maybe just being more transparent about, like I always find it quite funny when they tell on the news, like so and so of the government, you know, this PM or MP's cellphone bill last year was like $4000! (laughter) And I'm like 'what [the] hell, why weren't they on Vodafone[1]?!' (laughter) ... that kind of thing, it's almost like there seems to be a lot of wastage and

I think that's in any organisation, there are always going to be things that are a bit wasted and it's a huge organisation, the government, so they obviously need to figure some things out, but yeah, a bit more transparency around what they're spending my taxes on."

These comments suggest that a lack of specific taxes paid into unemployment insurance or superannuation may be behind some of this lack of clarity about where tax dollars go. As Chapter Two noted, how the welfare state is funded may well shape public attitudes towards social citizenship (Wilensky, 1976, 2002; Kangas, 1995).

It is also possible that New Zealanders do not really understand the term 'redistribution'. Figure 7.4 shows that a remarkably similar proportion (37–38%) of NZES respondents supported the proposition more 'government spending on low income earners' in both 1990 and 2005, which sits in contrast with the diminished support for redistribution discussed earlier. In fact, at least a third of NZES respondents considered greater spending on low income assistance important throughout this 15-year period and those who supported *less* spending remained a small minority.

Although the secondary axis of Figure 7.4 indicates no covariance between agreement that the government should spend more on low

Figure 7.4: Government spending on low income earners (agree only, LH) by unemployment rate, total social expenditure and Gini coefficient (RH), percentage

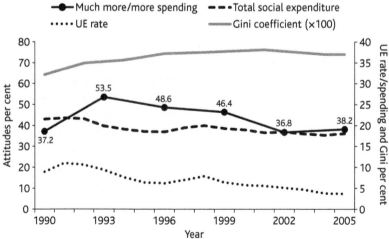

Sources: New Zealand Election Study; OECD; Reserve Bank

income earners and income inequality (as measured by the Gini coefficient), attitudinal trends do appear to be associated with both the unemployment rate and total social expenditure. Support for spending more on low income earners rose sharply in the early 1990s as the abolition of the Family Benefit, benefit cuts, the Employment Contracts Act and increased user-charges in healthcare and education all had a significant impact on low income families. Having peaked at 53.5% in 1993, support fell as improvements to both income assistance and tax credits for low income families were implemented in the mid-1990s and the economy began to recover. The biggest fall in support (by 9.6 percentage points), however, came in the Labour-coalition's first term, after which levels of agreement stayed more or less steady. Without data after 2005, it is difficult to assess the impact of the Labour-coalition's Working for Families strategy but the significant fall in support between 1999 and 2002 and a substantial 6.2 percentage point increase in the number of respondents who wanted *less* spending across this period suggests some New Zealanders thought that Labour-led governments were doing too much for low income families *prior* to Working for Families being implemented.

Despite overall support being similar in both 1990 and 2005, there is again some evidence the public rolled over and accepted the limits of government responsibility in this policy area. Left support for more spending on low income earners fell from 65.1% to 50.1% across 15 years, while the Centre increased only from 25.2% to 39.2% and the Right stayed around 21–22%. Most of the Left's fall in support occurred under Labour-led governments, especially in their first term, and this group's support also increased by the smallest amount across the 1990s. That half of Left respondents wanted the government to assist low income earners in 2005 suggests that this group still considered low income assistance to be important but they also appear to have been most strongly reassured by the Labour-coalition's relatively modest policies for low income earners, despite government unwillingness to explicitly talk about redistribution.

Among the youngest NZES respondents support *rose*, if only from 38.5% to 41.4%, across 15 years. In fact, there was remarkably little change across all age groups and only the 31–45s decreased their level of support overall. The oldest respondents increased their agreement from 39% to 44.5% between 1990 and 2005; this represented not only the largest absolute increase but it ensured this group remained the most likely to agree that the government should spend more on low income earners in 2005. Attitudes also stayed fairly steady across the 15-year period among those on low incomes (43–44%)

and middle incomes (around 32%). But high income earners became *more* supportive of spending on low income assistance over time, with agreement increasing 15.3% to 22.4%. However, low income earner support fell by 11.2 percentage points during the 2000s while the other two groups were relatively steady. Low income earners were still twice as likely in 2005 to agree with more spending than high income earners but the gap between the two groups narrowed because of the increased support among those on high incomes.

The increased desire for spending on low income assistance found among high income earners challenges the argument that responses to this proposition are shaped by self-interest. The qualitative study also included high income earners who were troubled about inequality. Notably, a focus group with wage/salary earners discussed in some detail the recent case of a New Zealander who died in 2007 when a power company cut off the supply that kept her home oxygen machine running because of an unpaid bill (see NZH, 2010). A high income earner participant questioned: "how could a family within New Zealand, where someone's working, not afford to be able to afford to pay their power bill?", while another on a similar income indicated that: "You had three people in that household, all earn, working full time on minimum wage and [I'm] still ... not surprised at all if the power bill didn't get paid". These types of discussion suggest that responses regarding redistribution may be driven more by values orientations, rather than simply whether the person responding will benefit from policy changes or not. Orton and Rowlingson (2007) note, however, that the idea that policy outcomes should be 'fair' may not be primarily motivated by concerns about making *incomes* more equal.

Although NZES responses suggest attitudes towards spending on low income assistance respond to changes in the economy and government expenditure, it is important to note that the qualitative study highlighted a lack of reliable information about policy, either in the present day or historically. Members of a benefit recipient focus group, for instance, were unaware that wage regulation during the post-World War II period had ensured a family wage sufficient for a male breadwinner and his family to live on (Cheyne et al, 2008). Once informed about this, they were asked whether the job at a discount retail outlet held by one of the participants paid such a living wage. They agreed it did *not* but failed to perceive this as any greater challenge than those faced by the generation before them. Indeed, some participants actively resisted the idea that families were better off at a time when there had been greater levels of equality within

New Zealand society. Yet responses to other questions contradicted this position with a benefit recipient noting, for instance, how benefits used to be adjusted for inflation and were thus more adequate for supporting a family than today. It is true that citizens on benefits and low incomes have always struggled, even during the so-called 'golden age' of the welfare state (Castles, 1996). But a lack of knowledge about past policies and conditions means some participants had no reference point from which to compare the current situation, making it difficult for them to imagine social rights no longer promoted by the government. Dean's (2012) British research involving past and present recipients of the means-tested Working Tax Credit for low wage workers, who were confused as to its purpose and how it was calculated, highlights how a lack of knowledge can also contribute to a sense of powerlessness.

Moreover, in some cases attitudes towards government intervention were shaped by a belief that community-based solutions would be more effective. A Māori focus group participant talked about how the Māori Women's Welfare League developed during the 1960s as a way for communities to help themselves rather than wait for government assistance. A middle-aged benefit recipient further lamented:

> "You know when I was a kid in the '50s and '60s, the family were there ... you had that community support because your cousin or your uncle ... there was always someone around who knew you, who could get you out of trouble or give you a shilling to get home on the bus or buy you a pie if you were hungry or whatever. Now that's progressively gone and we're not responsible for each other now ... You know, it's become institutional rather than communal."

The levels of support for government spending on low income assistance documented in Figure 7.4 may be mediated by these broader views about the benefits of community-based versus government interventions in an ethnically-diverse country like New Zealand where political discourse about socio-economic status and ethnicity are intimately intertwined.

To conclude, New Zealand support for redistribution and for government spending on low income earners grew through the 1990s but then declined during the 2000s, despite historically high levels of income inequality. A lack of recent data makes it difficult to be certain, but it seems likely that attitudes increased in response to roll-back reforms that reduced government expenditure when economic conditions were poor and then fell once the economy had improved and expenditure increased. The announcement of Working for Families in 2004 certainly did not arrest a decline in support for redistribution (or a desire for tax cuts), while support for more spending on low income earners remained relatively steady. This is the case even though Chapter Four found covariance between the implementation of Working for Families and increased support for government responsibility for jobs and wage controls. Notably, there was no covariance between spending on low income assistance and New Zealand's high levels of income inequality, despite the next section suggesting a majority of New Zealanders believed income gaps were too large in the late 2000s.

Redistribution — weakened but not dead?

The New Zealand findings reflect similar trends apparent in the UK and Australia. Table 7.2 shows that around the same proportion (42–44%) of BSA respondents believed 'government should redistribute income from the better-off to those who are less well-off' in both 1985 and 2012. But agreement with this proposition grew through the late 1980s, peaking at 50% in 1990. It then diminished steadily until the mid-2000s. Sefton et al (2009) argue that the redistributive effect of the British welfare state under Labour was similar to that evident during the recession of the early 1990s (a period of high unemployment when more redistribution might be expected) but the Labour government was wary of framing initiatives as redistributive and shifted away from out-of-work benefits towards in-work benefits and public services for the deserving poor over this period (Hills, 1998; Taylor-Gooby, 2005). Nonetheless, the roll-out phase does not appear to have irrevocably changed attitudes. Support for more redistribution

Table 7.2: Attitudes towards redistribution (agree/strongly agree only*), percentage

	1985	1987	1990	1993	1996	1998	2001	2004	2007	2010	2012
Government should redistribute income from the better-off to those who are less well-off											
United Kingdom	44	46	50	45	44	39	38	32	33	36	42

	1987	1990	1993	1996	1998	2001	2004	2007	2010
Income and wealth should be redistributed towards ordinary working people									
Australia	46	42	51	47	50	56	51	51	51

Sources: Australian Election Study (cited in McAllister & Pietsch, 2011); British Social Attitudes Survey.

increased slightly between 2010 and 2012, as the Conservative-Liberal Democrat coalition government eroded the working tax credit system and targeted the near universal Child Benefit to favour two-earner households (Levitas, 2012).

Although we do not have NZES data for the 2010s and thus cannot assess whether New Zealanders rolled over on the issue of redistribution, the same overall pattern of fluctuation evident in the British data was reflected in Figure 7.3, which considered NZES respondents' views of redistribution versus the rich keeping more of their incomes. The New Zealand Values Study (NZVS) asked the same question as the BSA about redistributing from the better-off to the less well-off across a limited number of years. Not only did New Zealand report similar levels of support to the UK across this period, but the roll-back phase – which saw levels of inequality grow rapidly – appears to have provoked support for redistribution in both countries, while the opposite was true when Labour governments took power (Perry and Webster, 1994; Perry, unpubl data).

AuSSA respondents were asked the same question used in the BSA only between 2003 and 2009; agreement that the government should redistribute income from the better-off to those who are less well-off also fell across this period, from 44% to 40%. However, Wilson and Meagher (2007) argue that Australians are less supportive of redistribution when it is framed as from those better-off to those less well-off than when offered a similar proposition that 'income and wealth should be redistributed towards ordinary working people'. Figure 7.2 shows that AES respondents support for the latter fluctuated by a small amount each election year, until the mid-2000s when support steadied and around half agreed with redistribution.

There are several possible reasons why no radical shifts were evident in Australian support. First, inequality grew more slowly in Australia than New Zealand and the UK between the mid-1980s and late 2000s (OECD, 2011). All three countries adopted similar neoliberal tax policies but the Australian Labor government also introduced a progressive Fringe Benefits Tax on business expenses and significantly increased financial assistance for low income families from 60% to 140% of the OECD average between 1980 and 1994 (McClelland and St John, 2006; Lewis et al, 2010). The Liberal-National coalition increased the rate for the family tax benefit and cash payments for many families, liberalised income tests and cut tax six years in a row from 2000, further contributing to Australia's income support for families being among the most generous in the OECD during the 2000s (McClelland and St John, 2006; Harding et al, 2009; OECD,

2013). Australia was also the last country of the three to introduce GST in 2000 and, when it did, basic food items were excluded (Quiggin, 2004). By the end of the 2000s, Australia's top income tax rate also remained higher than that of the UK and New Zealand (Joumard et al, 2012).

Nevertheless, despite these differences and in contrast to views about spending versus tax, the level of support for redistribution was relatively similar in all three countries and this appeared to move in the *opposite* direction to policy. These fluctuations over time certainly offer hope that New Zealand attitudes towards redistribution have not been irrevocably altered by neoliberal discourses about low tax and personal culpability, as the main findings presented in this section suggest.

Income inequality

No covariance was found between diminishing support for attitudes towards spending on low income earners and a decline in income inequality. Could it be that inequality had little influence on views about low income assistance because New Zealanders no longer considered inequality to be a problem? Table 7.3 finds no support for this claim. A majority of NZES respondents agreed that 'differences in income in New Zealand are too large' and support for this proposition grew moderately by 3.1 percentage points between 2008 and 2011, a period when inequality continued to climb after a minor reprieve in the mid-2000s. Notably, however, the number of respondents *disagreeing* that income differences were too large also increased by 5.6 percentage points over the same time period. Given much weaker support for redistribution and more spending on low income earners (see Figures 7.3 and 7.4), respondents either did not consider these activities to be the best solutions to income inequality or they were confused about the link between the two.

Although more NZES respondents acknowledged income inequality to be a significant problem in New Zealand in 2011 than in 2008, Table 7.3 indicates that the proportion who agreed that

Table 7.3: Attitudes towards income differences (agree/strongly agree only), percentage

	2008	2011
'Differences in income in New Zealand are too large'	57.5	60.6
'Large income differences are necessary for New Zealand's prosperity'	17.6	21.2
'Government should take measures to reduce differences in income levels'	–	58.5

Source: New Zealand Election Study.

'large income differences are *necessary* for New Zealand's prosperity' grew by 3.6 percentage points over the same three years. As with the proposition about reduced tax as a means to solve New Zealand's economic problems, it is unclear how respondents interpreted this question, but it seems likely the term 'prosperity' was associated with the country's economic situation. The ISSP asked a similar question in 1999 and almost a third (30%) of respondents then agreed large differences in income were necessary for New Zealand's prosperity, so this rise in support began long before the economic weakened and National came to power (Gendall et al, 2000). However, the number who *disagreed* with the same proposition also increased by 7.5% to 50.4% between 2008 and 2011, suggesting that the National government formed in 2008 had a polarising effect on attitudes.

That a majority of NZES respondents did *not* consider income differences necessary in the late 2000s sits in tension with the previous section's finding that only about two fifths of NZES respondents supported redistribution, a key route for overcoming such disparities. In 2011, NZES respondents were also asked whether 'government should take measures to reduce differences in income levels' and Table 7.3 shows that 58.5% of respondents agreed. Support again appears to have grown since 2009 when the ISSP asked a similar question and only 40% of respondents thought it was the government's responsibility to 'reduce the differences in income between people with higher incomes and those with lower incomes', down from 50% in 1999 (Gendall et al, 2000; Gendall and Murray, 2010).

More than twice as many NZES respondents supported the proposition that the government should reduce differences in income levels than favoured redistribution on the continuum discussed in Figure 7.3, highlighting again that New Zealanders do not necessarily make the connection between redistribution and income inequality. While the use of a 7-point scale for one question and not the other requires cautious comparison, the word 'redistribution' appears to harden attitudes towards possible government policies to address income inequality. British research has certainly found that support for redistributive policies tends to diminish when words like 'redistribution', 'poverty' and the 'poor' are used directly (Rowlingson et al, 2010). Given the limited data, however, it is difficult to know if the New Zealand findings *reflect* the Labour-coalition's lack of an effective communicative discourse around redistribution or if the government's decision to place a limited, focus on redistribution from 1999 without using the 'R-word' was an astute political move attuned to public opinion (Cheyne et al, 2008).

One way of assessing this is to consider the views of the Left; if that group was not interested in redistribution, then Labour would not want to promote this as a government activity. In 2011, the Left not only remained more likely than other groups on the ideological spectrum to agree that income differences are too large, but its support grew significantly from 72.5% to 85.3% over the three years National was in power. Right support stayed steady (around 42%) but Centre support *declined* slightly from 59.1% to 57.6%. This latter finding is clearly troubling, given the importance of this group electorally. Left agreement that income differences are necessary for the country's prosperity increased from 5.9% to 9.1% between 2008 and 2011, but obviously very few of this group endorsed such a view in 2011. But Centre support grew from 15.6% to 22.5%, while Right agreement increased from 29.1% to 34.6%. Together, these represent a significant minority bloc of voters who believe inequality is necessary.

Between 2008 and 2011, the belief that income differences are too large grew among low income earners (from 64.8% to 73.3%), middle income earners (58.7% to 64.1%) and especially high income earners (26.1% to 44%). All income groups were thus increasingly aware of income gaps. Yet, the idea that income differences are *necessary* grew only among those on low incomes (from 17.3 to 23.6%) and middle incomes (15.1% to 19.6%). Surprisingly, it *fell* dramatically among those on high incomes (30.4% to 21.4%), suggesting this group became both more concerned about and less tolerant of income inequality under National. Nonetheless, there remained a clear hierarchy when it comes to the government doing something to fix these income differences, with low income earners offering the highest support (71.5%) and high income earners the least (41.2%) in 2011. This suggests proximity and self-interest still played a role in shaping low income attitudes.

It is more concerning that only around half (50–57%) of the respondents aged under 45 believed income differences are too large in 2011, having changed little since 2008. Support among those aged 46–60 also stayed steady but sat around 60%, while agreement increased significantly from 62.5% to 72.1% among the oldest group over three years. Yet, although all age groups were more likely to believe inequality is *necessary* for the country's prosperity in 2011 compared to 2008, support increased from 17.8% to 24.6% among the oldest group compared to a rise from 17.8% to 20.7% among the youngest. In 2011, however, 63.1% of the oldest respondents supported the proposition that the government should do something to resolve income differences compared to only 55–58% among those aged 60 or younger. These differences are not great but they suggest that believing income inequality is necessary does not necessarily preclude support for government intervention, at least among older people who have a historical reference point for past redistributive policies.

The limited NZES data available does not allow us to consider whether New Zealanders became more intolerant of income inequality across the three phases of neoliberalism but other data suggests there was early concern about this issue, even if it had begun diminishing by the late 1980s (Heylen cited in Crothers, 1988; RCSP, 1988a). Gendall and Murray's (2010) analysis of ISSP data also found that New Zealanders' preference for a society where most people sit in the middle and few sit at the top or bottom remained fairly steady between 1992 and 2009 but their views of its actual shape changed significantly: only 37% thought New Zealand society had a small elite at the top and most people at the bottom in 2009, compared to 62% in 1992, while the number who believe New Zealand society has most people in the middle more than doubled over the same time to 34% in 2009. ISSP respondents thus believed society had become more like their ideal, despite growing levels of income inequality over the past three decades. This may be linked to the fact that 80% of such respondents considered themselves middle class in 2009, a 5 percentage point increase over 1999 (Gendall et al, 2000; Gendall and Murray, 2010). This, of course, represents a challenge to Left politics, which have traditionally been driven by working class priorities, and helps explain why the Labour-coalition government focused on policies benefiting 'middle class' voters.

The qualitative study attempted to explore New Zealanders' perceptions of the hierarchies within society in a different way. Having responded to the statement 'welfare recipients are treated like second class citizens' (see Chapter Five), participants were asked what other groups they thought to be 'second class' and why. In addition, they were asked to consider whether *they* themselves felt like a 'first class citizen', which was defined in terms of feeling as if they were valued and equal citizens of New Zealand. Notably, 24% of qualitative participants said that New Zealand citizens need to have their basic needs met to feel first class. A benefit recipient articulated this as: "Clean air, clean water, roof over their head. [A] standard of living which meets the basic needs, food, shelter, clothing". A sizeable minority thus believed a basic level of economic and social security was necessary to participate and feel equal in New Zealand. Another 23% of participants indicated that money was crucial to feeling first class, in the sense that a certain level of income was necessary to have your basic needs met and to participate, although a further 8% said explicitly that money was *not* important, if that meant being rich was necessary to feeling first class. While this focus on basis *needs* might be said to be in line with neoliberal rhetoric, it is notable that respect/kindness (30%) was the most commonly named condition required to feel first class; feeling valued (20%) and belonging (10%) were also mentioned. These concepts tap into a 'thicker' interpretation of social citizenship than simply material needs being met.

It is perhaps more interesting, particularly given the ISSP findings noted above, that some participants, particularly those on high incomes, resisted the concepts of 'first' and 'second' class completely. They often reframed the question in giving their response, as one retired participant did: "Oh, I don't like classing ... People are either good citizens or not I think". It became clear many interpreted 'class' rather narrowly in terms of occupational or income-based divisions, which they felt uncomfortable discussing given the dominant myth of New Zealand 'egalitarianism' (Sharp, 1997). Only one participant, a middle-aged high income earner, explicitly talked about New Zealand "moving towards an increasingly class-based society". A younger high income earner illustrates a more common response; when asked if he felt like a first class citizen in New Zealand, he said: "Absolutely not, I mean, I would say I'm thoroughly average ... in all respects, you know, I'm neither rich nor poor, I'm neither particularly bright nor, nor totally dumb. You know, I think, yeah, I'm just totally average". When asked what people would need to feel first class, his resistance became even clearer:

> "I actually don't know if I'd want to feel first class in the sense that, well, first class in the sense of being proud of my achievements and in that way maybe, you know, for the modest achievements that I've ... every time I write a good report I feel pride and if that's being a first class citizen, yes, then I feel number one. You know ... that I certainly feel good in that way, if I think about, you know, if I have a barbecue in the back yard and have friends around, yes, I feel great. If first class means feeling better than someone else I don't know whether we want, whether we want first class citizens."

While this participant's relative socio-economic privilege led him to interpret being first class in terms of pride and wellbeing, other wage/salary earners did not see themselves as first class because they felt disadvantaged in the current political context. A low income earner said:

> "... it's quite hard to phrase this. I'm basically white middle class and in a lot of ways I sort of feel that (pause) there's (pause) you're not entitled to – people on a Community Services Card, for example, are entitled to more, entitled to cheaper healthcare. People who earn more can get insurance so you're sort of in the middle ... so you can't afford the insurance and you're not entitled to the Community Services Card for the, you know, for the cheaper health care – I'm just talking healthcare here, but it flows over."

Although talking about socio-economic issues, this participant associates understandings of first and second class status with ethnicity and she felt penalised for being 'white'. This is not entirely surprising, given New Zealand's bicultural political context where targeting based on socio-economic status and ethnicity often overlaps (Humpage, 2006). But many participants found it difficult to identify themselves as first class because they negatively associated it with superiority or class consciousness, while others said they felt first class exactly because they wished to resist such hierarchies or divisions. Although similar findings were evident in earlier British research asking the same kinds of questions (Dean and Melrose, 1999), it is possible some of this group's resistance to being first class is linked to an awareness and sense of discomfort with recent growth in income inequality, particularly given New Zealand's historical myth of egalitarianism. Even if few participants named redistribution as the answer to this problem, this provides some hope for social citizenship advocates. Yet competing interpretations of what being first class meant to my participants suggests few interpreted citizenship in a Marshallian sense.

Overall, there was a slight growth in the number of NZES respondents agreeing that 'differences in income are too large' between 2008 and 2011, with a clear majority believing this to be the case in the latter year. While the proportion who agreed that such large income differences are *necessary* to New Zealand's prosperity also increased slightly, the proportion *disagreeing* increased twice as fast and half of the NZES respondents did not believe inequality to be necessary to the country's economic prosperity in 2011. In addition, almost the same number who believed 'income gaps are too large' wanted the government to take action to reduce these differences in 2011. This challenges the view that New Zealanders have come to endorse the neoliberal rhetoric of individual responsibility and choice as the main drivers behind individual success, even if the limited historical evidence suggests tolerance of income inequality *has* grown over time.

A responsive public?

British and Australian data offers greater opportunity to examine the long-term patterns in support for redistribution than possible in New Zealand. Table 7.4 indicates that the number of BSA respondents agreeing that 'differences in income are too large' increased in the late 1980s as the roll-back reforms by the British Conservative government were first implemented, then stayed steady through the 1990s before falling rapidly in the early 2000s once Labour came to power. Support for the same proposition did increase by 10 percentage points between 2004 and 2009, meaning around three quarters of all respondents agreed in both the latter year and 1987. But Sefton (2009) cautions that a sharp rise in actual income inequality means this finding indicates a tolerance of higher levels of inequality, with attitudes shifting most significantly among Labour voters. However, the number of BSA respondents agreeing that large differences in people's incomes are necessary for Britain's prosperity *declined* from 27% to 18% between 1987 and 1999 before then rising again to 25% in 2004. In 2010, 53% of Britons also agreed that it is 'the responsibility of government to reduce the differences in income between people with high incomes and those with low incomes' with BSA data showing that support for this proposition fluctuated over time, rising through the roll-back phase of neoliberalism and then falling through the 2000s until economic conditions worsened in the latter part of this decade.

Cautious analysis of the Australian data, which draws upon two slightly different survey questions, finds support for the idea that income differences are too large also increased across the 1990s, albeit from a lower level and even though the Labor government made

Table 7.4: 'Differences in income are too large' (agree/strongly agree only), percentage

	1987	1991	1992	1999	2003	2004	2005	2009
United Kingdom	76	82	–	82	–	65	–	75
Australia*	61	–	63	68	84	–	82	72

Note: * From 2003 the Australian question was 'the gap between those with high incomes and those with low incomes is too large'.

Sources: Australian Survey of Social Attitudes; British Social Attitudes Survey; International Social Survey Programme (cited in Meagher & Wilson, 2008).

some early attempts to contain inequality. Support fell after 2003, at first slowly when the Liberal-National coalition government was in power and then by 10 percentage points between 2005 and 2009. Given Australians did not face the same level of economic downturn, spending cuts and entitlement restrictions as found in the UK, it is no surprise that Australian support did not increase in the late 2000s when Labor came to power in 2007. In regards to whether the government should reduce income differences, Australian data is limited to the 2000s but support increased from 43% to 58% between 2003 and 2007, then fell to 50% in 2009. Meagher and Wilson (2008) speculate that rising perceptions of inequality are generated mostly from experiences of the labour market, where income gaps widened most and where the middle class may look up to high income earners, such as executives gaining 'golden handshakes' and lavish bonuses that are not regarded as rightful earning, instead of struggling low income earners below them. This is likely true for the other two countries as well.

Overall, New Zealanders were less likely to agree that income differences are too large in 2011 than Britons or Australians in the late 2000s, potentially indicating that New Zealanders are more tolerant of inequality despite New Zealand's comparatively poor position on this indicator. Yet what little data is available in New Zealand supports the argument that attitudes shift with the economic/political context as they appear to do in the other two countries. Moreover, New Zealanders offered slightly higher support than their counterparts in the UK and Australia for the idea that the government should reduce inequality in the late 2000s/early 2010s, even if a majority did so in all three countries. These facts make it difficult to argue that New Zealand's comparatively high level and rapid growth in income inequality saw its citizens harden their attitudes towards this problem more than their liberal welfare state counterparts.

Conclusion: the principle of equality lives on

The public attitudes towards tax, redistribution and inequality discussed in this chapter have rounded out earlier analysis by considering whether neoliberalisation has shaped views on the principle of equality. Although Chapter Six highlighted considerable continuing support for healthcare, education and superannuation and government spending in these areas, discussion here has highlighted how this sits in tension with a desire for tax cuts and a relatively weak interest in forms of redistribution, despite continuing awareness that income inequality is a significant problem. However, Table 7.5 indicates that public support around these three key issues has tended to fluctuate over time in response to government activity.

During the roll-back phase of neoliberalism, support for increased tax and more spending increased in all three countries, although this shift was far weaker in Australia. The New Zealand analysis also highlighted that support for tax cuts is not as strong when this policy shift is framed as a trade-off with more social spending, instead of as a means of resolving New Zealand's economic problems. However, at the same time support for the idea that the government should

Table 7.5: Attitudinal trends regarding tax, redistribution and inequality across three phases of neoliberalism in New Zealand, the United Kingdom and Australia

	New Zealand	United Kingdom	Australia
Reforms	**1984–1990: Labour** Regressive tax cuts, GST introduced **1990–1999: National** Abolished universal family benefit, improved low income assistance/ tax credits only from mid-1990s	**1979–1997: Conservative** Regressive tax cuts, increases to VAT Retained universal child benefit	**1983–1996: Labor** Mix of regressive and progressive tax reform, GST blocked Abolished universal child benefit but poorest families compensated through taxes and benefits
Increase tax and spend more*	↑	↑	↑
Redistribute to less well off **	↓	↓	↔***
Income differences too large	–	↑	↑
	1999–2008: Labour Coalition Minor progressive tax reform 1999 but tax cuts in 2008 Improved family support/tax credits for low/middle income working families from 2005	**1997–2010: Labour** Regressive tax cuts from 2000 Significant increase in family tax credits and other policies for low/middle income families in work	**1996–2007: Liberal-National Coalition** Multiple tax cuts but GST introduced in 2000 Improved family tax credits and other policies for low/ middle income families
Increase tax and spend more	↓	↓	↑
Redistribute to less well off	↑	↓	↔
Income differences too large	–	↓	↑

(continued)

Table 7.5: Attitudinal trends regarding tax, redistribution and inequality across three phases of neoliberalism in New Zealand, the United Kingdom and Australia (continued)

	New Zealand	United Kingdom	Australia
	2008+: National Tax cuts in 2009, 2010, 2011 Reduced tax credits for working families	**2010+: Conservative- Liberal Democrat Coalition** Regressive tax cuts from 2012 Increased targeting of tax credits/ assistance for families, including child benefit	**2007+: Labor** Regressive tax cuts 2009 and 2010 Increased targeting of family tax benefits but working families and single parents a focus of stimulus package
Increase tax and spend more	–	↑	↓
Redistribute to less well off	–	↑	↔
Income differences too large	↑	–	↓

* Note the slightly differing wording of the question highlighted in Table 7.1.

** New Zealand discussion of this issue in Figure 7.3 focused on a slightly different proposition but I have used the same question as asked in the UK and Australia for this comparison.

*** This represents 'steady' support, as defined in Table 1.1.

redistribute income from the well-off to the less well-off diminished during the 1990s in both New Zealand and the UK, suggesting that poor economic conditions and austerity measures reduced the public's sense that redistribution was feasible. Support for a similar proposition about redistribution towards ordinary working people stayed relatively steady overall in Australia, despite support increasing in the early 1990s. Britons and Australians were well aware that income differences grew during this period and the little data available in New Zealand suggests the same, giving the impression that neoliberal ideas about inequality had an impact on public beliefs.

It has also been noted that the New Zealand and British Labour governments implemented some important redistributive policies in the 2000s but neither wished to frame these explicitly as forms of redistribution and both implemented regressive tax cuts during their time in power. It might be expected that the public would thus shift away from seeing the government as having an appropriate role in reducing inequality. Support for increasing tax and spending more did decrease over this period in both countries and support for redistribution also fell across the 2000s in the UK as Britons became less likely to believe that income gaps were too large. Australian support for redistribution increased across the same period, as did support for more tax and spending and for the proposition that income differences are too large, within the differing political context set by the Liberal–National government. This latter finding suggests that the various tax incentives provided for the middle class by this regime did not completely satisfy the Australian public.

Despite the British findings just highlighted, there is little evidence of a significant and permanent change in attitudes across time. During the roll-over phase of neoliberalism, support for both increased tax and spending and redistribution to the less well-off increased once again, with the latter returning to around the level evident in 1985. Lacking New Zealand data, it can only be speculated that the National government's first term had a similar effect, supported by the fact that there was an increased belief that income gaps were too large. However, it is important to acknowledge that neither New Zealand's recession nor austerity spending restrictions were as significant as those experienced in the UK. The fact that Australia responded to increased spending by the Labor government formed in 2007 with a decline in support for more tax and spending, again indicates that attitudes respond to government activity. At the same time, support for redistribution stayed steady and there was a decline in the proportion of Australians believing that income differences were too large. This suggests that many thought these issues were less of a concern under Labor and as the economy weakened.

Thus, once again, hope for the future of social citizenship is found in the fact that although many citizens may be uncertain about exactly how (and if) the government can resolve income inequality, they still consider it to be a problem and only a minority consider it *necessary* for a country's prosperity. There is also only limited evidence that New Zealand's radical experience of neoliberalism in the 1990s, which saw inequality rise more quickly than in the other countries, made its citizens more accepting than those in the UK and Australia. While there was hardly any great enthusiasm for redistribution, most New Zealanders still believed that the government has a responsibility in this area and this, arguably, suggests some remaining support for the principle of equality in 2011.

Skilling (2013) highlights, however, that New Zealanders appear to endorse equal opportunity over equal outcomes. Thus they tend to offer only weak support for 'outcomes-focused' spending on redistribution and, as Chapter Five noted, benefits for the unemployed yet they strongly support 'opportunity-based' spending on health and education (see Chapter Six). Such a focus on equality of opportunity has not only been long-standing in New Zealand but has been widely promoted by Third Way thinkers (Sharp, 1997; Giddens, 1998). It has also been reinforced by the growing moral division between the deserving and undeserving poor, overshadowing the class-based divisions that traditionally underpinned concern about income inequality (Taylor-Gooby, 2013). These arguments make it easier to understand the tensions that exist across the four key policy areas discussed in this book, explored further in the final chapter.

Note
[1] A major telecommunications company.

EIGHT

The future of social citizenship

Framed as a hegemonic, all-powerful ideology, neoliberalism is said to have become the 'common sense of the times'. That a global financial crisis *caused* by neoliberal economics did not seriously challenge its dominance appeared to confirm this view (Harvey, 2010; Callinicos, 2010; Crouch, 2011). It is thus timely to evaluate to what degree and in what ways neoliberalism has shaped attitudes towards social citizenship over the past three decades. The preceding four empirical chapters explored a range of propositions tapping into New Zealand views about the right to decent work and wages, economic and social security, healthcare, education and superannuation, as well as the principle of equality. Analysis has illustrated that support for social citizenship survived into the 21st century, even if most New Zealanders would not use or recognise the term 'social citizenship' as defined by Marshall (2000). Nonetheless, in summarising key attitudinal trends across three phases of neoliberalisation and across three countries, the first section of this chapter provides evidence that New Zealand rolled over and endorsed (or at least came to accept) neoliberal values in key policy areas, most notably social security. The book concludes by considering how these findings can inform advocates wishing to galvanise public support for social citizenship in the 21st century and beyond.

Neoliberalism's coherent yet diverse impact on public attitudes

Drawing upon Peck and Tickell's (2002) scholarly work, this book conceived neoliberalisation as implemented first through a phase of neoliberal retrenchment that attempted to roll-back the welfare state. Public dissatisfaction, however, contributed to the emergence of a second, roll-out phase whereby efforts to moderate the social outcomes of neoliberalism helped embed its fundamental economic agenda. This book has contended that a third, roll-over phase of neoliberal governance then emerged. In the context of a global financial crisis, this initially spurned some aspects of neoliberalism but, in the longer term, continued to normalise a neoliberal economic agenda alongside further welfare state retrenchment (although to differing degrees in varied political settings). As this section illustrates, the New Zealand case study in this book provides evidence that public attitudes have rolled over in *some but not in all* policy areas. Despite considerable coherence in neoliberalisation's impact in all three countries studied, New Zealanders also appear to have accepted some neoliberal values to a greater extent than their British and Australian counterparts.

Roll-back neoliberalism

New Zealand's first phase of radical and rapid reform initially provoked a significant increase in support for many values associated with social citizenship. Following deregulation and privatisation in the late 1980s and early 1990s, the belief that trade unions are necessary to protect workers and that there should be state ownership of key assets grew between 1990 and 1993. Support for government responsibility for ensuring a decent standard of living for the unemployed and for spending in this area also *increased* as National significantly reframed unemployment as a personal problem in its first term. Little covariance between attitudes and shifts in unemployment rate suggest that regressive *policy* changes diminishing social citizenship encouraged support for the idea that the government was responsible for protecting citizens from life risks. Certainly New Zealanders increasingly favoured more government spending on low income earners between 1990 and 1993, while support for more spending on health and education increased rapidly until 1996, when New Zealand's first coalition government finally improved investment in these areas. These overall findings are in line with the common reading that New Zealand's endorsement of Mixed Member Proportional Representation in 1993 was an indicator of significant public dissatisfaction with the initial phase of roll-back reforms.

Attitudes supporting an inclusive social citizenship did, however, harden across the remaining years of the decade. Although trade unions mobilised significant public resistance against the Employment Contracts Act in the early 1990s, by 1999 far fewer New Zealanders agreed that it should be repealed. The beliefs that 'trade unions are necessary' and that 'unions have too much power' also fell away sharply after 1993. Support further declined for the ideas that 'big business has too much power', 'government should fully or partially own key assets' and 'wages should be controlled by legislation'. By the end of the 1990s, import controls and the idea that the government should be responsible for providing jobs were the only economic propositions where support increased. Despite their initial reservations, therefore, the attitudes of New Zealanders appeared to largely move in line with the neoliberal economic agenda promoted by both Labour and National governments from 1984.

In social policy, responses were more ambivalent. Fewer New Zealanders supported free healthcare and free education during 1990s but they increasingly wanted both higher tax and higher spending in both policy areas. Moreover, despite significant regressive tax reforms in 1985 and 1987, a growing proportion of New Zealanders agreed that tax should be reduced, both as a way to solve New Zealand's economic problems and as a trade off against spending on health and education. These mixed desires created an electoral dilemma for the incoming Labour-led government. It could not consider regressive changes in superannuation given that support for government responsibility for ensuring a decent standard of living for the elderly remained extremely high and there was public rejection of both the targeting of New Zealand superannuation and compulsory private superannuation during the 1990s. In contrast, support for the proposition that the government should ensure a decent standard of living for the unemployed was higher in 1999 than in 1990 but fell steadily from 1993. This is despite slightly fewer New Zealanders believing that need is caused by laziness and a lack of willpower across the decade. Support for redistribution and for more spending on low income earners also diminished, even though poverty and income inequality grew rapidly as the 1990s progressed.

Overall, the strengthening support for propositions relating to social citizenship in the face of neoliberalism was relatively short-lived in New Zealand. The evidence suggests that British support for social citizenship was more sustained. Both Curtice's (2010) and Bartle et al's (2011) analyses indicate that the public moved decidedly to the *Left* under the leadership of both Margaret Thatcher *and* John Major. As in New Zealand, 'a pro-welfare state backlash occurred almost immediately. Visible cutbacks were quite unpopular, and by the mid-1980s levels of support for public programs had returned to roughly the levels of the early 1970s' (Pierson, 1994, p 147). Yet, after 11 years of Conservative reform, the desire for more health and education spending continued to grow, and significantly more Britons wanted to increase tax and spend more on health, education and social benefits. Support for the proposition that the government should ensure healthcare for the sick and a decent standard of living for the elderly also remained remarkably steady. In addition, the hardening of attitudes towards the unemployed was not as significant as in New Zealand. British support for the government ensuring a decent standard of living for the unemployed and for more spending on unemployment benefits declined moderately but there was little change in the number of those who thought the unemployed could find a job if they really wanted. However, after initially climbing in the early 1990s, support for redistribution had by 1996 fallen back to the same level reported in 1985. As noted earlier, this represented a hardening of attitudes towards redistribution given an increased belief that income differences were too large, even if support for the idea that the government should reduce such differences grew across the same period.

Schmidt (2002) argues that the Conservative government did not fully achieve Thatcher's stated objective of persuading the British public that the government could and should do less than during the post-war period but the Conservatives were more successful in convincing Britons of the need for economic reform than in other policy areas. Yet the attitudinal evidence suggests agreement with the principles and policies of social citizenship was again more sustained in the UK than New Zealand. Support for government responsibility for providing jobs initially decreased significantly but, by the time Labour took power in 1996, it was at almost the same level as in 1985. Moreover, support for wage controls grew over the same period and Britons not only recognised that union power had been diminished but they increasingly agreed that unions were necessary to protect workers. Concern about big business having too much power also grew between the mid-1980s and 1996. Britons thus appeared to be less receptive to the radical economic reforms implemented than New Zealanders, at least in the medium term.

What then of Australia, whose reforms were more incremental and implemented by a *Labor* government between 1983 and 1996? Support for the proposition that the government should ensure healthcare for the sick and a decent standard of living for the old initially declined between 1985 and 1990 but a growth in support saw virtually all Australians agree with both propositions by 1996. This is not surprising given that Labor's Medicare system was becoming established and private superannuation became mandatory in 1992 and the public desire for spending on health, education and retirement tended to shift with government activities in each policy area during this period. Importantly, few Australians wanted more spending on social services instead of less tax, the direct opposite of the trends found in the UK. Labor's continued focus on social policy thus appears to have alleviated public concern and provided space for tax cuts to become more electorally important than in New Zealand where support for reduced tax was also rising. Despite a gradual increase in the belief that income differences are too large, support for redistribution fluctuated, contrasting with the hardening found in New Zealand and the UK.

In addition, after an initial decline in support, *more* Australians agreed that the government should ensure a decent standard of living for the unemployed in 1996 than in 1985. Support for spending on unemployment benefits also initially decreased then returned to a level similar to that of the mid-1980s. These findings are comparable with those in New Zealand but contrast with the UK. This is interesting because the Australian Labor government continued to play a far greater role in protecting Australians from the negative outcomes of economic change than New Zealand's National government. However, by 1996, fewer Australians agreed that the government should provide a job for everyone and fewer were concerned that unions had too much power, even without neoliberal industrial relations reforms being complete at this point. There was, however, growing concern about the power of big business and about the privatisation of state assets during this period.

The impact the initial implementation phase of neoliberalism had on public attitudes thus depended on the variant and speed of retrenchment. New Zealand attitudes appear to have been most negatively shaped by the extremity and speed of its roll-back reforms, while Australia's more incremental approach saw attitudes remain far steadier and, importantly, more supportive of propositions suggesting they still considered both decent employment and assistance for unemployed to be social rights. But in all cases, attitudinal shifts were mixed. Only in going beyond this early stage of reform can a better sense of neoliberalism's long-term impact on public opinion be gained.

Roll-out neoliberalism

Although not true for all policy areas, there is evidence that the roll-out phase of neoliberalism further embedded neoliberal values into the New Zealand public's psyche, especially when it comes to their perceptions of the unemployed. Attitudes towards this group hardened across a range of propositions more during the 2000s than the 1990s. The Labour-coalition government's own toughening of work obligations for the unemployed from the mid-2000s appears to have been overshadowed by a purported concern with social inclusion and a case management approach aiming to help the unemployed adjust to the neoliberal labour market. The qualitative data highlighted considerable ambivalence about all types of unemployed people being subject to work obligations and differing interpretations of what these might involve. But by 2008, three quarters of New Zealanders thought that the unemployed should have to work for their benefit in some way.

This lack of empathy for the unemployed sat alongside declining support for the proposition that the government should take responsibility for jobs between 1999 and 2005, although New Zealand was the only country of the three where a *majority* agreed with this proposition by the late 2000s. The public's focus on wages, rather than decent employment, in the 2000s largely matched that of the Labour-coalition. The renationalisation of a small number of key assets also appears to be associated with increased support for public ownership of key assets across the 2000s. However, public concerns about employment were not completely quelled by the Employment Relations Act's modest modifications to the deregulated labour market regime implemented in 1991. After an initial rise between 1999 and 2002, concern about trade union power declined, while more New Zealanders agreed that trade unions were necessary and wages should be controlled by legislation, after 2002.

There was also covariance between Labour-led government's policies – particularly the Primary Health Organisation (PHO) system and interest-free student loans – and increased support for core welfare state services. More New Zealanders supported free healthcare, particularly after 2005, while a greater number also wanted free education and greater education spending between 1999 and 2002 before support fell slightly. This sat in tension with an increasing desire for reduced taxes as a way to solve the country's economic problems until 2008, which explains why tax cuts became such a key electoral issue. However, the Working for Families In-Work Tax Credit may have softened the desire for reduced taxes when the proposition made it clear that this would be at the expense of less spending on health and education: support grew rapidly between 2002 and 2005 but then fell once Working for Families was implemented. This policy strategy, however, did little to bolster support for redistribution of income and wealth, which declined over the 2000s, as did support for more spending on assistance for low income earners.

In many ways, New Zealand attitudes followed the same trajectory evident in the UK under British Labour between 1996 and 2010. The British public took a decisive turn to the Right during this time (Sefton, 2009; Curtice, 2010; Padgett and Johns, 2010; Bartle et al, 2011). In particular, Labour's attempts to shore up confidence in the welfare system by 'talking tough', reframing welfare in terms of 'rights and responsibilities' and focusing on benefit fraud, are thought to have hardened attitudes towards the social security system and benefit recipients (Hills, 1998; Taylor-Gooby, 2005). Support for the proposition that the government should ensure a decent standard of living for the unemployed no longer appeared to shift with economic conditions, although agreement that the government should provide jobs continued to do so. Except for child benefits, overall support fell for spending on benefits. High levels of inequality and poverty remained in reality but fewer people thought income gaps were too large and fewer supported redistribution to the less well-off by the time Labour left power. As Orton and Rowlingson (2007) note, the British Third Way focused on providing better rewards for hard work and effort among poor groups without promoting empathy for the unemployed or challenging the socio-economic differences between social groups.

British attitudes towards government responsibility for ensuring healthcare for the sick and a decent standard of living for the elderly stayed relatively steady but support for more spending on health and education declined as Labour invested significantly in these areas. Similarly, fewer supported increased taxation to fund increased spending on health, education and social benefits. Yet, unlike New Zealand and Australia, there was no corresponding increase in a public desire for tax cuts. Regarding economic policy, support for government responsibility for providing jobs for everyone initially *increased* significantly between 1996 and 2000 then fluctuated, while an overwhelming majority supported minimum wages in 1999. Support for state ownership of public services, however, fell slightly despite the increased use and failure of some of Labour's public-private partnerships. This contrasts with the increased support for state ownership seen in New Zealand.

In the same year that Labour came to power in the UK, the Liberal-National government was formed in Australia. Australian attitudes towards benefit recipients having more work obligations and spending on the unemployed remained steady but, just as in the other countries, public support for a decent standard of living for the unemployed being ensured by the government declined. Australians did not, therefore, respond to the conservative Liberal-National government's increased focus on targeting and conditionality by softening their views of the unemployed, as New Zealanders did in the early 1990s. Australians were generally reserved about redistribution but greater number supported this and thought income gaps were too large during the Liberal-National period. Wilson and Meagher (2007) argue that this government's policies followed Australian expectations of the welfare state quite closely, including being tougher on the unemployed and supporting assistance for low and middle-income families but without major cuts to benefit levels or welfare services. During the 1990s and 2000s, the public responded to relatively limited spending in health, education and pensions by desiring more spending and giving greater weight to social rather than economic issues, the opposite of trends reported in the 1980s (Norton, 2004).

Views on government responsibility for providing jobs certainly stayed fairly steady but there was increased concern about the power of big business and privatisation. Those believing that union power had grown also declined. This suggests that, like New Zealanders and Britons, Australians did not completely 'buy' the neoliberal economic agenda endorsed (to varying degrees) by governments the world over. Similar to the American and British evidence of policy mood swings discussed in Chapter Two, Wilson et al (2012) found a latent liberal[1] or even social-democratic mood gained strength during the Liberal-National years, most likely as a balancing response to that government's perceived fiscal and social conservatism.

Between the mid-to-late 1990s and the late 2000s, therefore, New Zealanders and Britons became less concerned about social policy but Australians became more so. The completion of industrial relations and privatisation reforms saw Australians belatedly react against government policy in a way similar to that evident in New Zealand and the UK in the early 1990s. Public attitudes towards the unemployed hardened across all three countries, however, despite being led by different governments. The political rhetoric had a slightly different hue in the UK and New Zealand compared to Australia but all three governments during this period situated the unemployed as less deserving than other citizens and, having done so, were able to increase the level of conditionality that this group faced with little public resistance. In this way, the roll-out period embedded not only most components of the neoliberal economic agenda, but also a key shift away from endorsing the right to economic and social security.

Labor was not in power during this period in Australia, challenging the view that the Third Way politics associated with roll-out neoliberalism in liberal welfare states was critical to this shift. Wilson et al (2013) note that Australia has always had a stronger conservative streak stemming from the greater presence of Catholicism than New Zealand (and presumably most of the UK) and this saw more paternalistic, family-centred rewards for middle class support. But it remains that the Liberal-National government adopted many of the same political tactics (for instance, rewarding deserving lower and middle class workers through tax credits) that Labour governments used to reframe social citizenship in the 2000s as it also attempted to maintain electoral popularity during a time of relative prosperity.

Roll-over neoliberalism

To fully assess the impact of neoliberalism on public attitudes towards social citizenship, this book has argued that it is necessary to consider how public opinion reacted to policy implemented after the global financial crisis of 2008–09 because this represented a further 'weak point' in neoliberalism. However, its impact differed in the three countries, leading to variegated policy responses. The UK embarked on a harsh programme of retrenchment and broad-ranging spending cuts framed by a strong communicative austerity discourse. Zero budgets were presented three years in a row in New Zealand but key social expenditures were prioritised. In contrast, modest spending increases were possible in Australia because of the impact of the global financial crisis was weaker: neopaternalist social security policies continued nonetheless.

Although New Zealand's reforms were not as regressive or immediate as the UK's, this new phase of neoliberalism still detrimentally affected public attitudes towards social citizenship. Views about the unemployed had already progressively hardened since the mid-1990s but the three-year period between 2008 and 2011 saw the largest *ever* increases in support for the unemployed working for their benefits and for the belief that people live in need due to laziness/lack of willpower. There was also a significant fall in support for the idea that the government should ensure a decent standard of living for the unemployed. Given National's effective communicative discourse around welfare dependency, these findings are not surprising, but it is significant that New Zealanders in the early 1990s responded to a similar discourse and economic context by *increasing* their support for the same proposition. For these reasons, Table 8.1, which considers whether New Zealand public attitudes rolled over in the long term across the four policy areas, finds that this *was* the case in regards to social security.

The deservingness discourse central to National's welfare dependency rhetoric was also important for shaping attitudes towards redistribution. 2008–11 data is not available but Table 8.1 notes that public support for redistribution fell overall between 1990 and 2005. The beliefs that income differences are too large *and* they are necessary for the country's prosperity both increased during National's

Table 8.1: Have New Zealanders 'rolled over'?

Social security	**YES** Support for government ensuring a decent standard of living for the unemployed fell moderately overall and significantly between 2008 and 2011 Support for the unemployed work for their benefits grew significantly overall
Tax, redistribution and inequality	**YES** Support for more taxation on the rich and redistribute fluctuated but fell significantly overall Agreement that large income differences are necessary grew Support for reduced tax when asked in relation to social spending fluctuated but grew slightly overall
	NO Support for more spending on low income earners was similar in 1990 and 2005 Agreement that income differences were too large grew Support for reduced tax to solve NZ's economic problems fell slightly overall but grew steadily between 1993 and 2008, then fell significantly between 2008 and 2011
Economic policy relating to employment	**PROBABLY** Support for government taking responsibility for providing jobs fluctuated but was similar in 1990 and 2011 Support for import controls fluctuated but fell significantly overall and between 2008 and 2011 Support for wage controls fell overall but increased after 2002 Agreement that trade unions had too much power fluctuated and fell significantly overall with the largest ever increase between 2008 and 2011 Agreement that big business had too much power fell significantly overall but increased after 2005
	NO Agreement that trade unions were necessary to protect workers was similar in 1990 and 2011 but increased between 1999 and 2008 Support for full/partial government ownership of key assets fluctuated but grew overall
Healthcare, education and superannuation	**PROBABLY NOT** Support for government ensuring a decent standard of living for elderly was significant and steady 1990–2008 overall but fell moderately between 2008 and 2011 Support for more spending on superannuation overall fluctuated but was similar in 1990 and 2011 Support for free healthcare fell slightly overall and significantly 2008-11 but grew between 2002 and 2008 Support for more spending on health fluctuated but was similar in 1990 and 2011 Support for free education fell significantly with the largest ever decrease between 2008 and 2011 but increased 2005–08 Support for more spending on education fluctuated but was similar in 1990 and 2011

first term, suggesting media coverage about growing inequality and poverty during this period may have raised the visibility of this issue but did little to convince New Zealanders that the principle of equality was achievable. However, there was no unending desire for tax cuts; support for reduced taxes to solve New Zealand's economic problems fell dramatically once these were implemented after 2008.

Table 8.1 also offers only mixed evidence that attitudes towards the right to decent employment and wages permanently changed over time. The belief that trade unions are necessary remained relatively stable between 1990 and 2011. Support for government responsibility for providing jobs declined slightly between 2008 and 2011 but only to return to its 1990 level. The New Zealand public unexpectedly reported the largest *increase* in concern that trade unions have too much power across 21 years between 2008 and 2011, despite National making only minor regressive changes to industrial relations in its first term. The belief that trade unions are necessary, however, stayed steady and concern that big business has too much power continued to grow between 2008 and 2011, as did support for public ownership of key assets. New Zealanders did not, therefore, appear to be particularly receptive towards National's 'business friendly' approach. Support for import controls did weaken significantly overall and especially between 2008 and 2011. While this form of government intervention to protect the domestic labour market was no longer considered viable, support for wage controls – which was in decline until 2002 – continued to increase after National's return to power.

Although significant fluctuations over time indicate that declining support for core welfare state services after National regained power are likely reversible, there is no reason to be complacent. Having increased rapidly between 2005 and 2008, support for free education fell rapidly between 2008 and 2011 (support for more spending was steadier). I have, nonetheless, argued that the interest-free tertiary loans policy likely satiated wider public support for this policy. Support for free healthcare and more spending on health also decreased after 2008, but again this is probably because the PHO system met public desires for government responsibility in this area. National appears to have been aware that public attitudes towards all such propositions tend to shift with government activity and thus avoided any major retrenchment of core welfare state services that would be electorally unpopular. However, the 2008–11 period brought the first significant fall in support for government responsibility for ensuring a decent standard of living for the elderly (alongside a decline in support for more spending on superannuation). Given that National made no major policy shifts, Chapter Seven argued that this was probably associated with Labour's 2011 election rhetoric and raised concern that sustained support for economic security in old age may be weakening.

Taylor-Gooby (2013) suggests that the rapid, radical reforms of the Conservative-Liberal Democratic coalition government formed in 2010 were an attempt to make permanent the spending cuts attempted during the 1990s. While this kind of shock treatment strategy was to some extent successful in shifting New Zealand attitudes during the roll-back period, the limited evidence available makes it difficult to assess the impact of significant cuts in spending on health and education on British attitudes. Support for government responsibility for ensuring healthcare for the sick increased, probably in response to reforms of the National Health Service (NHS), and that for ensuring a decent standard of living for the elderly stayed steady. Data from 2012 indicates a slight softening of attitudes towards the unemployed, possibly as a delayed effect emerging from the recession or the austerity measures implemented (Pearce and Taylor, 2013). But Clery (2012a) reports that attitudes initially moved in line with the direction of the Coalition government's policy, being less supportive of government responsibility for ensuring social security for the unemployed and even for the elderly. Support for spending on all types of benefits also fell and the social security system was increasingly viewed as encouraging dependence. However there was virtually no change in responses to propositions suggesting benefits are too generous, that most people are fiddling the system, that cutting benefits would damage too many lives and that the government should redistribute to the less well-off. This suggests that the British public were not entirely convinced by the new government's harsh communicative discourse around welfare dependency. It is possible the tough economic climate made public views more hesitant but in the long term, Mulheirn and Masters (2013) believe a crisis of legitimacy in the British social security system was largely masked by steady economic growth between 1993 and 2007. It became evident, however, in the period of austerity and cost cutting that followed.

Based on limited empirical evidence, this book argues that Australians did not shadow their counterparts in the UK and New Zealand in the late 2000s. Overall, Labor's minor modifications after 2007 fit relatively well with public opinion, which supported the reversal of industrial relations legislation (but resulted in a significant increase in concern that unions have too much power) and greater spending on health and education (as indicated by a significant drop in support for more tax and more social spending). Labor only slightly modified the Liberal–National Coalition's discourse around welfare dependency and there was less concern about economic downturn, so it is not surprising that support for government responsibility for the unemployed continued to decline between 2007 and 2009, while the desire for benefit recipients to be given more work obligations remained steady. Interestingly, concern about income gaps being too large decreased significantly but support for redistribution remained steady. It is possible Australians were aware that the redistributive impact of family policy remained higher than many other countries during this period, just as it had in the long term (Joumard et al, 2012).

Conclusion: (mostly) rolled over

Chapter Two noted that neoliberalism's power as an ideological tool partially lies in its contradictory and adaptable nature. Its discourses are mostly oppositional to those framing the Keynesian welfare state but governments across all three phases of neoliberalism tapped into a normative distinction between the deserving and undeserving poor that has been long-standing in liberal welfare states. Chapter Two also indicated that early public opinion surveys found some ambivalence about social security (Coughlin, 1980; Page and Shapiro, 1992; Svallfors, 2012). This book has demonstrated that attitudes towards the unemployed hardened further as all three countries situated this group as undeserving of entitlement to social rights without meeting an increasing range of work-related conditions.

This growing convergence occurred even though New Zealand's social security reforms overall were less consistent than those of the other two countries, at least until 2010, and Australia's initial social security reforms were balanced by Labor's view that the government should still play some role in ensuring jobs. It is possible that a contributory component to the UK's unemployment assistance may explain why British support for the unemployed being ensured a decent standard of living by the government remained higher in the UK than New Zealand and Australia (see also Duffy et al, 2013). But this contributory component is rather weak and does not change the fact that public opinion in all *three* countries moved in line with neoliberal reforms to the greatest degree in the policy area where the shift from a Keynesian to neoliberal welfare state was less about old ideas being replaced by new ones and was more a practice of accretion and refashioning of existing principles around individualism and egalitarianism (Dean, 2007; Mulheirn and Masters, 2013).

Neoliberalism's power is also said to lie in its ability to change people's conception of self-interest by reducing support for social rights among those who have the most to gain from an expansive welfare state. In the case of New Zealand benefit recipients this process is incomplete, for they remained most likely to support propositions associated with the right to economic and social security and least likely to agree with ideas that reflect neoliberal welfare dependency rhetoric. However, the hardening of attitudes towards the unemployed occurred most quickly among this group over the 21 years studied, particularly during the 2000s. This suggests benefit recipients were especially receptive to Labour's 'work-first' approach framing the 'passive' welfare system as part of the problem. Although notions of self-interest were already weakening in this policy area, benefit recipient attitudes about welfare benefits making people lazy and dependent and about the unemployed working for their benefits also hardened rapidly between 2008 and 2011 as the level of conditionality they faced grew. British Labour's 'no rights without responsibilities' rhetoric similarly appeared to be internalised by the unemployed whom it targeted (Sefton, 2003, 2009; Barnes and Tomaszewki, 2010; Curtice, 2010). In the long term, such negative policy learning among benefit recipients may eventually diminish this group's ability to mobilise, as found in the United States (Soss, 1999; Mettler, 2002; Campbell, 2003).

Moreover, a unique feature of this book has been to distinguish between unemployed benefit recipients subject to forms of conditionality and other citizens who receive less conditional forms of social security. Notably, recipients of New Zealand Superannuation and the Student Allowance appear to have been particularly receptive to a strengthening of the deservingness discourse which framed them as legitimate dependents on state support but the unemployed as undeserving of such assistance. This trend was most evident under the Labour-coalition government and in regards to the idea that the government should ensure a decent standard of living for the unemployed. Such divisions among different types of social security recipients are clearly not conducive to developing a shared sense of solidarity among recipients of government income support that could potentially mobilise them against the social security reforms implemented in both New Zealand and the UK during the roll-over phase and the continuing neopaternalism found in Australia.

This book has found little evidence that New Zealand's historical myth of egalitarianism – which it shared with Australia – positively shaped attitudes towards redistribution of income and wealth (Castles, 1996). Income inequality grew faster in New Zealand than the other two countries from the mid-1980s onwards and a growing number of New Zealanders acknowledged income differences were too large by 2011. But public support for redistribution remained comparatively low and fewer New Zealanders thought income differences were too large than Britons or Australians, even if the proportion of New Zealanders believing income differences were *necessary* was similar to that reported in the UK and Australia. Once again, the process of neoliberalisation may have reshaped self-interest, in the sense that low income earners no longer necessarily favoured policies that would benefit them. Although still offering stronger agreement that income differences are too large in 2011, the proportion of low income New Zealanders who thought redistribution was the solution to this problem fell over time and particularly during the 2000s. This was the case even though low income earners are most likely to benefit from the Labour-coalition's redistributive Working for Families strategy from 2005. More low income earners than other groups also came to believe income differences are necessary between 2008 and 2011 when National's rhetoric endorsed similar ideas. However, this group's support for spending on low income assistance was far steadier, suggesting that it is the *term* 'redistribution' that has little contemporary currency. It may also matter who low income earners are comparing themselves to when thinking about income inequality in regards to such propositions (Orton and Rowlingson, 2007).

It has been further argued that, despite being concerned about income inequality and low wages, New Zealanders were unclear *how* the government might resolve these problems. This is because fundamental aspects of neoliberal economics policy have been accepted or endorsed in New Zealand, the UK and, to a lesser extent, Australia. Support for the policy levers aiming to help protect the domestic labour market – namely import and wage controls – weakened considerably under neoliberalisation. Findings suggest New Zealand's early and aggressive deregulation of the labour market, and its greater economic vulnerability following these reforms, made New Zealanders less able or willing to envision a return to Keynesian economic policies. They also became more accepting of big business dominance than their counterparts in other countries. Their views were, however, largely in line with a mild softening of key economic reforms in the 2000s, while the experience of privatisation appears to have increased support for public ownership in both New Zealand and Australia in a way not seen in the UK. Chapter Four argued that the normalising of neoliberal economics was thus significant but incomplete, particularly in Australia where economic reforms were made more incrementally and with greater consideration of their social outcomes.

Elsewhere, the public has tended to respond to perceived improvement or retrenchment in policies relating to employment, core welfare state services and tax by adjusting their levels of support. In this sense, public attitudes towards social citizenship may have diminished overall between the mid-1980s and the early 2010s but there is insufficient evidence that they have rolled over coherently and permanently in any of the three countries. Although not necessarily framed in terms of defending social rights at the time, the New Zealand public mobilised against marketisation and targeting through the union movement and local level protests. This resulted in significant policy reversals. Formal political processes were also used to send a message that many New Zealanders did not agree with the general policy direction of neoliberalism, leading to a change in New Zealand's electoral system. It is therefore troubling that more recent rounds of retrenchment have not provoked the same strength of reaction and the resistance evident clearly does not represent a form of push-back neoliberalism.

This is not surprising given support for social citizenship and the policies that institutionalised them were generally weaker among younger New Zealanders when comparing the attitudes of younger people in 1990 with those in the 21st century. My argument that the public has rolled over and accepted neoliberalisation is bolstered by the fact that, in many cases, younger New Zealanders offered lower support in the late 2000s or 2010s than the same age (<30) cohort in 1990. In particular, redistribution appeared to be less important to younger people in 2011. Spending on low income assistance garnered more support, however, suggesting that the term 'redistribution' has little resonance among younger New Zealanders. Only a significant minority also thought that the government should ensure a decent standard of living for the unemployed. In addition, while a strong majority of this group still believed that the government should ensure a decent standard of living for the elderly, younger New Zealanders reported the largest decline in support between 2008 and 2011. They may thus have been particularly susceptible to Labour's attempts to debate the age of eligibility for New Zealand superannuation. This is perhaps surprising given this entitlement's symbolic value is distant rather than proximate to young adults but political debate did, to some degree, revolve around issues of intergenerational justice (Soss and Schram, 2007; Duffy et al, 2013). The political impact is unlikely to be immediate, given the overwhelming belief that the elderly deserve government assistance, but this finding causes some concern for the future.

In other cases, however, the argument that New Zealand attitudes rolled over because young adults do not value social citizenship rights is harder to make. They still saw both trade unions and government as having a role in ensuring decent employment and wages. Younger people also appeared to have been more satisfied than older New Zealanders by the multiple tax cuts implemented between 2008 and 2011. More significantly, the PHO system was associated with an especially positive impact on younger New Zealanders' attitudes towards free healthcare in the 2000s, while the interest-free tertiary loan policy may explain this group's rapid increase in support for free education during this period. The movement in young people's support for *spending* in health and education was not outstanding but these findings suggest that having an historical reference point via personal memories of the Keynesian welfare state is not *necessary* for sustaining support for social citizenship. It is possible that young people view themselves more as 'consumers' than 'citizens' in this context but expectations of the welfare state remained high. As such, the New Zealand findings are more ambiguous than those reported in the UK, where there is said to be a growing divide between older and younger Britons associated with either the experience of growing up under Thatcherism in the 1980s and 1990s or a long-term decline in support for the welfare state that increasingly falls short of their rising expectations (Sefton, 2003; Hall, 2012; Duffy et al, 2013).

Evidence that public attitudes rolled over, however, is more apparent when we consider attitudinal trends among New Zealanders positioning themselves on the Left, who have traditionally supported policies and principles associated with social citizenship, and the Centre voters who often shape election results. Notably, a long-standing ideological divide on the issue of social security narrowed because the Left were the only group to offer *less* support for the government ensuring a decent standard of living for the unemployed across 21 years, even if the Left remained twice as likely to agree as the Right in 2011. The biggest fall in Left support for this proposition occurred during the 2000s, helping to explain the lack of resistance to the Labour-coalition government's regressive reforms of social security in the 2000s and suggesting that what being 'Left' means has changed among the public as well as within the Labour Party. I have argued that the extent of the Labour-coalition's hardening in social security policy may have been blurred by its initial softening of conditionality and its rhetoric of social inclusion. Given that attitudes towards the unemployed also hardened significantly among the ideological Centre, however, there was clearly no electoral need for Labour to promote the right to economic and social security for this group.

This was not the case in other areas of social policy. When it comes to the principles of free healthcare, free education and a decent standard of living for the elderly, ideological differences not only remained but there appears to be greater consensus about their value across the ideological spectrum. Only support for free health declined faster among the Left than other groups, while the same was true among the Centre for free education. However, strong support for increased spending in these areas and for superannuation suggests these issues remained electorally important.

Support for redistribution has also traditionally been associated with the Left and this group continued to offer the highest levels of support for related propositions across the ideological spectrum. However, agreement with both redistribution and spending on low income earners fell fastest among the Left, particularly from the 2000s onwards. This group may have recognised that Working for Families assisted low income earners, but the Left appear to have responded to the Labour-coalition's reluctance to frame it as redistributive by viewing redistribution as less important than in the past. The Left's desire for tax cuts, however, did weaken after Working for Families was introduced and few of this group desired reduced tax by the time multiple tax cuts had been implemented in 2008–2011. That around a third of the Centre still supported reduced tax by 2011 and they more quickly came to agree that income gaps are needed for New Zealand's prosperity than other New Zealanders nonetheless suggests that tax may well return as an electoral issue in the future.

In regards to economic policy, the Left has traditionally been associated with working class issues of wages and employment conditions and support for the trade union movement. This is still true; notably, the Left were the only group for whom the Employment Contracts Act did not appear to provoke increased agreement that trade unions have too much power and its belief that trade unions are necessary remained fairly steady. In 2011, moderately fewer of the Left agreed that the government should provide jobs than in 1990 but support for both import and wage controls had declined significantly. This suggests that the Left was increasingly reluctant to see the government as responsible for employment but still saw a role for trade unions advocating for workers' rights. This is surprising given many advances for workers have come through government policy rather than industrial relations negotiations in recent years.

Left concern about big business having too much power did decline over 21 years but its level of support remained the highest in 2011 and strong Left support for public ownership of key assets also persisted.

In sum, ideological differences regarding social citizenship narrowed across the 21-year period studied. This finding is in line with British empirical evidence that Labour's own supporters reported the biggest swing to the Right from the mid-1990s, narrowing the gap between their opinions and those of Conservative supporters, particularly regarding the unemployed. It also supports arguments that shifts in Labour Party policy have acted as a weathervane for attitudes for its supporters. But it is important to note that the narrowing of ideological gaps in New Zealand was not always because the Left hardened its views; sometimes Right attitudes softened and opinion on many issues fluctuated, particularly among those at the Centre. Ideological gaps also *widened* for a few propositions: trade unions are necessary to protect workers; reduced taxes to solve New Zealand's economic problems; free education; and differences in income in New Zealand are too large. Chapter One further noted how the ideological preferences of New Zealand Election Study respondents fluctuated over time, just as views about social citizenship do. This does not necessarily challenge the claim that the Labour Party's accommodation of neoliberal values changed what it means to be Left. But only in regards to social security is there any overwhelming evidence that this shift occurred.

Importantly, although understandings of self-interest may be changing among benefit recipients, low income earners and the Left and younger New Zealanders may not support key aspects of social citizenship as much as they did in the early 1990s, these groups have not simply been 'brainwashed' by the process of neoliberalisation. Not only have attitudes shifted in some policy areas more than others, but in many cases there is evidence of a policy mood that tends to shift over time in response to the direction of government policy. This occurs both within sub-groups and across the New Zealand population. Moreover, New Zealanders may have chosen to elect neoliberal governments, but they also demanded a greater focus on social policy from them and endorsed an MMP representation system that provides space for traditional Left views to continue to be articulated and sometimes implemented through smaller political parties. Expectations of the state also remain strong. Similar to Dean and Melrose's (1999) British findings, the New Zealand participants in the qualitative study commonly drew upon contractarian perspectives prioritising an individualistic conception of the social order, whereby some individual freedoms are given up for a measure of protection against the predations and irresponsibilities of others. But this represented 'a contract that is quite full and substantive, not rather empty and minimalist' (Dean and Melrose, 1999, p 129) and in New Zealand included continuing support for health, education, wage regulation and nationalisation. This was articulated through solidaristic repertoires offering an altruistic, collectivist view of the social order where risk is pooled to provide security against external threats.

Together these kinds of 'resistances, refusals, and blockages' contribute to the 'grit' that Clarke (2004: 44) believes challenges the 'Big Story' of global neoliberalisation. They indicate the value of social citizenship advocates promoting progressive policy options that actively seek to encourage greater public support for social citizenship, creating the kind of electoral pressure that could destabilise neoliberalism in the future. It is to this task of advancing social citizenship that the book now turns.

Understanding the past to change the future

The hybrid policy configuration that has emerged over the past three decades represents neoliberalism's failure to *completely* transform the welfare state along market and individualist lines. The welfare state may have survived, but Taylor-Gooby (2008, 2012, 2013) nonetheless believes that recent policy trends undermine the values essential for continuing political support for social citizenship. He identifies three conditions required to advance the welfare state: generous and inclusive provision, leading to a focus on collective rather than individual perspectives in future policy; effectiveness, in terms of delivering the outcomes desired; and feasibility, ensuring the electoral support needed for sustainability. At present, he believes meeting any two of these conditions precludes the third, creating a welfare state trilemma hindering progressive reform. Taylor-Gooby (2012) thus promotes a multi-pronged progressive strategy seeking to shift public discourse in a more supportive direction. Taking his lead, I now use the book's findings about the relationship between policy and public attitudes to assess proposals for galvanising support for social citizenship in New Zealand and beyond.

Challenging the deserving/undeserving dichotomy

The first priority must be to challenge the dominant neoliberal discourses (individual responsibility, welfare dependency and making work pay) that have enhanced the historical dichotomy between the deserving and undeserving, not only between taxpayers and benefit recipients, but also between benefit recipients and those receiving other forms of income assistance (Clarke, 2004). These binaries encourage a sense of distrust between different types of citizens and in the social security system's ability to accurately target those in need. They also raise questions as to whether citizens will have their own needs met when they are vulnerable and that services will work efficiently when needed (Taylor-Gooby, 2008, 2012).

Contributory social insurance schemes have been advocated as one way to strengthen the link between the contributions and obligations of citizens and reduce the stigmatisation of those receiving assistance (Horton and Gregory, 2009; Taylor-Gooby, 2012; Mulheirn and Masters, 2013). Chapter Two highlighted research evidence suggesting this might be true in some cases. It was also noted that attitudes towards the government ensuring a decent standard of living for the unemployed were softer in the UK, where unemployment assistance partly based on a contributory scheme already exists, than in New Zealand and Australia where unemployment benefits are funded through general taxation. But other British attitudes regarding social security have hardened nonetheless; this is not surprising, given social insurance programmes usually have a second-tier system for those unable to contribute that maintains the deserving/undeserving dichotomy. New Zealand also has little institutional history with contributory programmes.

In that the qualitative data identified how New Zealanders may conceive the social security system to be a problem because they are aware that it stigmatises benefit recipients, it may be more useful to encourage a belief that social security has a *positive* impact on the lives of benefit recipients by explicitly articulating the contributions they make to society in return for the right to economic and social security (Roche, 1992; Johansson and Hvinden, 2005). In this context, Horton and Gregory (2009) promote making working-age benefit entitlements conditional on social participation, with sanctions for those who refuse to engage in activities that make a social contribution. They wish to reinforce reciprocal relationships by refocusing conditionality away from participation in paid work, which promotes moralistic divisions and individual interest. The qualitative data suggested that New Zealand support for work obligations may be partially driven by an interest in benefit recipients contributing to the 'public good', with some believing caring obligations would meet this criterion. Such a proposal, however, focuses only on benefit recipients, thus reinforcing the idea that this group's citizenship rights are more conditional than those of other citizens (Handler, 2004). It would also be difficult to ensure that the participation activities required of benefit recipients are realistically understood by most people as making a social contribution (Horton and Gregory, 2009; Taylor-Gooby, 2012).

Such contributions would certainly need to go well beyond the new 'social obligations' introduced by the New Zealand National government in 2013, which require benefit recipients to search and prepare for work and enrol their children in early childhood education and in primary healthcare (Wynd, 2013). Ben-Ishai (2012) argues that we should reorient the individualism of neoliberalism, reconceiving social citizenship as a status that grants individuals not only the right to freedom from material constraints on autonomy (defined in terms of the capacity to live one's life according to one's own plans), but also the right to access services and resources needed to foster and develop the capacity to act autonomously. She finds that the obligations required under 'workfare' do not fulfil this promise but highlights promising North American service delivery case studies which do.

The National government chose to focus its 2013 obligations squarely on the undeserving unemployed because its consultation on the 1998 Code of Social and Family Responsibility demonstrated that proposing similar obligations for *all* citizens could cause public resistance. This 'grit', to use Clarke's (2004) term, could be capitalised upon by encouraging debate about what members of the *public* believe their responsibilities to be. Chapter Five highlighted how the participants in the qualitative study talked about both individual and community responsibilities in ways that challenged neoliberal discourses. Chapter Four further noted an interest in greater corporate responsibility; a significant increase in support for public ownership of key assets may also be associated with the perception that multinational corporations do not take responsibility for maintaining jobs in New Zealand. Although not explicitly discussed by participants, environmental responsibilities should be part of the discussion because they resonate strongly with many people (particularly the young) and because environmental pressures place real constraints on the extension of social citizenship rights (Roche, 1992; Gough, 2012).

Roche (1992) certainly stresses that debate about citizen responsibilities must consider intergenerational obligations. Marshall's (2000) view of social citizenship focused on the contemporary generation but the future of the welfare state relies on present generations recognising and accepting new social duties that allow future generations to make social rights claims, even when there is little likelihood of compensation or reciprocation by rights claims against future generations. The Labour-coalition government's New Zealand Superannuation Fund, which ring-fenced budget surpluses to ensure the future funding of universal superannuation, is a policy of this order but it lacked an effective communicative discourse explaining how it aimed to ensure pensions for the future generation. There was thus little public outcry when National paused payments into the fund from 2008. Despite the overwhelming belief that the government should ensure a decent standard of living for the elderly, only less than half of New Zealanders supported increasing the eligibility age for New Zealand Superannuation in 2011. This suggests that there is limited understanding or acceptance of these intergenerational responsibilities in New Zealand.

Greater universalism would also challenge the deserving/undeserving dichotomy. Removing limits to the number of hours that parents must work before receiving New Zealand's Working for Families In-Work Tax Credit, for instance, would break down the distinction between benefit recipients and workers when receiving family assistance (St John and Rankin, 2009). Both the Labour and Green parties have indicated they will address this current discrimination if they form a government in 2014 (Green Party, 2013; King, 2013). Labour's need to distinguish itself from National, which became extremely difficult as the roll-over phase of neoliberalism incorporated many aspects of Third Way politics, may thus open the way for a potential advance of social citizenship. Lobby groups will need to ensure this issue stays on the agenda but Chapter Four found some covariance between increased support for wage controls and the announcement of Working for Families. This suggests at least some New Zealanders believe government intervention of this type is appropriate; it just remains to convince them that this is the case for all families with children, regardless of their income source, and then vote accordingly. The Expert Advisory Group for Solutions on Child Poverty's (2012) recommendation that New Zealand adopt a universal child benefit for children under six, with targeted payments for older children, could support this argument by increasing the proximity and visibility of child assistance among New Zealanders. The recommendation has been endorsed by the Green Party (2013) and history suggests that small steps towards advancing social citizenship may not necessarily be the last ones; improvements in healthcare affordability and accessibility started with increased government subsidies for children under six in 1996 but the Labour-coalition government's desire to stay in power saw these eventually benefit all age groups through the PHO system.

In the longer term, St John and Rankin (2009) promote both refundable and non-refundable tax credits that would flatten and simplify the tax scale without having to raise top tax marginal rates, which may not be politically viable in the long term, given the fluctuating nature of attitudes towards reduced tax (particularly among the ideological Centre). Proposals for a universal basic income ensuring that no one falls below a minimum level of income, whether they engage in paid work or other forms of participation, would go even further to remove distinctions between the deserving and undeserving. Treating every individual as having the same unconditional right would reframe citizenship as a status not a contract and encourage a sense that everyone shares the same social risks (van Parijs, 1992; Goldsmith 1997; Rankin 1997; Handler, 2004). However, a 2011 universal basic income proposal by a well-known businessman and former government economist failed to ignite interest during the election (Morgan and Guthrie, 2011). As Rankin (1997) suggests, many New Zealanders may not conceive income taxes and benefits as part of the same fiscal system. Growing support for wage controls, which I believe are misinterpreted in terms of tax credits, suggests some interest in government intervention but the New Zealand public need to be given clear examples of which types of intervention will make a difference in the 21st century.

Building greater reciprocity

The title of Handler and Hasenfeld's (2006) North American book *Blame welfare, ignore poverty and inequality* accurately describes the political situation in New Zealand. A hardening of attitudes towards the unemployed has been accompanied by a reluctance to support redistribution, which is not surprising given that neoliberal governments have avoided using this term while strategically using tax cuts and credits to appease public concerns about low wages. Working for Families – New Zealand's most visible and proximate redistributive programme across all three phases of neoliberalism – had no obvious effect on attitudes towards redistribution or spending on low income earners, nor did it radically diminish the desire for tax cuts. This may be because New Zealanders recognised that it was unlikely significantly to reduce income inequality and poverty in the long term. But the Labour-coalition also failed to name it as a redistributive policy and instead used it to distinguish between the deserving and undeserving.

This is problematic because Taylor-Gooby (2008) contends that, in addition to trust and social inclusion, the welfare state relies on citizens valuing both horizontal redistribution (between groups at differing life stages) and vertical redistribution (between the rich and poor). Income inequality is thought to discourage the solidarity needed to sustain social citizenship rights by creating social distance between those able to meet their own needs privately and the poor, who are increasingly distrustful of governments that allow income gaps to grow (Orton and Rowlingson, 2007). British research thus identifies the need to find new ways of talking about the negative outcomes of neoliberalisation; the word 'poverty', for instance, provokes images of starving children far-distant geographical or historical locations, and absolute rather than relative poverty (Castell and Thompson, 2007; Orton and Rowlingson, 2007). But, given that New Zealanders are still concerned with decent jobs and wages, yet offer weaker support for redistribution and more spending on low income workers, a focus on *pre*distribution may be even more useful in harnessing support for social citizenship (Taylor-Gooby, 2012).

Predistribution was a key arm of the Keynesian welfare state, enabled through tripartite negotiations ensuring decent wages across New Zealand and Australia and in many British industries. Legislative interventions to set minimum wages continue in this tradition, although recent 'living wage' campaigns suggest these are insufficient to ensure a decent living standard for many workers. More controversial, but potentially more effective, measures to curb wages at the top income levels through to remuneration system and maximum wage legislation reform could also be implemented (Handler, 2004; Taylor-Gooby, 2012, 2013). Taylor-Gooby (2012) argues that predistribution would deal with inequality at its source and thus lessen the need for redistribution but risks failing to strengthen inclusivity and solidarity between those in secure work and those in less stable jobs. He believes it may also encounter electoral and public opinion obstacles if seen to strengthen sectional interests. This could include trade unions interests, however, a clear majority of New Zealanders still believe unions are necessary to protect workers and the backlash against WorkChoices in Australia shows unions can still mobilise the public against regressive legislation threatening the opportunity for unions to negotiate predistributive measures.

Redistribution and predistribution are central to ensuring a sense of reciprocity among citizens but less traditional means should not be overlooked. Chapter Five noted how participants in the qualitative study who were from Māori and Pasifika backgrounds resisted or reinterpreted a neoliberal individual responsibility discourse because they could not understand responsibility outside a collectivist framework. Reciprocity is a significant value underpinning the social orders of both Māori and Pasifika communities and, given that they together make up almost a quarter of the New Zealand population and Māori have a special relationship with the state as indigenous peoples, this value is slowly beginning to be reflected in policy. The Whānau Ora approach to social service delivery introduced in 2010, for instance, builds upon Māori collective notions of reciprocity and interdependence at the level of the extended family to improve the effectiveness of state-led social services (Humpage, 2012). It thus explicitly focuses on how citizens relate to *each other*, rather than simply their rights or obligations as individuals. Such a conceptualisation of reciprocity may sit uncomfortably with traditional, state-focused understandings of social citizenship and does pose some risks but may be part of a broader New Zealand strategy to ensure the sustainability of social citizenship by helping it 'make sense' to an ethnically diverse population.

Growing trust through universalism and devolution

Chapter Two highlighted research evidence suggesting that the public tend to support universal social programmes more than targeted ones because they are visible and proximate to a wider range of citizens. The findings in this book are more mixed. Support for government responsibility for ensuring a decent standard of living for the elderly remained extremely high over the three phases of neoliberalism in New Zealand, the only country of the three studied to offer universal superannuation, but this was also the case in the UK and Australia where mandatory earnings-related superannuation schemes are supplemented by state means-tested pensions and, in the UK, a low flat-rate national insurance pension. This tells us something about the long-standing normative framing of the elderly. Universalism *did* appear to make a difference when it comes to healthcare. British support for government responsibility for ensuring healthcare for the sick was consistently higher than that in Australia, where the same question was asked, suggesting the higher level of universalism embodied by the British NHS compared to Australian Medicare had an impact upon attitudes. Moreover, New Zealand's PHO system, which increased fee subsidies and improved access to primary healthcare, also appears to have had a positive impact on public attitudes towards free healthcare.

It is important, however, that support for free healthcare grew even though most primary healthcare services are no longer delivered by state-level bureaucracies but have been decentralised to a wide range of private practitioners and community organisations. Public support for core welfare state services tended to be lower in Australia, where there is a long tradition of churches, charitable organisations and informal support systems playing a significant role in service provision, in comparison to New Zealand and the UK where this was less the case (Davey, 2001; Wright et al, 2011). This suggests that decentralised service provision may reduce the visibility and traceability of government responsibilities regarding social citizenship. Nonetheless, one way to counter criticisms that universalism represents a return to the one-size-fits-all bureaucratic model of the post-war era is to stress that particularism can be accommodated through the devolution of funding to service providers catering to the specific needs of diverse groups of citizens. UMR Research (2009) found the general drivers of trust in New Zealand public services to be related to service experiences meeting expectations and staff being competent, keeping their promises and treating people fairly but Māori, Asian and Pacific People respondents particularly stressed the need for cultural sensitivity and for services that do not make people feel ashamed if they do not have the right information. Arguably, group-specific services are most likely to meet these needs and thus enhance trust in core welfare services.

In a decentralised context, citizens have been reframed as individual consumers abstracted from other social roles and positions. However, Chapter Six highlighted that the adoption of a consumer orientation by the participants in the qualitative study was uneven and often instrumentalist, with overwhelming support for compulsory education and emergency health services accompanying a common belief that user-pays was more appropriate (or fiscally necessary) in tertiary education and primary health care. Consumer rights have also provided a new means for empowering individual citizens in their encounters with public bureaucracies (Harris, 1999; Clarke, 2004; Clarke and Newman, 2006; Bode, 2008). Chapter Five noted how the consumer rights rhetoric evident in government departments encouraged some of the participants to believe that New Zealanders have *more* rights than responsibilities when compared with the past, even though this is clearly *not* the case in social security. This interpretation is troubling because consumer rights are far narrower than those related to one's status as a citizen but they *do* keep the language of rights and entitlement in the frame and situate individuals as *active* rather than passive agents. Taylor-Gooby (2008, 2012) acknowledges real limits in how far a sense of inclusion and participation can be promoted this way but also believes greater user engagement could help make services more responsive and thus build the public trust necessary for welfare states to function and maintain popular support.

Moving beyond state-centred social citizenship

This book has focused on the important role that government policy plays in articulating and institutionalising social rights. Despite fears that globalisation has diminished state power, the financial crisis highlighted that the nation-state remains the key site for policy-making (Callinicos, 2010; Gough, 2012). But Dean (2013) argues that a post-Marshallian concept of social citizenship must go *beyond* the state and be constituted in a variety of modes and across multiple sites. At the sub-national level, public concerns about and claims to social citizenship could be articulated and developed through experimental local social rights councils, which engage with governments and social service providers on behalf of local populations. Citizens' assemblies that promote informed, robustly-debated policy choices by citizens may also be ideally suited to New Zealand's small population and geographical size, which encourage a sense of intimacy and access in politics (Hayward, 2012). Dean (2013) further supports grass-roots movements (such as *Occupy*) that use new social media to promote the needs of marginalised social groups on a global stage. Such movements are increasingly important given that Crouch (2011) questions whether political parties and mainstream media are still 'fit for purpose' to act as intermediaries between public and political elites when both are dominated by the corporate interests whom neoliberalism benefits the most.

Social citizenship must also account for the fact that the state is no longer the sole provider of protection against risks in the 21st century (Harris, 1999; Johansson and Hvinden, 2005). Marshall (2000) originally conceived social citizenship as a status tied to the nation-state and this book has necessarily concentrated on attitudes and policies at the level of the nation-state, given that it is the jurisdiction where most policy relating to social citizenship is made and implemented. However, it has identified a high level of coherence in both the process of neoliberalisation and its impact upon attitudes across the three countries studied. The speed that financial instability then recession spread across the world certainly shows how integrated the global economy has become (Callinicos, 2010), while global environmental problems place real constraints upon economic growth and the future implementation of social rights (Harvey, 2010; Gough, 2012). These facts support an argument that social citizenship should be reframed as an issue of *global* dimensions (Roche, 1992; Johansson and Hvinden, 2005; Dean, 2013). Dean (2013) provides two useful instances whereby social citizenship can be advanced at a global level. First, concerted pressure could be placed upon the United Nations for the development of an international social security system. This is important because while social rights remain subordinate to other kinds of citizenship rights, and there is no distinctive forum for their expression or realisation, their creation or development depends upon the political process (Dean and Melrose, 1999).

Second, Dean (2013) believes global advocacy movements can promote social citizenship through the worldwide extension of basic income schemes, the reduction of working hours, the defence of public services and new forms of progressive taxation to fund poverty relief. Neoliberalisation is characterised by 'fast-policy' transfer, whereby policy ideas spread quickly across national boundaries. Peck et al (2012, p 284) ask: 'Is it possible to appropriate the circulatory systems of the fast-policy regime for alternative ends?' to systematically and strategically disseminate *progressive* forms of best practice. International bodies such as the Organisation for Economic Co-operation and Development and the World Bank have used country comparisons across a range of key economic indicators to convince nation-states to adopt and extend a neoliberal agenda (Craig and Porter, 2006). Analyses illustrating 'the paradox of redistribution' (that is, highly targeted welfare systems produce greater levels of poverty than universal ones) are a further example of how social citizenship advocates can use the extensive international social data available to challenge this same agenda (Korpi and Palme, 1998; Harrop, 2012). The trickier task is to convince both the public and political elites that poverty and inequality should be prioritised above economic growth but alongside environmental sustainability (Gough, 2012). We need to use what we know about public opinion to do so.

Conclusion: social citizenship in the context of neoliberalism

There is considerable coherence in the neoliberal project, its shifting nature and the way it has shaped public attitudes. The evidence presented in this book indicates that the public have rolled over and accepted key neoliberal tenets, highlighting the urgent need to disrupt and destabilise neoliberalism. Yet, while neoliberalism clearly does *matter*, its varied impact across time and space makes it difficult to argue that it has become an omnipotent 'common sense of the times' among the general public since the 1980s. Just as public opinion pioneers found, public attitudes remain complex rather than straightforward. Attitudes towards social security and, to a lesser extent, redistribution *have* progressively hardened but others have fluctuated depending on government activity, economic conditions, the proximity and visibility of policies and, importantly, alternative public discourses. If attitudes are not set in stone, then it is still possible to strive to galvanise support for the welfare state and rework social citizenship to protect citizens from the life risks they face in the 21st century.

Note

[1] Here 'liberal' is again used in the North American sense, meaning a progressive politics on the Left.

Appendix

This book analyses data from a range of different studies. The main ones include:

The New Zealand Election Study (NZES), a survey monitoring the democratic process in New Zealand. Since 1990, over 2000 respondents take part in each three-yearly nationwide survey. Data (including panel data in many years) are primarily collected using questionnaires which are posted to randomly-selected registered electors immediately following each election. In some years (1999 and 2002) telephone interviews were used addition to mailed questionnaires; in 2005 and 2011, some respondents completed the survey online. Given that New Zealand has compulsory voter registration, the sample is reasonably representative of the general population but oversampling has been undertaken for Māori every year since 1996 and young people in 2011. For more details about specific surveys: http://www.nzes.org/

The New Zealand Values Study (NZVS) is a nationwide, representative survey conducted as part of the World Values Survey programme which aims to capture the political and social attitudes and values of different populations. The New Zealand surveys have not been identical in format or methodology but systematically draw a sample from the electoral roll. This book utilises data from 1989 (N=1000, face-to-face interviews), 1993 (N=1272, postal questionnaire replicated in the International Social Survey Programme), 1998 (N=1201, postal questionnaire) and 2004 (N=954, postal questionnaire). A telephone survey was also conducted in 2004 (see Rose et al, 2005) but because this methodology is less comparable with the previous surveys, this book largely relies on unweighted, unpublished data from the postal survey kindly provided by Paul Perry. Note that the data was relatively representative in each year but over-sampling for Maori and selected low average household income meshblocks was conducted in 1998. More information about the World Values Survey is found at: http://www.worldvaluessurvey.org/

The International Social Survey Programme (ISSP) involves an annual survey of selected economic and social policy issues across 40 countries. The same questionnaire is used in every country but different modules are chosen each year in roughly seven year cycle. In

New Zealand, this administered through a nationwide postal survey drawing from the electoral roll. This book draws upon the 'Role of Government' module in 1997 (N=1206) and 2006 (N=1200) and the 'Social Inequality in New Zealand' module in 1999 (N=1118) and 2009 (N=935). The samples for each were reasonably representative but high income earners were still over-represented in the 2009 survey even after weighting. More information is found at: http://www.issp.org/

The New Zealand Attitudes and Values Survey (NZAVS) was commissioned by the Royal Commission on Social Policy to determine, amongst other things, the public's social policy preferences and the values underlying these preferences. It was conducted by the Department of Statistics in 1987 using a sub-sample of the Household Labour Force Survey to ensure high inclusion of sub-groups. The survey involved 3000 New Zealanders, with oversampling for Maori and benefit recipients. Notably, 47% of the sample said they received a Department of Social Welfare benefit or allowance in the 12 months preceding the survey, including the Family Benefit and New Zealand Superannuation. Detailed survey results are found in the first volume of the Royal Commission of Social Policy (1998a).

The Conditional and Contingent? New Zealand Social Citizenship in the Context of Neoliberalism study ('the qualitative study') was conducted by the present author in 2007 and 2008 to investigate contemporary public beliefs about social citizenship in New Zealand. 37 interviews and nine focus groups were undertaken with a total of 87 different New Zealand citizens aged 18 years or older in the Auckland and Christchurch regions. Participants were purposively selected based on income source, income level, gender, ethnicity and age. In the final sample, females and low-income earners were over-represented. A report offering more details about the methodology and findings is found at: http://www.artsfaculty.auckland.ac.nz/images/cms/files/Final%20Summary%20SC%20Report%20WEB%20identical%20copy%5B1%5D.pdf

The British Social Attitudes Survey (BSA Survey) has been conducted each year since 1983 to track changing social, political and moral attitudes in the UK. Over 3000 respondents take part each year having been selected via random probability sampling. This ensures the sample is representative of the British population. Respondents are interviewed in their homes using a standardised questionnaire. For more information: http://www.britsocat.com/ or http://www.natcen. ac.uk/our-research/research/british-social-attitudes/

The British Election Study (BES) is a large survey conducted at every general election since 1964 that investigates attitudes towards government and policy along with party choice, turnout, political participation and campaign dynamics. A combination of in-person/ CAPI, postal and internet surveys have been used but the main national probability survey of electors is conducted by face-to-face interview both before and after the election takes place. The most recent study in 2010 has a sample size of N=7569. More information is found at: http://www.essex.ac.uk/bes/ or http://www.besis.org/

The Australian Survey of Social Attitudes (AuSSA) is a biennial survey studying the social attitudes and behaviour of Australian citizens that began in 2003. It provides cross-sectional data based on a core questionnaire supplemented by changing modules driven by the needs of the social research community, including those from the International Social Survey Programme. Over 4000 Australians complete a postal questionnaire, having been selected using systematic random sampling from the electoral roll. More information is found at: http://aussa.anu.edu.au/index.php or http://www.ada.edu.au/social-science/browse/major-studies/australian-survey-of-social-attitudes

The Australian Election Study (AES) began in 1987 and explores political attitudes and behaviour in the Australian electorate at the time of the Australian Federal Election. This is largely based on a postal questionnaire but some surveys were completed by telephone or online in 2010. Stratified systematic random samples of at least 2000 respondents are based on the Commonwealth electoral roll. For more information: http://aes.anu.edu.au/ or http://www.ada.edu.au/social-science/browse/politics-and-elections/australian-election-study

References

Achterberg, P. and Raven, J. (2012) 'Individualisation: A double-edged sword: Does individualisation undermine welfare state support?', in R. van der Veen, M. Yerkes and P. Achterberg (eds) *The transformation of solidarity: Changing risks and the future of the welfare state*, Amsterdam: Amsterdam University Press, pp 49–68.

Adcock, C. (1981) 'Unemployment', *National Business Review,* 16 November, p 7.

Aimer, P. and Miller, R. (2002) 'New Zealand politics in the 1990s', in J. Vowles, P. Aimer, J. Karp, S. Banducci, R. Miller and A. Sullivan (eds) *Proportional representation on trial: The 1999 New Zealand general election and the fate of MMP*, Auckland: Auckland University Press, pp 1–15.

Alcock, P. and Craig, G. (2001) 'The United Kingdom: Rolling back the welfare state?', in P. Alcock and G. Craig (eds), *International social policy: Welfare regimes in the developed world*, Houndmills: Palgrave, pp 124–42.

Appelbaum, L. (2001) 'The influence of perceived deservingness on policy decisions regarding aid to the poor', *Political Psychology,* vol 22, no 3, pp 419–42.

Appleby, J. and Lee, L. (2012) 'Health care in Britain: Is there a problem and what needs to change?' in A. Park, E. Clery, J. Curtice, M. Phillips and D. Utting (eds) *British social attitudes: The 29th report,* London: Natcen Social Research, pp 80–98.

Appleby, J. and Phillips, M. (2009) 'The NHS: Satisfied now?', in A. Park, J. Curtice, K. Thomson, M. Phillips and E. Clery (eds) *British social attitudes: The 25th report,* London: Sage, pp 25–54.

Armstrong, J. (1999) 'Clark seeks votes of struggling middle NZ', *New Zealand Herald,* 8 November, p 1.

Arnold, D. (1990) *The logic of congressional action,* New Haven: Yale University Press.

Ashton, T. (1999) 'The health reforms: To market and back?', in J. Boston, P. Dalziel and S. St John (eds) *Redesigning the welfare state in New Zealand: Problems, policies, prospects,* Auckland: Oxford University Press, pp 134–53.

Barabas, J. (2009) 'Not the next IRA: How health savings accounts shape public opinion', *Journal of Health Politics, Policy and Law,* vol 34, no 2, pp 181–217.

Barnes, M. and Tomaszewski, W. (2010) 'Lone parents and benefits: An obligation to look for work?', in A. Park, J. Curtice, K. Thomson, M. Phillips, E. Clery and S. Butt (eds) *British social attitudes: The 26th report*, London: Sage, pp 193–216.

Barron, J. (2011) 'Election 2011: Party policies', *Interest.co.nz*, 24 July, http://www.interest.co.nz/news/54333/election-2011-party-policies-industrial-relations

Bartle, J., Dellepiane-Avellaneda, S. and Stimson, J. (2011) 'The moving centre: Preferences for government activity in Britain, 1950–2005', *British Journal of Political Science*, vol 41, no 2, pp 259–85.

Bauman, Z. (2001) *The individualized society*, Cambridge: Polity Press.

Bean, C. and Papadakis, E. (1998) 'A comparison of mass attitudes towards the welfare state in different institutional regimes, 1985–1990', *International Journal of Public Opinion Research*, vol 10, no 3, pp 211–36.

Beck, U. (1992) *Risk society: Towards a new modernity*, London: Sage.

Beck, U. (2000) *What is globalization?* Cambridge: Polity Press.

Beck, U. and Beck-Gernsheim, E. (2001) *Individualization: Institutionalized individualism and its social and political consequences*, London: Sage.

Ben-Ishai, E. (2012) *Fostering autonomy: A theory of citizenship, the state, and social service delivery*, University Park: Pennsylvania State University Press.

Bennett, A. (2013) 'Resounding vote against asset sales in referendum', *New Zealand Herald*, 13 December, http://www.nzherald.co.nz/nz/news/article.cfm?c_id=1&objectid=11172228.

Benson-Pope, D. (2006) 'Working New Zealand: Rollout of upfront work-focused services to all Work and Income service and contact centres', Paper to the Cabinet Policy Committee, Wellington, 26 October.

Beveridge, W. (1942) *Report of the Inter-Departmental Committee on Social Insurance and Allied Services*, London: His Majesty's Stationery Office.

Blair, T. (1996) 'Leader's speech', Labour Party Conference, Blackpool, http://www.britishpoliticalspeech.org/speech-archive.htm?speech=202.

Blekesaune, M. and Quadagno, J. (2003) 'Public attitudes towards welfare state policies: A comparative analysis of 24 nations', *European Sociological Review*, vol 19, no 5, pp 415–27.

Blumenfeld, S. (2010) 'Collective bargaining', in E. Rasmussen (ed) *Employment relationships: Workers, unions and employers in New Zealand*, Auckland: Auckland University Press, pp 40–55.

Blyth, M. (2002) *Great transformations: Economic ideas and institutional change in the twentieth century*, Cambridge: Cambridge University Press.

Bode, I. (2008) 'Social citizenship in post-liberal Britain and post-corporatist Germany: Curtailed, fragmented, streamlined, but still on the agenda', in T. Maltby, P. Kennett and K. Rummery (eds) *Social policy review 20: Analysis and debate in social policy, 2008,* Bristol: The Policy Press, pp 191–212.

Boston, J. (1999a) 'New Zealand's welfare state in transition', in J. Boston, P. Dalziel and S. St John (eds) *Redesigning the welfare state in New Zealand: Problems, policies, prospects*, Auckland: Oxford University Press, pp 3–19.

Boston, J. (1999b) 'The funding of tertiary education; Enduring issues and dilemmas', in J. Boston, P. Dalziel and S. St John (eds) *Redesigning the welfare state in New Zealand: Problems, policies, prospects*, Auckland: Oxford University Press, pp 197–217.

Boston, J., Levine, S., McLeay, E. and Roberts, N. (1996) *New Zealand under MMP: A new politics?,* Auckland: Auckland University Press/ Bridget Williams Books.

Boston, J. and McLeay, E. (1997) 'Forming the first MMP government: Theory, practice and prospects', in J. Boston, S. Levine, E. McLeay and N. Roberts (eds) *From campaign to coalition: The 1996 election*, Palmerston North: Dunmore Press, pp 207–46.

Boston, J. and St John, S. (1999) 'Targeting versus universality: Social assistance for all or just for the poor?', in J. Boston, P. Dalziel and S. St John (eds) *Redesigning the welfare state in New Zealand: Problems, policies, prospects*, Auckland: Oxford University Press, pp 93–113.

Bottomore, T. (1992) 'Citizenship and social class, forty years on', in T. H. Marshall and T. Bottomore (eds) *Citizenship and social class*, London: Pluto Press, pp 55–93.

Bourdieu, P. (1998) *Acts of resistance*, Cambridge: Polity Press.

Bourdieu, P. and Wacquant, L. (2001) 'NewLiberalSpeak: Notes on the new planetary vulgate', *Radical Philosophy,* vol 105, January/ February, pp 2–5.

Brand, U. and Sekler, N. (2009) 'Postneoliberalism: Catch-all word or valuable analytical and political concept? Aims of a beginning debate', *Development Dialogue,* vol 51, January, pp 5–13.

Brennan, M. (2005) 'Education under Howard: Divisive, politicised and quick-fix', in C. Aulich and R. Wettenhall (eds) *Howard's second and third governments*, Sydney: University of New South Wales, pp 117–34.

Brenner, N., Peck, J. and Theodore, N. (2010) 'Variegated neoliberalization: Geographies, modalities, pathways', *Global Networks,* vol 10, no 2, pp 182–222.

Brenner, N. and Theodore, N. (2002) 'Cities and the geographies of "actually existing neoliberalism"', *Antipode,* vol 34, no 3, pp 349–79.

Brooks, C. and Manza, J. (2007) *Why welfare states persist: The importance of public opinion in democracies,* Chicago: University of Chicago Press.

Bryson, L. (2001) *Australia: The transformation of the wage-earners' welfare state,* Houndmills: Palgrave.

Burchardt, T. and Propper, C. (1999) 'Does the UK have a private welfare class?', *Journal of Social Policy,* vol 28, no 4, pp 643–65.

Burstein, P. (2010) 'Public opinion, public policy and democracy', in K. Liecht and C. Jenkins (eds) *Handbook of politics: State and society in global perspective,* New York: Springer, pp 63–79.

Burton, B. (2010) 'Employment relations 2000–2008: An employer view', in E. Rasmussen (ed) *Employment relationships: Workers, unions and employers in New Zealand,* Auckland: Auckland University Press, pp 94–115.

Callinicos, A. (2010) *Bonfire of illusions: The twin crises of the liberal world,* Cambridge: Polity Press.

Cameron, D. and Clegg, N. (2010) *The coalition: Our programme for government,* London: HM Government.

Campbell, A. (2003) *How policies make citizens: Senior political activism and the American welfare state,* Princeton: Princeton University Press.

Campbell, G. (1990) 'Solo survivor', *Listener & TV Times,* 24 September, pp 20–21.

Carley, M. (2011) 'National minimum wage to be increased by 2.5%', *Eironline: European Industrial Relations Observatory Online,* http://www.eurofound.europa.eu/eiro/2011/04/articles/uk1104039i.htm.

Castell, S. and Thompson, J. (2007) *Understanding attitudes to poverty in the UK,* York: Joseph Rowntree Foundation.

Castles, F. (1996) 'Needs-based strategies of social protection in Australian and New Zealand', in G. Esping-Andersen (eds) *Welfare states in transition: National adaptations in global economies,* London: Sage, pp 88–115.

Castles, F. G. (2004) *The future of the welfare state: Crisis myths and crisis realities,* Oxford: Oxford University Press.

Cheyne, C., O'Brien, M. and Belgrave, M. (2008) *Social policy in Aotearoa New Zealand: A critical introduction* (4th edn), Melbourne: Oxford University Press.

Clark, J. (2010) 'Privatisation', in M. Thrupp and R. Irwin (eds) *Another decade of New Zealand education policy: Where to now?,* Hamilton: Wilf Malcolm Institution of Educational Research, University of Waikato, pp 201–14.

Clark, T. and Lipset, S. M. (1991) 'Are social classes dying?', *International Sociology,* vol 6, no 4, pp 397–410.

Clarke, H., Borges, W., Stewart, M., Sanders, D. and Whiteley, P. (2012) 'The politics of austerity: Modeling British attitudes towards public spending cuts', in N. Schofield, G. Caballero and D. Kselman (eds) *Advances in political economy: Institutions, modelling and empirical analysis,* Berlin: Springer, pp 265–87.

Clarke, H., Kornberg, A., McIntyre, C., Bauer-Kaase, P. and KaaseSource, M. (1999) 'The effect of economic priorities on the measurement of value change: New experimental evidence', *American Political Science Review,* vol 93, no 3, 637–47.

Clarke, J. (2004) 'Dissolving the public realm: The logics and limits of neo-liberalism', *Journal of Social Policy,* vol 33, no 1, pp 27–48.

Clarke, J. and Newman, J. (2006) *The managerial state: Power, politics and ideology in the remaking of social welfare,* London: Sage.

Clarke, J. and Newman, J. (2012) 'The alchemy of austerity', *Critical Social Policy,* vol 32, no 3, pp 299–319.

Clasen, J. (2005) *Reforming European welfare states: Germany and the United Kingdom compared,* Oxford: Oxford University Press.

Clasen, J. and Siegel, N. (2007) 'Comparative welfare state analysis and the 'dependent' variable problem', in J. Clasen and N. Siegel (eds) *Investigating welfare state change: The 'dependent' variable problem in comparative analysis,* Cheltenham: Edward Elgar, pp 3–12.

Clery, E. (2012a) 'Are tough times affecting attitudes to welfare?', in A. Park, E. Clery, J. Curtice, M. Phillips and D. Utting (eds) *British social attitudes: The 29th report,* London: NatCen Social Research, pp 1–26.

Clery, E. (2012b) 'Taking the pulse: Attitudes to the health service', in A. Park, E. Clery, J. Curtice, M. Phillips and D. Utting (eds) *British social attitudes 28,* London: NatCen Social Research, pp 141–50.

Cleveland, L. (1986) 'New Zealand political culture: A historical note', *Political Science,* vol 38, no 61, pp 61–9.

Collins, S. (1990) 'Privatisation: There is not much left', *New Zealand Herald,* 24 October, p 9.

Collins, S. (2006) 'Kiwis blame poor for being lazy', *New Zealand Herald,* 4 February, http://www.nzherald.co.nz/nz/news/article.cfm?c_id=1&objectid=10366826.

Cook, F. L. and Barrett, E. (1992) *Support for the American welfare state: The views of Congress and the public,* New York: Columbia University Press.

Cook, F. L. and Czaplewski, M. (2009) 'Public opinion and social insurance: The American experience', in L. Rogne, C. Estes, B. Grossman, B. Hollister and E. Solway (eds) *Social insurance and social justice: Social security, Medicare, and the campaign against entitlements*, New York: Springer, pp 251–78.

Cotterell, G. (2009) 'Making work pay? A comparative analysis of recent welfare reform in New Zealand and the United Kingdom', unpublished PhD thesis, University of Auckland, Auckland.

Coughlin, R. (1980) *Ideology, public opinion and welfare policy: Attitudes toward taxes and spending in industralised societies*, Berkeley: University of California.

Craig, D. and Cotterell, G. (2007) 'Periodising neoliberalism?', *Policy & Politics*, vol 35, no 3, pp 497–514.

Craig, D. and Porter, D. (2005) 'The Third Way and the third world: Poverty reduction and social inclusion strategies in the rise of "inclusive"liberalism', *Review of International Political Economy*, vol 12, no 2, pp 226–63.

Craig, D. and Porter, D. (2006) *Development beyond neoliberalism? Governance, poverty reduction and political economy*, New York: Routledge.

Crothers, C. (1988) 'Public views of the welfare state: The overseas literature and local studies', Paper written for the Royal Commission on Social Policy, Auckland: Department of Sociology, University of Auckland.

Crothers, C. and Vowles, J. (1993) 'The material conditions of voting', in J. Vowles and P. Aimer (eds) *Voter's vengeance*, Auckland: Auckland University Press, pp 95–109.

Crouch, C. (2011) *The strange non-death of neoliberalism*, Cambridge: Polity Press.

Curtice, J. (2010) 'Thermostat or weathervane? Public reactions to spending and redistribution under New Labour', in A. Park, J. Curtice, K. Thomson, M. Phillips, E. Clery and S. Butt (eds) *British social attitudes: The 26th report*, London: Sage, pp 19–38.

Dahlgreen, W. (2013) 'Nationalise energy and rail companies, say public', *YouGov*, 4 November, http://yougov.co.uk/news/2013/11/04/nationalise-energy-and-rail-companies-say-public/.

Dale, M. C., O'Brien, M. and St John, S. (2011) *Left further behind: How policies fail the poorest children in New Zealand*, Auckland: Child Poverty Action Group.

Dale, M. C., Wynd, D., St John, S. and O'Brien, M. (2010) *What work counts? Work incentives and sole parent families*, Auckland: Child Poverty Action Group.

Davey, J. (2001) 'New Zealand: The myth of egalitarianism', in P. Alcock and G. Craig (eds) *International social policy: Welfare regimes in the developed world,* Houndmills, Basingstoke: Palgrave, pp 85–103.

Davison, I., Cheng, D. and Harper, P. (2010) 'Thousands rally in support of Hobbit', *New Zealand Herald*, 25 October, http://www.nzherald.co.nz/nz/news/article.cfm?c_id=1&objectid=10682933.

Deacon, A. (1978) 'The scrounging controversy: Public attitudes towards the unemployed in contemporary Britain', *Social & Economic Administration,* vol 12, no 2, pp 120–35.

Deacon, A. (2005) 'An ethic of mutual responsibility? Toward a fuller justification for conditionality in welfare', in L. Mead and C. Beem (eds) *Welfare reform and political theory*, New York: Russell Sage Foundation, pp 127–50.

Dean, H. (2007) 'The ethics of welfare to work', *Policy & Politics*, vol 35, no 4, pp 573–89.

Dean, H. (2012) 'The ethical deficit of the United Kingdom's proposed Universal Credit: Pimping the precariat?', *The Political Quarterly,* vol 83, no 2, pp 353–59.

Dean, H. (2013) 'The translation of needs into rights: Reconceptualising social citizenship as a global phenomenon', *International Journal of Social Welfare Article*, vol 22, issue supplement S1, pp S32–49.

Dean, H. and Melrose, M. (1999) *Poverty, riches, and social citizenship*, New York: St. Martin's Press.

Dean, H. and Taylor-Gooby, P. (1992) *Dependency culture: The explosion of a myth*, Hemel Hempstead: Harvester Wheatsheaf.

Dean, J., Goodlad, R. and Rosengard, A. (2000) 'Citizenship in the new welfare market: The purposes of housing advice services', *Journal of Social Policy,* vol 29, no 2, pp 229–45.

Dekker, F. (2012) 'Labour flexibility and support for social security' in R. Van der Veen, M. Yerkes and P. Achterberg (eds) *The transformation of solidarity: Changing risks and the future of the welfare state,* Amsterdam: Amsterdam University Press, pp 69–90.

Department of Labour. (2013) 'Previous minimum wage rates', http://www.dol.govt.nz/er/pay/minimumwage/previousminimum.asp.

Department of Social Welfare (1998) 'Towards a Code of Social and Family Responsibility: The response report', Wellington: Department of Social Welfare.

Duch, R. and Stevenson, R. (2008) *The economic vote: How political and economic institutions condition election results*, Cambridge: Cambridge University Press.

Duffy, B., Hall, S., O'Leary, D. and Pope, S. (2013) *Generation strains: A Demos and Ipsos Mori report on changing attitudes to welfare*, London: Demos.

Duncan, G. (2007) *Society and politics: New Zealand social policy* (2nd edn), Auckland: Pearson Prentice Hall.

Dunleavy, P. and Husbands, C. (1985) *British democracy at the crossroads: Voting and party competition in the 1980s*, London: Allen & Unwin.

Dwyer, P. (1998) 'Conditional citizens? Welfare rights and responsibilities in the late 1990s', *Critical Social Policy*, vol 18, no 57, pp 493–517.

Dwyer, P. (2004a) *Understanding social citizenship: Themes and perspectives for policy and practice*, Bristol: Policy Press.

Dwyer, P. (2004b) 'Creeping conditionality in the UK: From welfare rights to conditional entitlements?', *Canadian Journal of Sociology*, vol 29, no 2, pp 265–87.

Eardley, T., Saunders, P. and Evans, C. (2000) *Community attitudes towards unemployment, activity testing and mutual obligation*, Sydney: Social Policy Research Centre, University of New South Wales.

Edelman, M. (1971) *Politics as symbolic action; mass arousal and quiescence*, Chicago: Markham Publishing.

Edelman, M. (1977) *Political language: Words that succeed and policies that fail*, New York: Academic Press.

Edlund, J. (1999) 'Trust in government and welfare regimes: Attitudes to redistribution and financial cheating in the USA and Norway', *European Journal of Political Research*, vol 35, no 3, pp 341–70.

Edwards, P. K. and Sayers Bain, G. (1988) 'Why are trade unions becoming more popular? Unions and public opinion in Britain', *British Journal of Industrial Relations,* vol 26, no 3, pp 311–26.

Elizabeth, V. and Larner, W. (2009) 'Racializing the "social development" state: Investing in children in Aotearoa/New Zealand', *Social Politics*, vol 16, no 1, pp 132–58.

Elola, J. (1996) 'Health care system reforms in Western European countries: The relevance of health care organization', *International Journal of Health Services*, vol 26, no 2, pp 239–51.

Erikson, R., Mackuen, M. and Stimson, J. (2002a) 'Public opinion and policy: Causal flow in a macro system model', in J. Manza, F. L. Cook and B. Page (eds) *Navigating public opinion: Polls, policy and the future of American democracy*, Oxford: Oxford University Press, pp 33–53.

Erikson, R., MacKuen, M. and Stimson, J. (2002b) *The macro policy*, Cambridge Cambridge: University Press.

Espiner, G. (2010) 'Dealing to dole bludgers', *North & South,* vol 290, pp 94–5.

Esping-Andersen, G. (1990) *The three worlds of welfare capitalism*, Cambridge: Polity Press.

Esping-Andersen, G. (2002) 'Towards the good society, once again?', in G. Esping-Andersen, D. Gallie, A. Hemerijck and J. Myles (eds) *Why we need a new welfare state*, Oxford: Oxford University Press, pp 1–25.

Esser, I. (2009) 'Has welfare made us lazy? Employment commitment in different welfare states', in A. Park, J. Curtice, K. Thomson, M. Phillips and E. Clery (eds) *British social attitudes: The 25th report*, London: Sage and NatCen Social Research, pp 79–105.

Etzioni, A. (1998) 'Introduction', in A. Etzioni (ed) *The essential communitarian reader*, Oxford: Rowman & Littlefield Publishers, pp ix–xxiii.

Expert Advisory Group on Solutions to Child Poverty (2012) *Solutions to child poverty in New Zealand: Evidence for action*, Wellington: Office of the Children's Commissioner.

Forma, P. (1997) 'The rational legitimacy of the welfare state: Popular support for ten income transfer schemes in Finland', *Policy & Politics*, vol 25, no 3, pp 235–49.

Fraser, N. and Gordon, L. (1994) 'Civil citizenship against social citizenship?', in B. van Steenbergen (ed) *The condition of citizenship*, London: Sage, pp 108–26.

Freedland, M. (2001) 'The marketisation of public services', in C. Crouch, K. Eder and D. Tambini (eds) *Citizenship, markets and the state*, Oxford: Oxford University Press, pp 90–110.

Friedman, M. (1962) *Capitalism and freedom*, Chicago: University of Chicago Press.

Gallie, D. and Alm, S. (2000) 'Unemployment, gender and attitudes to work' in D. Gallie and S. Paugam (eds) *Welfare regimes and the experience of unemployment in Europe*, Oxford: Oxford University Press, pp 109–33.

Gamson, W. (1992) *Talking politics*, Cambridge: Cambridge University Press.

Gelissen, J. (2002) *Worlds of welfare, worlds of consent? Public opinion on the welfare state*, Leiden: Brill Academic Publishers.

Gendall, P., Michaels, V. and Pegg, C. (2007) *The role of government*, Palmerston North: Massey University.

Gendall, P. and Murray, N. (2010) *Social inequality in New Zealand*, Palmerston North: Massey University.

Gendall, P., Robbie, P. and Douglas, R. (1997) *The role of government and work orientation*, Palmerston North: Massey University.

Gendall, P., Robbie, P., Patchett, S. and Bright, N. (2000) *Social inequality in New Zealand*, Palmerston North: Massey University.

Giddens, A. (1991) *Modernity and self-identity: Self and society in the late modern age*, Cambridge: Polity Press.

Giddens, A. (1994) *Beyond left and right: The future of radical politics*, Cambridge: Polity Press.

Giddens, A. (1998) *The Third Way: The renewal of social democracy*, Cambridge: Polity Press.

Gilbert, N. (2002) *Transformation of the welfare state: The silent surrender of public responsibility*, Oxford: Oxford University Press.

Gitlin, T. (1995) *The twilight of common dreams: Why America is wracked by culture wars*, New York: Metropolitan Books.

Glennie, H. (1990) 'State contracts: When doctors fall out', *New Zealand Herald*, 8 November, p 9.

Gold, H. and Webster, A. (1990) *New Zealand values today: The popular report of the November 1989 New Zealand study of values*, Palmerston North: Alpha Publications.

Goldsmith, M. (1997) 'Universal basic income and a social wage', *Social Policy Journal of New Zealand*, vol 9, November, pp 1–8.

Goot, M. and Watson, I. (2012) 'WorkChoices: An electoral issue and its social, political and attitudinal cleavages', in J. Pietsch and H. Aarons (eds) *Australia: Identity, fear and governance in the 21st century*, Canberra: ANU E Press, pp 133–70, http://epress.anu.edu.au?p=210621.

Gough, I. (2011) 'From financial crisis to fiscal crisis', in K. Farnsworth and Z. Irving (eds) *Social policy in challenging times: Economic crisis and welfare systems*, Bristol: Policy Press, pp 49–64.

Gough, I. (2012) 'Reply to Michael Hill', *Social Policy & Administration*, vol 46, no 5, pp 582–95.

Graefe, P. (2006) 'Social economy policies as flanking for neoliberalism: Transnational policy solutions, emergent contradictions, local alternatives', *Policy & Society*, vol 23, no 3, pp 69–86.

Grant, R. (2004) *Less tax or more social spending: Twenty years of opinion polling*, Canberra: Information and Research Services Parliamentary Library, Commonwealth of Australia.

Green Party (2013) *Children's policy – every child counts*, https://www.greens.org.nz/policy/childrens-policy-every-child-matters.

Green-Pedersen, C., Van Kersbergen, K. and Hemerijck, A. (2001) 'Neo-liberalism, the "Third Way" or what? Recent social democratic welfare policies in Denmark and the Netherlands', *Journal of European Public Policy*, vol 8, no 2, pp 307–25.

Gu, J. (2011) *Comparing the cost effectiveness of Australia's work for the dole with the UK's New Deal for Young People*, Melbourne: Department of Econometrics and Business Statistics, Monash University.

Gusmano, M. K., Schlesinger, M. and Thomas, T. (2002) 'Policy feedback and public opinion: The role of employer responsibility in social policy', *Journal of Health Politics, Policy and Law,* vol 27, no 5, pp 731–72.

Hall, P. (2002) 'The comparative political economy of the "Third Way"', in O. Schmidtke (ed) *The Third Way transformation of social democracy: Normative claims and policy initiatives in the 21st century,* Aldershot: Ashgate, pp 31–58.

Hall, Stuart. (1988) 'The toad in the garden: Thatcherism among the theorists', in C. Nelson and L. Grossberg (eds) *Marxism and the interpretation of culture,* London: Macmillan Education, pp 35–57.

Hall, Stuart. (2005) 'New Labour's double-shuffle', *Review of Education, Pedagogy and Cultural Studies,* vol 27, no 4, pp 319–35.

Hall, Suzanne. (2012) *21st century welfare: Seventy years since the Beveridge Report,* London: Ipsos MORI Social Research Institute.

Ham, C. (2009) *Health policy in Britain* (6th edn), Houndsmills: Palgrave Macmillan.

Handler, J. (2004) *Social citizenship and workfare in the United States and Western Europe: The paradox of inclusion,* Cambridge: Cambridge University Press.

Handler, J. and Hasenfeld, Y. (2006) *Blame welfare, ignore poverty and inequality,* Cambridge: Cambridge University Press.

Harding, A., Ngu Vu, Q. and Payne, A. (2009) 'A rising tide? Income inequality, the social safety net and the labour market in Australia', in J. Corbett, A. Daly, H. Matsushige and D. Taylor (eds) *Laggards and leaders in labour market reform: Comparing Japan and Australia,* London: Routledge, pp 123–39.

Harker, L. (2006) 'Delivering on child poverty: What would it take?', Report for the Department for Work and Pensions, London: Department for Work and Pensions.

Harper, J. (2013) 'Experts predict Australia Post will be privatised within five years', *Herald Sun,* 11 July, http://www.heraldsun.com. au/business/experts-predict-australia-post-will-be-privatised-within-five-years/story-fni0dcne-1226677891939.

Harré, L. (2010) 'Collective bargaining – right or privilege?', in E. Rasmussen (ed) *Employment relationships: Workers, unions and employers in New Zealand,* Auckland: Auckland University Press, pp 24–39.

Harris, J. (1999) 'State social work and social citizenship in Britain: From clientalism to consumerism', *British Journal of Social Work,* vol 29, no 6, pp 915–37.

Harrop, (2012) *The Coalition and universalism,* London: Fabian Society.

Hartevalt, J. and Robinson, M. (2011) 'Key rules out retirement age lift', *Stuff*, 27 October, http://www.stuff.co.nz/national/politics/5862270/Key-rules-out-retirement-age-lift.

Hartevalt, J. and Vance, A. (2011a) 'Superannuation debate part of election deal', *Stuff*, 6 December, http://www.stuff.co.nz/national/politics/6089778/Superannuation-debate-part-of-election-deal.

Hartevalt, J. and Vance, A. (2011b) 'Stark choice between two major parties', *Dominion Post*, 25 November, http://www.stuff.co.nz/dominion-post/news/politics/election-2011/6031287/Stark-choice-between-two-major-parties.

Hartman, Y. (2005) 'In bed with the enemy: Some ideas on the connections between neoliberalism and the welfare state', *Current Sociology,* vol 53, no 1, pp 57–73.

Harvey, D. (2007) *A brief history of neoliberalism*, Oxford: Oxford University Press.

Harvey, D. (2010) *The enigma of capital and the crises of capitalism*, London: Profile Books.

Hasenfeld, Y. and Rafferty, J. A. (1989) 'The determinants of public attitudes toward the welfare state', *Social Forces,* vol 67, no 4, pp 1027–48.

Hayek, F. V. (1944) *The road to serfdom*, Oxford: Routledge.

Hayward, J. (2012) 'Citizens' assemblies and policy reform in New Zealand', *Policy Quarterly*, vol 9, no 2, pp 70–5.

Hayward, J. and Rudd, C. (2000) 'Metropolitan newspapers and the election', in J. Boston, S. Church, S. Levine, E. McLeay and N. Roberts (eds) *Left turn: The New Zealand general election of 1999*, Wellington: Victorial University Press, pp 89–104.

Heclo, H. (2001) 'The politics of welfare reform', in R. Blank and R. Hashins (eds) *The new world of welfare*, Washington, D.C: Brookings Institution Press, pp 169–200.

Held, D. (2006) 'Culture and political community – National, global and cosmopolitan' in P. Spender and H. Wollman (eds) *Nations and nationalism: A reader*, New Brunswick: Rutgers University Press, pp 317–27.

Hemerijck, A., Vandenbroucke, F., Andersen, T., Pochet, P., Degryse, C., Basso, G. and Taylor-Gooby, P. (2012) 'The welfare state after the Great Recession', *Intereconomics: Review of European Economic Policy,* vol 47, no 4, pp 200–29.

Henman, P. (2007) 'Governing individuality', in C. Howard (ed) *Contested individualization: Debates about contemporary personhood*, New York: Palgrave Macmillan, pp 171–86.

Heylen Research Centre. (1988) *Corporatisation and privatisation: A summary of public opinion*, Wellington: Heylen Research Centre.

Heylen Research Centre. (1991) *Social issues survey*, Wellington: Heylen Research Centre.

Higgins, J. (1997) 'No longer a burning social issue? Employment assistance policy and the closure of the unemployment debate in New Zealand', *Journal of Sociology*, vol 33, no 2, pp 137–52.

Hills, J. (1998) *Thatcherism, New Labour and the welfare state*, London: Centre for Analysis of Social Exclusion, London School of Economics.

Hills, J. (2002). 'Following or leading public opinion? Social security policy and public attitudes since 1997', *Fiscal Studies*, vol 23, no 4, pp 539–58.

Horton, T. and Gregory, J. (2009) *The solidarity society*, London: Fabian Society.

Huber, E. and Stephens, J. (2001) *Development and crisis of the welfare state: Parties and policies in global markets*, Chicago: Chicago University Press.

Humpage, L. (2005) 'Experimenting with a "whole of government" approach: Indigenous capacity building in New Zealand and Australia', *Policy Studies*, vol 26, no 1, pp 47–66.

Humpage, L. (2006) 'An "inclusive" society: A "leap forward" for Māori in New Zealand?' *Critical Social Policy*, vol 26, no 1, pp 222–42.

Humpage, L. (2008) 'Relegitimating neoliberalism? Performance management and indigenous affairs policy', *Policy & Politics*, vol 36, no 2, pp 1–17.

Humpage, L. (2012) 'Understanding Māori and Pasifika attitudes towards employment and the unemployed', *New Zealand Sociology*, vol 27, no 2, pp 28–52.

Humpage, L. and Craig, D. (2008) 'From welfare to welfare-to-work' in N. Lunt, M. O'Brien and R. Stephens (eds) *New welfare, New Zealand*, Melbourne: Thompson, pp 41–9.Huseby, B. (1995) 'Attitudes towards the size of government', in O. Borre and E. Scarborough (eds) *The scope of government*, Oxford: Oxford University Press, pp 87–118.

Inglehart, R. (1997) *Modernization and postmodernization: Cultural, economic and political change in 43 societies*, Princeton: Princeton University Press.

Ipsos MORI. (2013) 'Attitudes to trade unions 1975–2011', http://www.ipsos-mori.com/researchpublications/researcharchive/poll.aspx?oItemID=94.

Jacobs, L. and Shapiro, R. (2002) 'Politics and policymaking in the real world: Crafted talk and the loss of democratic responsiveness', in J. Manza, F. L. Cook and B. Page (eds) *Navigating public opinion: Polls, policy and the future of American democracy*, Oxford: Oxford University Press, pp 54–75.

Jaeger, M. (2006) 'Welfare regimes and attitudes towards redistribution: The regime hypothesis revisited', *European Sociological Review*, vol 22, no 2, pp 157–70.

Jenson, J. and Papillon, M. (2001) *The changing boundaries of citizenship: A review and a research agenda*, Montréal: Canadian Policy Research Network.

Jenson, J. and Saint-Martin, D. (2003) 'New routes to social cohesion? Citizenship and the social investment state', *Canadian Journal of Sociology*, vol 28, no 1, pp 77–99.

Jessop, B. (1999) 'The changing governance of welfare: Recent trends in its primary functions, scale, and modes of coordination', *Social Policy & Administration*, vol 33, no 4, pp 348–59.

Jessop, B. (2002) *The future of the capitalist state*, Cambridge: Polity Press.

Johansson, H. and Hvinden, B. (2005) 'Welfare governance and the remaking of citizenship in J. Newman (ed) *Remaking governance: Peoples, politics and the public sphere*, Bristol: Policy Press, pp 101–18.

Joumard, I., Pisu, M. and Bloch, D. (2012) 'Tackling income inequality: The role of taxes and transfers', *OECD Journal: Economic Studies*, vol 2012, no 1, pp 1–36.

Kangas, O. (1995) 'Attitudes on means-tested social benefits in Finland', *Acta Sociologica*, vol 38, no 4, pp 299–310.

Kelsey, J. (1993) *Rolling back the state: Privatisation of power in Aotearoa/ New Zealand*, Wellington: Bridget Williams Books.

Kelsey, J. (1997) *The New Zealand experiment: A world model for structural adjustment?*, Auckland: Auckland University Press/Bridget Williams Books.

Kelsey, J. (2002) *At the crossroads: Three essays*, Wellington: Bridget Williams.

Key, J. (2008) *ReStart to help people made redundant*, 15 December, http://www.beehive.govt.nz/release/restart-help-people-made-redundant.

Key, J. (2010) 'Hobbit movies to be made in New Zealand', 27 October, http://johnkey.co.nz/archives/1062-Hobbit-movies-to-be-made-in-New-Zealand.html.

Key, J. (2012) 'Mighty River Power IPO to go ahead early next year', 3 September, http://www.beehive.govt.nz/release/mighty-river-power-ipo-go-ahead-early-next-year.

Keynes, J. M. (1936) *The general theory of employment, interest, and money*, New York: Harcourt Brace and World.

King, A. (2013) 'Ryall's fairy dust at work again', 4 October, http://www.labour.org.nz/media/ryalls-fairy-dust-work-again.

Korpi, W. and Palme, J. (1998) 'The paradox of redistribution and strategies of equality: Welfare state institutions, inequality and poverty in the western countries', *American Sociological Review*, vol 63, no 5, pp 661–87.

Korpi, W. and Palme, J. (2003) 'New politics and class politics in the context of austerity and globalization: Welfare state regress in 18 countries, 1975–95', *American Political Science Review*, vol 97, no 3, pp 425–46.

Kumlin, S. and Svallfors, S. (2007) 'Social stratification and political articulation: Why attitudinal class differences vary across countries', in S. Mau and B. Veghte (eds) *Social justice, legitimacy and the welfare state*, Aldershot: Ashgate, pp 19–46.

Larner, W. (2000) 'Neo-liberalism: Policy, ideology, governmentality', *Political Economy*, vol 63, Autumn, pp 5–25.

Larner, W. and Butler, M. (2005) 'Governmentalities of local partnership: The rise of a "partnering state" in New Zealand', *Studies in Political Economy*, vol 75, Spring, pp 85–108.

Larsen, C. A. (2006) *The institutional logic of welfare attitudes: How welfare regimes influence public support*, Aldershot: Ashgate.

Lawson, R., Todd, S. and Evans, S. (2006) *New Zealand in the 21st century: A consumer lifestyles study*, Dunedin: Consumer Research Group.

Leitner, H., Sheppard, E., Sziarto, K. and Maringanti, A. (2007) 'Contesting urban futures: Decentering neoliberalism', in H. Leitner, J. Peck and E. Sheppard (eds) *Contesting neoliberalism: Urban frontiers*, New York: Guilford Press, pp 1–25.

Le Grand, J. (2003) *Motivation, agency and public policy: Of knights and knaves, pawns and queens*, Oxford: Oxford University Press.

Levine, S. and Roberts, N. (2000) 'Voting behaviour in 1999', in J. Boston, S. Church, S. Levine, E. McLeay and N. Roberts (eds) *Left turn: The New Zealand general election of 1999*, Wellington: Victoria University Press, pp 161–74.

Levine, S. and Roberts, N. (2003) 'New Zealand votes: An overview', in J. Boston, S. Church, S. Levine, E. McLeay and N. Roberts (eds) *New Zealand votes: The general election of 2002*, Wellington: Victoria University Press, pp 15–27.

Levitas, R. (2012) 'The just's umbrella: Austerity and the big society in coalition policy and beyond', *Critical Social Policy,* vol 32, no 3, pp 320–42.

Lewis, P., Garnett, A., Treadgold, M. and Hawtrey, K. (2010) *The Australian economy: Your guide,* Frenchs Forest: Pearson Australia.

Lewis-Beck, M. (1988) *Economics and elections: The major Western democracies,* Ann Arbor: University of Michigan Press.

Lipset, S. M. (1963) *The first new nation: The United States in historical and comparative perspective,* New York: Basic.

Lister, R. (2003a) *Citizenship: Feminist perspectives,* Basingstoke: Macmillan.

Lister, R. (2003b) 'Investing in the citizen-workers of the future: Transformations in citizenship and the state under New Labour', *Social Policy & Administration,* vol 37, no 5, pp 427–43.

Lunt, N. (2006a) 'Sickness and Invalid's Benefits: New developments and continuing challenges', *Social Policy Journal of New Zealand,* vol 27, no 26, pp 77–99.

Lunt, N. (2006b) 'Employability and New Zealand welfare restructuring', *Policy & Politics,* vol 34, no 3, pp 473–94.

Lunt, N. (2008) 'From welfare state to social development: Winning the war of words in New Zealand', *Social Policy & Society,* vol 7, no 4, pp 405–18.

MacKuen, M., Erikson, R. and Stimson, J. (1989) 'Macropartisanship', *American Political Science Review,* vol 83, no 4, pp 1124–42.

MacLeavy, J. (2011) 'A "new politics" of austerity, workfare and gender? The UK coalition government's welfare reform proposals', *Cambridge Journal of Regions, Economy & Society,* vol 4, no 3, pp 355–67.

Maharey, S. (1999a) 'A road to a better future', Address to Bell Gully Government Relations seminar, Auckland, 27 October.

Maharey, S. (1999b) 'Economic prosperity must also provide social justice', *New Zealand Herald,* 4 November, p A17.

Manza, J. and Cook, F. L. (2002) 'The impact of public opinion on public policy: The state of the debate', in J. Manza, F. L. Cook and B. Page (eds) *Navigating public opinion: Polls, policy and the future of American democracy,* Oxford: Oxford University Press, pp 17–32.

Marsh, I., Meagher, G. and Wilson, S. (2005) 'Are Australians open to globalisation?', in S. Wilson, G. Meagher, R. Gibson, D. Denemark and M. Western (eds) *Australian social attitudes: The first report,* Sydney: University of New South Wales Press, pp 240–57.

Marshall, T. H. (2000) 'Citizenship and social class', in C. Pierson and F. Castles (eds) *The welfare state reader,* Cambridge: Polity Press, pp 32–41.

Marston, G. and McDonald, C. (2007) 'Assessing the policy trajectory of welfare reform in Australia', *Benefits,* vol 15, no 3, pp 233–45.

Matthews, J. S. and Erickson, L. (2005) 'Public opinion and social citizenship in Canada', *Canadian Review of Sociology & Anthropology,* vol 42, no 4, pp 373–401.

Matthews, J. S. and Erickson, L. (2008) 'Welfare state structures and the structure of welfare state support: Attitudes towards social spending in Canada, 1993–2000', *European Journal of Political Research,* vol 47, no 4, pp 411–35.

Mau, S. (2003) *The moral economy of welfare states: Britain and Germany compared,* London: Routledge.

Mau, S. and Veghte, B. (2007) 'Introduction: Social justice, legitimacy and the welfare state' in S. Mau and B. Veghte (eds) *Social justice, legitimacy and the welfare state,* Aldershot: Ashgate, pp 1–16.

McAllister, I. (1997) 'Political culture and national identity', in B. Galligan, I. McAllister and J. Ravenhill (eds) *New developments in Australian politics,* Melbourne: Macmillan Education Australia, pp 3–21.

McAllister, I. and Pietsch, J. (2011) *Trends in Australian political opinion: Results from the Australian election study, 1987–2010,* Canberra: Australian National University.

McClelland, A. and St John, S. (2006) 'Social policy responses to globalisation in Australia and New Zealand, 1980–2005', *Australian Journal of Political Science,* vol 41, no 2, pp 177–91.

McQueen, H. (1990) 'Education spending in NZ lags behind most OECD countries', *National Business Review,* 19 October, p 13.

Mead, L. (1997) 'Welfare employment', in L. Mead (ed) *The new paternalism: Supervisory approaches to poverty,* Washington, D.C: Brookings Institution Press, pp 39–88.

Meagher, G. and Wilson, S. (2007) 'Are unions regaining popular legitimacy in Australia?', in D. Denemark, G. Meagher, S. Wilson, M. Western and T. Phillips (eds) *Australian social attitudes 2: Citizenship, work and aspirations,* Sydney: University of New South Wales Press, pp 195–216.

Meagher, G. and Wilson, S. (2008) 'Richer, but more unequal: Perceptions of inequality in Australia 1987–2005', *Journal of Australian Political Economy,* vol 61, June, pp 220–43.

Mendes, P. (2005) 'Welfare reform and mutual obligation', in C. Aulich and R. Wettenhall (eds) *Howard's second and third governments,* Sydney: University of New South Wales, pp 135–51.

Mendes, P. (2009) 'Is social inclusion just a new buzzword? A half time report card on the social welfare policies of the Rudd Government', *Practice Reflexions,* vol 4, no 1, pp 27–39.

Mettler, S. (2002) 'Bringing the state back in to civic engagement: Policy feedback effects of the G.I. Bill for World War II veterans', *American Political Science Review,* vol 96, no 2, pp 351–65.

Mettler, S. and Soss, J. (2004) 'The consequences of public policy for democratic citizenship: Bridging policy studies and mass politics', *Perspectives on Politics,* vol 2, no 1, pp 55–73.

Ministerial Committee on Poverty. (2011) *Poverty Committee framework,* Wellington: Ministerial Committee on Poverty.

Ministry of Foreign Affairs and Trade. (2013) 'Trade relationships and agreements', http://mfat.govt.nz/Trade-and-Economic-Relations/2-Trade-Relationships-and-Agreements/index.php

Ministry of Social Policy. (2001) *The social development approach: Overview,* Wellington: Ministry of Social Policy.

Ministry of Social Development. (2012) *Children's action plan: Identifying, supporting and protecting vulnerable children,* Wellington: New Zealand Government.

Mishra, R. (1990) *The welfare state in capitalist society,* Hemel Hempstead: Harvester Wheatsheaf.

Mishra, R. (1999) *Globalization and the welfare state,* Cheltenham: Edward Elgar.

Morgan, G. and Guthrie, S. (2011) *The big kahuna: Turning tax and welfare in New Zealand on its head,* Wellington: Public Interest Publishers.

Mudge, S. L. (2011) 'What's left of Leftism?: Neoliberal politics in western party systems, 1945–2004', *Social Science History,* vol 35, no 3, pp 337–80.

Mulheirn, I. and Masters, J. (2013) *Re-engineering contributory welfare: Social security for a networked age.* London: Social Market Foundation.

Murray, C. (1984) *Losing ground: American social policy, 1950–1980,* New York: Basic Books.

Myles, J., and Quadagno, J. (2002) 'Political theories of the welfare state', *Social Service Review,* vol 75, no 1, pp 34–57.

Nadeau, R., Blais, A., Nevitte, N. and Gidengil, E. (2000) 'It's unemployment, stupid! Why perceptions about the job situation hurt the Liberals in the 1997 election', *Canadian Public Policy,* vol 26, no 1, pp 77–93.

Nadeau, R. and Lewis-Beck, M. (2001) 'National economic voting in U.S. presidential elections', *Journal of Politics,* vol 63, no 1, pp 159–81.

Nannestad, P. and Paldam, M. (2000) 'Into Pandora's box of economic evaluations: A study of the Danish macro VP-function, 1986–1997', *Electoral Studies,* vol 19, no 2–3, pp 123–40.

Nash, R. and Harker, R. (2005) 'The predictable failure of school marketisation: The limitations of policy reform', in J. Codd and K. Sullivan (eds) *Education policy directions in Aotearoa New Zealand,* Melbourne: Thomson/Dunmore Press, pp 201–17.

National Party. (2008) 'Election campaign advert', *New Zealand Herald,* 7 November, p A12.

National Party. (2011) 'Building a brighter future', http://www.national.org.nz/Policy.aspx.

New Zealand Government. (1996) *1996 coalition agreement between New Zealand First and the National Party of New Zealand,* Wellington: New Zealand Government.

New Zealand Government. (2001) *Pathways to opportunity: From social welfare to social development,* Wellington: New Zealand Government.

New Zealand Government. (2007) 'Social Security Amendment Act', http://www.legislation.govt.nz/act/public/2007/0020/latest/DLM408545.html.

New Zealand Government. (2010) 'Social Assistance (Future Focus) Bill', http://www.legislation.govt.nz/bill/government/2010/0125/9.0/whole.html.

New Zealand Herald. (1981a) 'Survey to assess hardship', *New Zealand Herald,* 9 November, p 2.

New Zealand Herald. (1981b) 'Govt family policy "inadequate"', *New Zealand Herald,* 29 October, p 10.

New Zealand Herald. (1981c) 'Young "despair"', *New Zealand Herald,* 6 November, p 2.

New Zealand Herald. (1990a) 'Benefit abuse in sights', *New Zealand Herald,* 29 September, p 5.

New Zealand Herald. (1990b) 'Proposals on benefits floated', *New Zealand Herald,* 10 October, p 3.

New Zealand Herald. (1990c) 'Labour accused of smears', *New Zealand Herald,* 3 October, p 4.

New Zealand Herald. (1990d) 'MP reiterates fee pledge', *New Zealand Herald,* 28 September, p 14.

New Zealand Herald. (1999) 'Where they stand: The five major parties on the big issues', *New Zealand Herald,* 22 November, p A10.

New Zealand Herald. (2008a) 'Long-term handouts harmful for depression patients – psychiatrist', *New Zealand Herald,* 12 November, p A6.

New Zealand Herald. (2008b) 'Turia puts focus on poor at policy launch', *New Zealand Herald*, 15 October, p A5.

New Zealand Herald. (2010) 'Muliaga family to sue over mum's death', *New Zealand Herald*, 27 June, http://www.nzherald.co.nz/nz/news/article.cfm?c_id=1&objectid=10654826.

New Zealand Herald. (2012) 'NZ private health insurance uptake hits 6-year low', *New Zealand Herald*, 23 May, http://www.nzherald.co.nz/business/news/article.cfm?c_id=3&objectid=10807807.

Norton, A. (2004) 'Liberalism and the Liberal Party of Australia', in P. Boreham, G. Stokes and R. Hall (eds) *The politics of Australian society: Political issues for the new century* (2nd edn) Frenchs Forest: Pearson Education Australia, pp 22–36.

O'Brien, M. (2008) *Poverty, policy and the state: Social security reform in New Zealand*, Bristol: Policy Press.

O'Connor, J. S. and Robinson, G. (2008) 'Liberalism, citizenship and the welfare state', in W. van Oorschot, M. Opielka and B. Pfau-Effinger (eds) *Culture and welfare state: Values and social policy in comparative perspective*, Cheltenham: Edward Elgar, pp 29–49.

Organisation for Economic Co-operation and Development. (2011) *Society at a glance: OECD social indicators*, Paris: Organization of Economic Cooperation and Development.

Organisation for Economic Co-operation and Development. (2012) *Social spending after the crisis: Social expenditure (SOCX) data update 2012*, Paris Organization of Economic Cooperation and Development.

Organisation for Economic Co-operation and Development. (2013) *OECD StatExtracts: Social expenditure*, http://stats.oecd.org/Index.aspx?datasetcode=SOCX_AGG.

Orloff, A. S. (1993) 'Gender and the social rights of citizenship: The comparative analysis of gender relations and welfare states', *American Sociological Review*, vol 58, no 3, pp 303–28.

Orton, M. and Rowlingson, K. (2007) *Public attitudes to economic inequality*, Warwick: Warwick University.

Padgett, S. and Johns, R. (2010) 'How do political parties shape public opinion? Britain in a European perspective', in A. Park, J. Curtice, K. Thomson, M. Phillips, E. Clery and S. Butt (eds) *British social attitudes: The 26th report*, London: Sage, pp 39–64.

Page, B. and Jacobs, L. (2009) *Class war? What Americans really think about economic inequality*, Chicago: University of Chicago Press.

Page, B. and Shapiro, R. (1983) 'Effects of public opinion on policy', *American Political Science Review*, vol 77, no 1, pp 175–90.

Page, B. and Shapiro, R. (1992) *The rational public: Fifty years of trends in Americans' policy preferences*, Chicago: University of Chicago Press.

Parker, D. (2004) 'The UK's privatisation experiment: The passage of time permits a sober assessment', CESifo Working Paper no 1126, Munich: Centre for Economic Studies/Ifo Institute.

Paske, H. and Ray, P. (1981a) 'The state of welfare', *The Listener & TV Times,* 14–20 November, pp 16–17.

Pearce, N. and Taylor, E. (2013) 'Government spending and welfare: Changing attitudes towards the role of the state', in A. Park, C. Bryson, E. Clery, J. Curtice and M. Phillips (eds) *British social attitudes: The 30th report*, London: NatCen Social Research, pp 33–61.

Pearson, D. (2002) 'Theorizing citizenship in British settler societies', *Ethnic & Racial Studies,* vol 25, no 6, pp 989–1012.

Peck, J., Theodore, N. and Brenner, N. (2009) 'Postneoliberalism and its malcontents', *Antipode,* vol 41, no s1, pp 94–116.

Peck, J., Theodore, N. and Brenner, N. (2012) 'Neoliberalism resurgent? Market rule after the Great Recession', *South Atlantic Quarterly,* vol 111, no 2, pp 265–88.

Peck, J. and Tickell, A. (2002) 'Neoliberalizing space', *Antipode,* vol 34, no 3, pp 380–404.

Peck, J. and Tickell, A. (2007) 'Conceptualizing neoliberalism, thinking Thatcherism', in H. Leitner, J. Peck and E. Sheppard (eds) *Contesting neoliberalism: Urban frontiers*, New York: Guilford Press, pp 26–50.

Perry, B. (2010) *Household incomes in New Zealand: Trends in indicators of inequality and hardship 1982 to 2009*, Wellington: Ministry of Social Development.

Perry, P. and Webster, A. (1994) *Value changes from 1989 to 1993 in New Zealand: A research note,* Palmerston North: Massey University.

Perry, P. and Webster, A. (1999) *New Zealand politics at the turn of the millennium: Attitudes and values about politics and government,* Auckland: Alpha Publications.

Peters, M. and Olssen, M. (1999) 'Compulsory education in a competition state', in J. Boston, P. Dalziel and S. St John (eds) *Redesigning the welfare state in New Zealand: Problems, policies, prospects*, Auckland: Oxford University Press, pp 70–92.

Pfau-Effinger, B. (2005) 'Culture and welfare state policies: Reflections on a complex interrelation', *Journal of Social Policy,* vol 34, no 1, pp 3–20.

Pierson, C. and Castles, F. G. (2002) 'Australian antecedents of the Third Way', *Political Studies,* vol 50, no 4, pp 683–702.

Pierson, P. (1993) 'When effect becomes cause: Policy feedback and political change', *World Politics,* vol 45, no 4, pp 595–628.

Pierson, P. (1994) *Dismantling the welfare state? Reagan, Thatcher, and the politics of retrenchment*, Cambridge: Cambridge University Press.

Pierson, P. (2001) *The new politics of the welfare state*, Oxford: Oxford University Press.

Pierson, P. and Hacker, J. (2005) *Off center: The Republican revolution and the erosion of American democracy,* New Haven: Yale University Press.

Piven, F. and Cloward, R. (1971) *Regulating the poor: The functions of public welfare* New York: Random House.

Plant, R. (2004) 'Ends, means and political identity', in R. Plant, M. Beech and K. Hickson (eds) *The struggle for Labour's soul: Understanding Labour's political thought since 1945*, London: Routledge, pp 105–19.

Porter, D. and Craig, D. (2004) 'The Third Way and the third world: Poverty reduction and social inclusion in the rise of "inclusive" liberalism', *Review of International Political Economy,* vol 11, no 2, pp 387–423.

Pusey, M. and Turnbull, N. (2005) 'Have Australians embraced economic reform?', in S. Wilson, G. Meagher, R. Gibson, D. Denemark and M. Western (eds) *Australian social attitudes: The first report*, Sydney: University of New South Wales Press, pp 161–81.

Putnam, R. (2000) *Bowling alone: The collapse and revival of American community*, New York: Simon & Schuster.

Quiggin, J. (1998) 'Social democracy and market reform in Australia and New Zealand', *Oxford Review of Economic Policy,* vol 14, no 1, pp 77–95.

Quiggin, J. (2004) 'Economic policy', in R. Manne (ed) *The Howard years*, Melbourne: Black Inc Agenda, pp 169–90.

Quin, P. (2009) *New Zealand health system reforms*, Parliamentary paper, 29 April, Wellington: New Zealand Parliament.

Ramia, G. and Wailes, N. (2006) 'Putting wage-earners into wage-earners' welfare states: The relationship between social policy and industrial relations in Australia and New Zealand', *Australian Journal of Social Issues,* vol 41, no 1, pp 49–68.

Rankin, K. (1997) 'A new fiscal contract? Constructing a universal basic income and a social wage', *Social Policy Journal of New Zealand*, vol 9, November, pp 1–12.

Rasmussen, E. and Anderson, D. (2010) 'Between unfinished business and an uncertain future', in E. Rasmussen (ed) *Employment relationships: Workers, unions and employers in New Zealand*, Auckland: Auckland University Press, pp 208–23.

Rasmussen, E., Hunt, V. and Lamm, F. (2006) 'New Zealand employment relations: Between individualism and social democracy', *Labour & Industry,* vol 17, no 1, pp 19–40.

Rasmussen, E. and Lamm, F. (2005) 'From collectivism to individualism in New Zealand employment relations', in M. Baird, R. Cooper and M. Westcott (eds) *Proceedings of the 19th conference of the Association of Industrial Relations Academics of Australia and New Zealand*, Sydney: Association of Industrial Relations Academics of Australia and New Zealand, pp 479–86.

Rawlinson, K. and Quine, O. (2013) 'Hundreds celebrated Margaret Thatcher's death – few had lived through her reign', *The Independent*, 9 April, http://www.independent.co.uk/news/uk/politics/hundreds-celebrated-margaret-thatchers-death--few-had-lived-through-her-reign-8566594.html.

Reserve Bank. (2013) 'Key graphs', http://www.rbnz.govt.nz/statistics/key_graphs/.

Roberts, J. and Codd, J. (2010) 'Neoliberal tertiary education policy', in M. Thrupp and R. Irwin (eds) *Another decade of New Zealand education policy: Where to now?*, Hamilton: Wilf Malcolm Institute of Educational Research, University of Waikato, pp 99–110.

Roche, M. (1992) *Rethinking citizenship: Welfare, ideology and change in modern society*, Cambridge: Polity Press.

Room, G. (2000) 'Commodification and decommodification: A developmental critique', *Policy & Politics*, vol 28, no 3, pp 331–51.

Roper, B. (2005) *Prosperity for all? Economic, social and political change in New Zealand since 1935*, Melbourne: Cengage Learning.

Roper, B. (2011) 'The fifth (Key) National government's neoliberal policy agenda: Description, analysis and critical evaluation', *New Zealand Sociology*, vol 26, no 1, pp 12–40.

Rose, E., Huakau, J., Sweetsur, P. and Casswell, S. (2005) *Social values: A report from the New Zealand Values Study 2005*, Palmerston North: Massey University.

Rowlingson, K., Orton, M. and Taylor, E. (2010) 'Do we still care about inequality?', in A. Park and E. Clery (eds) *British social attitudes: The 27th report*, London: NatCen Social Research, pp 1–2.

Royal Commission on Social Policy. (1988a) *The April report: Report of the Royal Commission on Social Policy* (Vol. 1), Wellington: Royal Commission on Social Policy.

Royal Commission on Social Policy. (1988b) *The April report: Report of the Royal Commission on Social Policy* (Vol. III), Wellington: Royal Commission on Social Policy.

Royal Commission on Social Policy. (1988c) *The April report: Report of the Royal Commission on Social Policy* (Vol. IV), Wellington: Royal Commission on Social Policy.

Royal Commission on Social Security. (1972) *Social security in New Zealand: Report of the Royal Commission of Inquiry,* Wellington: Government Printer.

Rudman, B. (1999) 'Vote result with change work world', *New Zealand Herald,* 24 November, p A20.

Sanders, D. (2000) 'The real economy and the perceived economy in popularity functions: How much do voters need to know? A study of British data, 1974–97', *Electoral Studies,* vol 19, no 2–3, pp 275–94.

Saunders, P. (1994) 'Rising on the Tasman tide: Income inequality in New Zealand and Australia in the 1980s', *Social Policy Journal of New Zealand,* vol 2, July, pp 1–15.

Schmidt, V. (2001) 'The politics of economic adjustment in France and Britain: When does discourse matter?', *Journal of European Public Policy,* vol 8, no 2, pp 247–64.

Schmidt, V. (2002) 'Does discourse matter in the politics of welfare state adjustment?', *Comparative Political Studies,* vol 8, no 1, pp 168–93.

Schmidtke, O. (2002) 'Transforming the social democratic left: The challenges to Third Way politics in the age of globalization', in O. Schmidtke (ed) *The Third Way transformation of social democracy: Normative claims and policy initiatives in the 21st century,* Aldershot: Ashgate, pp 3–27.

Schoen, C., Osborn, R., Bishop, M. and How, S. (2007) *The Commonwealth Fund 2007 international health policy survey in seven countries,* New York: The Commonwealth Fund.Sefton, T. (2003) 'What we want from the welfare state', in K. Thomson (ed) *British social attitudes: The 20th report: Continuity and change over two decades,* London: Sage and NatCen Social Research, pp 23–51.

Sefton, T. (2009) 'Moving in the right direction? Public attitudes to poverty, inequality and redistribution', in J. Hills, T. Sefton and K. Stewart (eds) *Towards a more equal society? Poverty, inequality and policy since 1997,* Bristol: Policy Press, pp 223–44.

Sefton, T., Hills, J. and Sutherland, H. (2009) 'Poverty, inequality and redistribution', in J. Hills, T. Sefton and K. Stewart (eds) *Towards a more equal society? Poverty, inequality and policy since 1997,* Bristol: Policy Press, pp 21–45.

Selbourne, D. (2001) *The principle of duty,* Notre Dame: University of Notre Dame Press.

Selznick, P. (1998) 'Foundations of communitarian liberalism', in A. Etzioni (ed) *The essential communitarian reader,* Lanham: Rowman & Littlefield Publishers, pp 3–13.

Sennett, R. (1998) *The corrosion of character: The personal consequences of work in the new capitalism,* New York: W.W Norton.

Sharp, A. (1997) *Justice and the Māori: The philosophy and practice of Māori claims in New Zealand since the 1970s* (2nd edn), Auckland: Oxford University Press.

Shaver, S. (2001) 'Australian welfare reform: From citizenship to social engineering', *Australian Journal of Social Issues,* vol 36, no 4, pp 277–93.

Siltanen, J. (2002) 'Paradise paved? Reflections on the fate of social citizenship in Canada', *Citizenship Studies,* vol 6, no 4, pp 395–414.

Skilling, P. (2013) 'Egalitarian myths in New Zealand: A review of public opinion data on inequality and redistribution', *New Zealand Sociology,* vol 28, Special Issue, pp 104–31.

Skocpol, T. (1992) *Protecting soldiers and mothers: The political origins of social policy in the United States*, Cambridge: Harvard University Press.

Smyth, P. (2010) 'Changes and challenges' in A. McClelland and P. Smyth (eds) *Social policy in Australia: Understanding for action*, Melbourne: Oxford University Press, pp 128–42.

Soroka, S., Maioni, A. and Martin, P. (2013) 'What moves public opinion on healthcare? Individual experiences, system performance and media framing', *Journal of Health Politics, Policy and* Law, vol 38, no 5, pp 893–920.

Soroka, S. and Wlezien, C. (2004) 'Opinion representation and policy feedback: Canada in comparative perspective', *Canadian Journal of Political Science,* vol 37, no 3, pp 531–59.

Soroka, S. and Wlezien, C. (2005) 'Opinion-policy dynamics: Public preferences and public expenditure in the United Kingdom', *British Journal of Political Science,* vol 35, no 4, pp 665–89. Soss, J. (1999) 'Lessons of welfare: Policy design, political learning and political action', *American Political Science Review,* vol 93, no 2, pp 363–80.

Soss, J. and Schram, S. (2007) 'A public transformed? Welfare reform as policy feedback', *American Political Science Review,* vol 101, no 1, pp 111–127.

Springer, S. (2010) 'Neoliberalism and geography: Expansions, variegations, formations', *Geography Compass,* vol 4, no 8, pp 1025–38.

St John, S. (1999a) 'Superannuation in the 1990s: Where angels fear to tread?', in J. Boston, P. Dalziel and S. St John (eds) *Redesigning the welfare state in New Zealand: Problems, policies, prospects*, Auckland: Oxford University Press, pp 278–298.

St John, S. (1999b) 'Accident compensation in New Zealand: A fairer scheme?', in J. Boston, P. Dalziel and S. St John (eds) *Redesigning the welfare state in New Zealand: Problems, policies, prospects*, Auckland: Oxford University Press, pp 154–176.

St John, S. (1999c) 'Poverty, family finances and social security' in J. Boston, P. Dalziel and S. St John (eds) *Redesigning the welfare state in New Zealand: Problems, policies, prospects*, Auckland: Oxford University Press, pp 238–59.

St John, S. and Rankin, K. (2009) *Escaping the welfare mess?*, Auckland: Child Poverty Action Group.

Starke, P. (2008) *Radical welfare state retrenchment: A comparative analysis*, Basingstoke: Palgrave Macmillan.

Starke, P. (2013) 'Antipodean social policy responses to economic crises', *Social Policy & Administration*, vol 47, no 6, pp 647–67.

Stephens, J. (2010) 'The social rights of citizenship', in F. Castles, S. Leibfried, J. Lewis, H. Obinger and C. Pierson (eds) *The Oxford handbook of the welfare state*, http://www.oxfordhandbooks.com/view/10.1093/oxfordhb/9780199579396.001.0001/oxfordhb-9780199579396.

Stewart, K. (2009a) 'Introduction', in J. Hills, S. Tom and K. Stewart (eds) *Towards a more equal society? Poverty, inequality and policy since 1997*, Bristol: Policy Press, pp 1–18.

Stewart, K. (2009b) '"A scar on the soul of Britain": Child poverty and disadvantage under New Labour', in J. Hills, T. Sefton and K. Stewart (eds) *Towards a more equal society? Poverty, inequality and policy since 1997*, Bristol: Policy Press, pp 47–69.

Stimson, J. (1999) *Public opinion in America: Moods, cycles and swings* (2nd edn), Boulder, CO: Westview Press.

Stimson, J. (2004) *Tides of consent: How public opinion shapes American politics*, New York: Cambridge University Press.

Stone, A. (1990) 'Education, enterprise and jobs are at the top of Bolger's list', *New Zealand Herald*, 19 November, p 1.

Sullivan, A. and Vowles, J. (1998) 'Realignment? Māori and the 1996 election', in J. Vowles, P. Aimer, B. Susan and J. Karp (eds) *Voters' victory? New Zealand's first election under proportional representation*, Auckland: Auckland University Press, pp 171–91.

Svallfors, S. (1997) 'Worlds of welfare and attitudes to redistribution: A comparison of eight Western nations', *European Sociological Review*, vol, 13, no 3, pp 283–304.

Svallfors, S. (2003) 'Welfare regimes and welfare opinions: A comparison of eight Western countries', *Social Indicators Research*, vol 64, no 3, pp 495–520.

Svallfors, S. (2004) 'Class, attitudes and the welfare state: Sweden in comparative perspective', *Social Policy & Administration*, vol 38, no 2, pp 119–38.

Svallfors, S. (2006) *The moral economy of class. Class and attitudes in a comparative perspective*, Stanford: Stanford University Press.

Svallfors, S. (2007) 'Conclusion: The past and future of political sociology', in S. Svallfors (ed) *The political sociology of the welfare state: Institutions, social cleavages and orientations,* Stanford: Stanford University Press, pp 258–80.

Svallfors, S. (2010) 'Public attitudes', in F. Castles, S. Leibfried, J. Lewis, H. Obinger and C. Pierson (eds) *The Oxford handbook of the welfare state,* http://www.oxfordhandbooks.com/view/10.1093/oxfordhb/9780199579396.001.0001/oxfordhb-9780199579396.

Svallfors, S. (2012) 'Welfare states and welfare attitudes', in S. Svallfors (ed) *Contested welfare states: Welfare attitudes in Europe and beyond,* Stanford: Stanford University Press, pp 1–24.

Tattersfield, B. (1990) 'Fundamental split over solutions', *National Business Review,* 26 October, p 9.

Taylor, D. (2009) 'Australia's changing labour market', in J. Corbett, A. Daly, H. Matsushige and D. Taylor (eds) *Laggards and leaders in labour market reform: Comparing Japan and Australia,* London: Routledge, pp 23–44.

Taylor-Gooby, P. (1985) *Public opinion, ideology and state welfare,* London: Routledge & Kegan Paul.

Taylor-Gooby, P. (2005) 'The work-centred welfare state', in K. Thomson (ed) *British social attitudes: The 21st report: Continuity and change over two decades,* London: Sage and Natcen Social Research, pp 1–21.

Taylor-Gooby, P. (2008) *Reframing social citizenship,* Oxford: Oxford University Press.

Taylor-Gooby, P. (2012) *A left trilemma: Progressive public policy in the age of austerity,* London: Policy Network.

Taylor-Gooby, P. (2013) *The double crisis of the welfare state and what we can do about it,* Houndsmills: Palgrave.

Taylor-Gooby, P. and Stoker, G. (2011) 'The Coalition programme: A new vision for Britain or politics as usual?', *The Political Quarterly,* vol 82, no 1, pp 4–15.

Thomas, B. (2008) 'Nats party before the axe falls', *National Business Review,* 21 November, p 27.

3 News. (2011) 'New Zealand First policies at a glance', 22 November, http://www.3news.co.nz/New-Zealand-First-policies-at-a-glance/tabid/419/articleID/233627/Default.aspx.

Thrupp, M. (2007) 'Education's "inconvenient truth": Part one – persistent middleclass advantage', *New Zealand Journal of Teachers' Work,* vol 4, no 2, pp 77–88.

Thrupp, M. and Irwin, R. (2010) 'Introduction', in M. Thrupp and R. Irwin (eds) *Another decade of New Zealand education policy: Where to now?*, Hamilton: Wilf Malcolm Institute of Educational Research, pp xvii–xi.

Titmuss, R. M. (1970) *The gift relationship: From human blood to social policy*, London: Allen and Unwin.

Toynbee, P. and Walker, D. (2011) *The verdict: Did Labour change Britain?*, London: Granta Publications.

Turner, B. (2001) 'The erosion of citizenship', *British Journal of Sociology of Education*, vol 52, no 2, pp 189–209.

UMR Research. (2009) *Understanding the drivers of satisfaction and trust in public services: A qualitative study*, Wellington: State Services Commission.

Vandenbroucke, F. (2002) 'Foreword', in G. Esping-Andersen, D. Gallie, A. Hemerijck and J. Myles (eds) *Why we need a new welfare state*, Oxford Oxford University Press, pp viii–xxiv.

van der Veen, R. (2012a) 'Risk and the welfare state', in R. van der Veen, M. Yerkes and P. Achterberg (eds) *The transformation of solidarity: Changing risks and the future of the welfare state*, Amsterdam: Amsterdam University Press, pp 13–30.

van Oorschot, W. (2006) 'Making the difference in social Europe: Deservingness perceptions among citizens of European welfare states', *Journal of European Social Policy*, vol 16, no 1, pp 23–42.

van Oorschot, W. (2008) 'Popular deservingness perceptions and conditionality of solidarity in Europe', in W. Van Oorschot, M. Opielka and B. Pfau-Effinger (eds) *Culture and welfare state: Values and social policy in comparative perspective*, Cheltenham: Edward Elgar, pp 268–88.

van Oorschot, W., Opielka, M. and Pfau-Effinger, B. (2008) 'The culture of the welfare state: Historical and theoretical arguments', in W. van Oorschot, M. Opielka and B. Pfau-Effinger (eds) *Culture and welfare state: Values and social policy in comparative perspective*, Cheltenham: Edward Elgar, pp 1–26.

van Parijs, P. (1992) 'Competing justifications of basic income', in P. van Parijs (ed) *Arguing for basic income: Ethical foundations for radical reform*, London: Verco.

van Wanrooy, B. (2007) 'The quiet before the storm? Attitudes towards the new industrial relations system', in D. Denemark, G. Meagher, S. Wilson, M. Western and T. Phillips (eds) *Australian social attitudes 2: Citizenship, work and aspirations*, Sydney: University of New South Wales Press, pp 174–94.

Vis, B., van Kersbergen, K. and Hylands, T. (2012) 'To what extent did the financial crisis intensify the pressure to reform the welfare state?', in B. Greve (ed) *The times they are a changing? Crisis and the welfare state,* Chichester: John Wiley and Sons, pp 7–22.

Vowles, J. (2002) 'Did the campaign matter?', in J. Vowles, P. Aimer, J. Karp, S. Banducci, R. Miller and A. Sullivan (eds) *Proportional representation on trial: The 1999 New Zealand general election and the fate of MMP,* Auckland: Auckland University Press, pp 16–33.

Vowles, J. (2004) 'Patterns of public opinion', in J. Vowles, P. Aimer, S. Banducci and R. Miller (eds) *Voters' veto: The 2002 election in New Zealand and the consolidation of minority government,* Auckland: Auckland University Press, pp 117–33.

Vowles, J. (2012) 'Down, down, down: Turnout in New Zealand from 1946 to the 2011 election', Paper for presentation at the Annual conference of the New Zealand Political Studies Association, Wellington, 25–27 November.

Vowles, J. and Aimer, P. (1993) *Voters' vengeance: The 1990 election in New Zealand and the fate of the fourth Labour government,* Auckland: Auckland University Press.

Vowles, J., Aimer, P., Catt, H., Lamare, J. and Miller, R. (1995) *Towards consensus? The 1993 general election in New Zealand and the transition to proportional representation,* Auckland: Auckland University Press. Wacquant, L. (2012) 'Three steps to a historical anthropology of actually existing neoliberalism', *Social Anthropology,* vol 20, no 1, pp 66–79.

Waldegrave, T., Anderson, D. and Wong, K. (2003) *Evaluation of the short-term impacts of the Employment Relations Act 2000,* Wellington: Department of Labour.

Walker, B. (2007) 'The Employment Relations Amendment Act 2004', http://www.employment.org.nz/ERA%20Amendment%2024Mar07%5B1%5D.pdf.

Walsh, P. and Brosnan, P. (1999) 'Redesigning industrial relations: The Employment Contracts Act and its consequences', in J. Boston, P. Dalziel and S. St John (eds) *Redesigning the welfare state in New Zealand: Problems, policies, prospects,* Auckland: Oxford University Press, pp 117–33.

Waltman, J. and Marsh, C. (2007) 'Minimum wages and social welfare expenditures', *Policy Studies,* vol 28, no 2, pp 163–74.

Welfare Justice: The Alternative Welfare Working Group. (2010a) *Welfare justice for all: Reflections and recommendations: A contribution to the welfare reform debate,* Wellington: Caritas Aotearoa New Zealand.

Welfare Justice: The Alternative Welfare Working Group. (2010b) *Welfare justice in New Zealand: What we heard*, Wellington: Caritas Aotearoa New Zealand.

Welfare Working Group. (2010) *Long-term benefit dependency: The issues: Summary paper*, Wellington: Institute of Policy Studies.

Welfare Working Group. (2011) *Reducing long-term benefit dependency: Recommendations*, Wellington: Institute of Policy Studies.

Wendt, C., Mischke, M. and Pfeifer, M. (2011) *Welfare states and public opinion: Perceptions of healthcare systems, family policy and benefits for the unemployed and poor in Europe*, Cheltenham: Edward Elgar.

Whiteford, P. (2006) 'The welfare expenditure debate: "Economic myths of the left and right" revisited', *Economic & Labour Relations Review,* vol 17, no 1, pp 33–77.

Wilensky, H. (1976) *The new corporatism, centralization, and the welfare state*, Beverly Hills: Sage.

Wilensky, H. (2002) *Rich democracies: Political economy, public policy and performance*, Berkeley: University of California Press.

Wilkinson, K. (2010) '90-day trial period extended to all employers', 18 July, http://www.beehive.govt.nz/release/90-day-trial-period-extended-all-employers.

Wilkinson, K. (2012) 'Improvements to employment law announced', 14 May, http://www.national.org.nz/Article.aspx?articleId=38484.

Williams, F. (1989) *Social policy: A critical introduction*, Cambridge: Polity Press.

Wilson, A. (2013) 'United Kingdom: Industrial relations profile, *Eironline: European Industrial Relations Observatory Online*, http://www.eurofound.europa.eu/eiro/country/united.kingdom_2.htm.

Wilson, S. (2006) 'Not my taxes! Explaining tax resistance and its implications for Australia's welfare state', *Australian Journal of Political Science,* vol 41, no 4, pp 517–35.

Wilson, S. and Meagher, G. (2007) 'Howard's welfare state: How popular is the new social policy agenda?', in D. Denemark, G. Meagher, S. Wilson, M. Western and T. Phillips (eds) *Australian social attitudes 2: Citizenship, work and aspirations*, Sydney: University of New South Wales Press, pp 262–85.

Wilson, S., Meagher, G. and Hermes, K. (2012) 'A new role for government? Trends in social policy preferences since the mid-1980s', in J. Pietsch and H. Aarons (eds) *Australia: identity, fear and governance in the 21st Century*, Canberra: ANU E Press, pp 107–31, http://epress.anu.edu.au?p=210621.

Wilson, S., Spies-Butcher, B. and Stebbing, A. (2009) 'Targets and taxes: Explaining the welfare orientations of the Australian public', *Social Policy & Administration,* vol 43, no 5, pp 508–25.

Wilson, S., Spies-Butcher, B., Stebbing, A. and St John, S. (2013) 'Wage-earners' welfare after economic reform: Refurbishing, retrenching or hollowing out social protection in Australia and New Zealand?', *Social Policy & Administration,* vol 47, no 6, pp 623–46.

Wlezien, C. (1995) 'The public as thermostat: Dynamics of preferences for spending', *American Journal of Political Science,* vol 39, no 4, pp 981–1000.

Wright, V. (1981) 'Unaccountable unemployment', *The Listener & TV Guide,* 7–15 November, pp 20–22.

Wright, S., Marston, G., and McDonald, C. (2011) 'The role of non-profit organizations in the mixed economy of welfare-to-work in the UK and Australia', *Social Policy & Administration,* vol 45, no 3, pp 299–318.

Wynd, D. (2013) *Benefit sanctions: Creating an invisible underclass of children?* Auckland: Child Poverty Action Group.

Young, A. (2011) 'More poll gloom for Labour', *New Zealand Herald,* 3 November, http://www.nzherald.co.nz/nz/news/article.cfm?c_id=1&objectid=10763639.

Zaller, J. (1992) *The nature and origins of mass opinion,* Cambridge: University of Cambridge Press.

Zepke, N. and Robinson, J. (1979) *Goals of New Zealanders: A summary of replies from workshops organised during 1978 by the Commission for the Future,* Wellington: Commission for the Future.

Zimdars, A., Sullivan, A. and Heath, A. (2012) 'A limit to expansion? Attitudes to university funding, fees and opportunities', in A. Park, E. Clery, J. Curtice, M. Phillips and D. Utting (eds) *British social attitudes 28,* London: NatCen Social Research, pp 77–90.

Index

Note: page numbers in bold type refer to Tables.